Robert M. Young

Robert M. Young

Essays on the Films

Edited by LEON LEWIS

McFarland & Company, Inc., Publishers
Jefferson, North Carolina, and London

Frontispiece: Robert Young demonstrating the last leap in the concluding scene of *Roosters*.

LIBRARY OF CONGRESS CATALOGUING-IN-PUBLICATION DATA

Robert M. Young : essays on the films / edited by Leon Lewis.
    p.   cm.
Filmography: p.
Includes bibliographical references and index.

ISBN 978-0-7864-2063-6
softcover : 50# alkaline paper ∞

1. Young, Robert M. — Criticism and interpretation.
I. Lewis, Leon.
PN1998.3.Y65R63   2005
791.4302'33'092 — dc22   2005011459

British Library cataloguing data are available

©2005 Leon Lewis. All rights reserved

No part of this book may be reproduced or transmitted in any form or by any means, electronic or mechanical, including photocopying or recording, or by any information storage and retrieval system, without permission in writing from the publisher.

On the cover: (top to bottom) Young with Farrah Fawcett (*Extremities*); with Arie Verveen (*Caught*); with Ray Liotta and Tom Hulce (*Dominick and Eugene*) — Photofest

Manufactured in the United States of America

McFarland & Company, Inc., Publishers
  Box 611, Jefferson, North Carolina 28640
  www.mcfarlandpub.com

To John McElwee,
with deepest gratitude for
his enthusiatic participation in
and extraordinarily generous support of
the Appalachian State University Film Program

Contents

Introduction by Leon Lewis ... 1

1. Interview with Robert M. Young ... 9
   Edwin T. Arnold

2. *NBC White Paper, Cortile Cascino*, and the Assault on the Familiar ... 43
   Craig Fischer

3. Demanding Dignity: *Nothing But a Man* ... 58
   Bruce Dick and Mark Vogel

4. *¡Alambrista!* Walking the Illegal Tightrope ... 74
   Melissa E. Barth

5. From Cell to Celluloid: A Dramaturgical Note on Miguel Piñero's *Short Eyes* ... 87
   John Crutchfield

6. *Ballad of Gregorio Cortez:* A Traditional Tale for Postmodern Times ... 112
   Cecelia Conway

7. Love, Death and Healing: Some Psychoanalytic Themes in *Extremities* ... 133
   Roger James Stilling

8. "Don't Let Anybody Hurt Anybody": Working-Class Masculinity in *Dominick and Eugene* ... 149
   Alexander H. Pitofsky

9. Memory and History in *Triumph of the Spirit* 161
   Zohara Boyd and Rosemary Horowitz

10. "California Dreamin'": *Talent for the Game* 180
    Eugene L. Miller

11. Stereotypes Collide: Machismo and 191
    Marianismo in *Roosters*
    Holly E. Martin

12. Space and Sexuality in *Caught* 206
    Thomas McLaughlin

13. From Script to Screen: Adaptation of 219
    Richard Dresser's *Below the Belt*
    Dennis Bohr

Appendix A: Filmography 239
Appendix B: Chronology 242
The Contributors 245
Index 249

Introduction

In early January 2004, Robert M. Young, as he was completing the final editing process for *Human Error*, read an article in the *New York Times Sunday Magazine* about Sam Goldstein, at eighty the oldest working taxi driver in New York City. Young, at seventy-eight, was captivated by the concept of a conjunction of two veterans of their trade, and decided to hire Goldstein to drive him across the continent to the Sundance Film Festival in Utah, at which *Human Error* was scheduled to have its world premier. He planned to issue reports about the progress of his journey on a website he had set up, to pick up the film's three principal actors along the road, and to deliver the film from a parking space that the New York City Film Commission had rented in a prominent spot at the festival.

Sundance was started by Robert Redford in 1981 as a showcase for films made on a minimal budget by independent filmmakers, but has grown in prestige to the degree that it now serves as an important initial screening forum for films by major studios like Miramax and Sony, showing 125 full-length documentaries and feature films from the nearly 5000 submitted. In keeping with the prevalent pattern of his career, Young was depending on the strength of his film to attract the attention of distributors who might overlook a work that was not highly publicized by organizations with substantial budgets for production and publicity.

Although Young was unable to actually hire Goldstein, since he had to work on the editing of the film until the day before the festival opened and then fly directly to Utah, the high-spirited exuberance of his plan to capture some attention from hordes of celebrities and their flaks amidst a media frenzy is representative of the energy and inventiveness that has enabled him to work through five decades of truly independent filmmaking. In 1996, Young brought *Caught* to the Sundance Festival in a similar attempt to find

Robert Young (center) on the set of *Dominick and Eugene* (1988), with (from left) Mike Farrell, the producer; Arthur Coburn, the editor; and Curtis Clark, the cinematographer.

a distributor, and was able to interest Sony Classics in handling the film. "Sundance is for newcomers," Young said at that time, "but you *can* have experience and still be a newcomer and an upstart. I had to make the film the same way young people do." In order to finance that production, Young, at the age of 70, cashed in his IRA pension from the Directors Guild, a characteristic personal gesture that has been his method throughout his life as a filmmaker. And as an indication of his flexibility when his integrity is not compromised, Young has also been able to work within the remnants of the old studio system to direct films (like 1988's *Dominick and Eugene*) that were sufficiently successful, by standard commercial measures, to keep him always in demand as a writer and director if he chose to accept the various projects that were offered.

Young was born in 1924, the son of first-generation immigrants from Russia. His father, who Young feels would have liked to be a filmmaker himself, founded the DuArt Film Lab in New York after working as a film editor in the 1920s and 1930s. As a boy, Young put together mini-films from discarded stock. He recalls, "As long as I can remember, I wanted to make movies, but my father felt I was too unrealistic and idealistic to make it on my own and would need the protection of the family business." Consequently, Young entered the Massachusetts Institute of Technology to study chemical engineering and "fit into the lab business," but he was "rescued from that fate by the Japanese bombing of Pearl Harbor and my eighteenth birthday," and he joined the Navy as a photographer's mate.

Young spent two years in New Guinea and the Phillipines, where "the people around us, from different races and cultures, opened my eyes and mind to a world richer and more exciting than the one I had known." Upon his discharge from the Navy, Young entered Harvard, where he majored in English Literature, founded the Harvard Film Society, and with several classmates, put together a film about a Boston factory worker. Young wanted his films "to be about the world I was learning about," so he turned toward documentaries, "inexpensive to make and I could write, shoot, edit and learn about life and film as I went along." With two Harvard classmates, Young formed a film cooperative and found work at the Marineland Studios in Florida, where he used some of the proficiency he had acquired in the Navy to make a series of films specializing in on-and-underwater photography, frequently handling the camera himself.

When *Secrets of the Reef* (1956) earned acclaim as one of the outstanding films of the year, Young's reputation as a documentary filmmaker enabled him to move into the mainstream of that genre, and led to his hiring by the National Broadcasting Company to work on the prestigious NBC TV *White Paper* series. When NBC shelved his extraordinary film about a Sicilian community, *Cortile Cascino*, in 1962, Young realized that he could not depend on conventional means of production to do the kind of work he believed in; and in 1964, with his close friend Michael Roemer, he made *Nothing But a Man*, self-financed, self-produced and self-constructed in every way, a landmark film that set the course for his career.

Almost every film that Young has made since has been a challenge in aesthetic and economic terms. Typically, he stood with Miguel Piñero, when the playwright insisted on a Puerto Rican actor for the lead in *Short Eyes* (1978), defying the studio and risking the wrath of the Directors Guild when he supported Piñero, who wanted to use fellow inmates from the Tombs as actors. "It was a non-union film, so I got suspended from the Directors Guild and was never paid," Young said in an interview in 2003 when the film was re-released. "I even got fined $1,500—but I'd give my eye teeth to do it again."

Some of the films that he has completed have been marked by constant struggles with financiers and stars (a not uncommon condition for all filmmakers); some projects have been derailed after a considerable expenditure of time and effort; and some projects remain in the planning stage, perhaps permanently. Nonetheless, undiscouraged and enthusiastic to a degree that has awed co-workers and friends, Young is still ready to put into production several ideas that he has developed. As he stated in 1980 when he had completed *Rich Kids*, "I love making films. I wouldn't know what else to do. I love being on the set. What I like is being on the set before everyone arrives and imagining what's going to happen."

In 2001, Young's imagination was fired by the possibilities he saw in books by Cormac McCarthy. To develop an understanding of McCarthy's challenging work, he consulted some of the studies by Edwin T. Arnold, a pioneering McCarthy scholar. Always interested in learning more, Young contacted Arnold at Appalachian State University, and a friendship developed as they talked, first about McCarthy's books and then about film, when Young learned that Arnold was also a *cinéaste*, teaching film courses at Appalachian and publishing (with his colleague Eugene Miller) two books about the director Robert Aldrich, among other film essays.

Arnold was struck by Young's willingness to talk with what seemed like endless energy and enthusiasm about filmmaking, and by the obvious pleasure that animated Young when he had the opportunity to meet students who were interested in the film industry. During the fall of 2002, Arnold asked Young if he might like to spend some time at Appalachian, where students in film classes could see some of his films and ask him about his life and work. In spite of invitations from other universities and offers to present his work at film festivals as well as the demands of several film projects that he was working on simultaneously, Young immediately agreed. In the spring of 2003, he spent a week at Appalachian, joining classes that had seen some of his films, meeting students and other members of the university community, and participating in public presentations of his films. Because he was so open and available, and because his remarkably genial demeanor encouraged everyone who met him to want to share his company, Young was almost always involved with people during that week.

For those faculty members of the English department who are a part of Appalachian's film program, Young's visit was something of a revelation. Even the most ardent film experts found that they were familiar with only a few of Young's films. Newfound awareness of the scope and variety of Young's work, and of the circumstances of his direction of films ranging from those made completely on the industry's standard model to films relying entirely on individual initiative and invention, led to the realization of just how much Young had accomplished. Given the inspiring example of a man who, at 78, remained dynamically involved in his life's profession, and the awareness of how little sustained critical attention and appreciation Young had received, the possibility of a volume that examined his work from a variety of perspectives seemed like an idea too promising to let pass.

It is not possible, in a book of this size, to deal with all of Young's films in depth, and the subjects of the separate chapters depend as much on individual preference and areas of inquiry as on an estimation of which of Young's films are most important by one criterion or another. Robert Young himself would probably have chosen a somewhat different list if he were compelled to make a choice, but as each essay indicates, a strong case can be made for the inclusion of those films under close scrutiny. Still, films like *Rich Kids* (1980), which Robert Altman produced, with its fine ensemble acting; *Saving Grace* (1984), a lighthearted film about a pope who breaks out of Vatican confinement to truly serve his flock; or *The Plot Against Harry* (1989), which Young and Michael Roemer resurrected after the unfinished production was shelved in 1968, might merit a detailed discussion, as would many of Young's prize-winning documentaries and television features, such as *J. T.* (1971), *Solomon and Sheba* (1995), or the film of Ernest Hemingway's short story "Soldier's Home" (1976). The retrospect that this volume affords has the potential for opening the field both of the work that Young has done, and as a basis for understanding the areas in film that he continues to explore.

As far as individual choices are concerned, many of the selections had a compelling logic that was immediately obvious. John Crutchfield and Dennis Bohr, accomplished playwrights, write about Young's adaptations of plays by Miguel Piñero (*Short Eyes*) and Richard Dresser (*Below the Belt*). Bruce Dick, a Richard Wright scholar, and Mark Vogel, an expert on popular culture, collaborate on Young and Roemer's pioneering representation of African-American life, *Nothing But a Man*. Rosemary Horowitz and Zohara Boyd, who with Rennie Brantz have developed a Holocaust Studies Symposium at Appalachian, discuss *Triumph of the Spirit*. Cecelia Conway, a folklorist and documentary filmmaker, draws on her background in music to examine *The Ballad of Gregorio Cortez*. Holly E. Martin, a specialist in the ethnic literature of the American Southwest, explains the intricate social structure informing the rituals of *Roosters*. Thomas McLaughlin brings his solid background in literary theory and cultural studies to *Caught,* while Eugene L. Miller uses his impressive familiarity with American sports to discuss *Talent for the Game*. Melissa E. Barth's essay on *¡Alambrista!* is a reflection of her work in the Appalachian Equity Office and her extensive feminist scholarship. Alexander H. Pitofsky, an eighteenth century scholar, demonstrates his grasp of contemporary culture with his trenchant essay on Young's most commercially viable film, *Dominick and Eugene*. Craig Fischer, a film and popular culture historian, writes about the crucial NBC *White Paper* production of *Cortile Cascino,* one of the defining moments in Young's career.

Robert Young working with Ray Liotta and Tom Hulce on the set of *Dominick and Eugene*.

Roger James Stilling, a Shakespearean scholar, illuminates mythic patterns of meaning in *Extremities,* and Edwin T. Arnold, whose initial contact with Young was the genesis of the entire project, has compiled an engrossing and informative interview from his extensive conversations with Young, an interview that effectively conveys a sense of Young as a man who has inspired all of those who have worked on this volume.

Numerous accounts demonstrate how difficult it is to get a film financed and into production, and how much corporate and financial considerations control the production itself now that the famous "studio system" has essentially ceased to exist.

The long and distinctively individual nature of Robert M. Young's life in films shows how one determined director has managed to maintain — through five decades — a career that has not been dependent on anything other than his energy, invention and persistence as a filmmaker. This does not mean that Young has shunned "the system" when he could use it for his own purposes without completely compromising his social and aesthetic goals. As a man who has traveled extensively to and successfully worked in some of the more forbidding regions of the planet, Young has been able to adapt to conditions and circumstances that would have discouraged most people. Similarly, he has been able to rescue productions that were about to fall completely apart, a testament to his patience and flexibility and an example of Young's ability to work effectively in situations fraught with tension and anger. As numerous co-workers and friends have consistently maintained, in an industry where rampant egotism, selfish scheming and neurotic self-indulgence are standard fare, Young's endearing amiability and good nature are important aspects of his capacity to maintain a working relationship with "the system" and its denizens. If this has been a primarily positive exchange, it has inevitably had its costs, but the sum of Young's life in film stands as an almost unique example of how it has been possible to work with integrity and independence in a realm where such attributes are not necessarily taken as positive virtues. The narrative of Young's life as a filmmaker is rare enough to justify, almost by its singularity alone, a critical study and celebration of one man who — to borrow a phrase from Dylan Thomas's "Poem in October" — has always tried to make films that expressed his "heart's truth" regardless of the obstacles and impediments he has encountered.

1. Interview with Robert M. Young
Edwin T. Arnold

The following interview is a construct of many hours of talking with and listening to Bob Young. Our conversations went in many directions, thanks to Young's enthusiasm and recall. A life lived as fully and as well as his is impossible to structure without sometimes taking liberties with the order in which topics were discussed, and I regret that I have had to omit too many of his remarkable stories from this edited account. As the interview will show, Robert Young understands that representations of experience can only pretend to the truth of the experience itself, and such is the case with this interview. Our talks took place over a four-day period, September 8–11, 2003, at his summer home near Holderness, New Hampshire.

ETA: Since others in this book will be writing on specific films, I think I'd like to talk to you more about your career and why you make films than about the individual films themselves, although I'm sure they will come up in the conversation.

RY: Why I make films is a big question, maybe the biggest. I mean, to me, it's all about my life; it's not about movies, *per se*. While growing up, I loved reading stories and seeing movies. I had dreams of adventure. I loved Melville and Conrad, and I wanted to go into the world. I wanted to experience the kinds of things that Melville and Conrad described. So those basic attitudes about what I wanted to experience were very important in propelling me into making movies. I got interested in *things*, and making films allowed me to explore them.

ETA: You grew up in a kind of film family, didn't you?

RY: Right. My dad had been a film editor before he founded DuArt Film Laboratories in New York. I think my dad was a very creative guy, but he had to make a living and so he founded a film laboratory. I don't think that's where he should have been — he should have been making movies. Later, he was supportive enough of my plans, but he was opposed to my making movies; he wanted me to go into his business. He thought I was too idealistic to make it in the world of filmmaking. That's why I first went to M.I.T. He sort of pushed me in the direction of being an engineer, and that's not what I really wanted to be. So when World War II came along, it was really an opportunity for me to get out of M.I.T. and change my direction.

ETA: But you were interested in making movies as a teenager, before you went to M.I.T. and then into the military?

RY: Yes, I was interested. But I had no real plans at that time. I took a lot of still photography, and I loved movies, but it wasn't as if my goal was that clear. I was still just too young to know what I wanted to do with my life. But I thought, somehow, I might end up making movies. When I was 13 or 14, I edited some little films from footage that was around the house. I'd splice things together and put them in funny orders. But it wasn't really until I was in the Navy, after I'd been at M.I.T. — and I was a failure there; I was 16 when I went and was at the bottom of the class, on probation when I left — that I began to think seriously about becoming a filmmaker.

During my training, I went to Pensacola Flight School for photographers. It was curious how that happened, because I had cheated to get into the Navy. I was color-blind, and my eyes weren't good enough, but I cheated and I got in. And then, because I had been at M.I.T. for almost two years, I got almost a perfect score when I went into the Navy, and they selected me for Annapolis because I was in good health and my eyes, theoretically, were perfect. And that scared the hell out of me because I knew that I was going to be found out. I didn't want to go to Annapolis. I wanted to be a hero and be in the war and experience all of that. So when I had my choice of schools, I chose to be a photographer's mate because I had this glamorous idea that I'd be a photographer's mate gunner and fly in airplanes. And I was, sort of. I did fly in dive bombers and torpedo bombers and PBYs doing reconnaissance. I was doing photography, but it wasn't the kind of thing I was really looking forward to.

Finally, I had kind of an epiphany when I was in the Admiralty Islands, which is north of New Guinea. I was attached to a group that was doing film and laboratory work for a squadron on this island from where they were doing reconnaissance. And I had this conversion experience, it reminded me of Jonathan Edwards, where I *knew*, in one moment I *knew*, that I was going to make movies. I don't know what the actual catalyst was, but one of the things that had affected me strongly was seeing the black guys who were in the Navy and were limited to working in the Officers' Club, washing dishes and serving and all that. That really troubled me, and I wrote a story, probably the first real story I ever did. It was about a black man, a musician I think, whose feelings were hurt by something that happened on a New York subway. It was a very internal kind of a story, and I still have images of it in my head.

But that's when I said I was going to make movies, and there was just no question about it. And I never changed my mind from that point. It was such a strong conviction that *this* was what I was going to do. I certainly wasn't going back to M.I.T. It was only after the war, when I went to Harvard, that I started reading Eisenstein and realized that I wanted to do it all — writing, photography, editing. I wanted to be a complete filmmaker. I think this is before that term was actually used very much. But I didn't think in terms of being a director or a cinematographer: I thought it was absolutely imperative to do *everything*. I didn't see how you could make films without understanding it all. I loved movies, but I didn't think that the movies I had seen dealt with a lot of the things that I thought they *ought* to be dealing with, like these black guys in the Officers' Club. I felt very keenly about those kind of social issues, and I thought film was a way to approach them.

But I also became very interested in the indigenous people whom I had met while I was in the service. For example, when I was shipped out to the Pacific, we landed at a place along the coast of New Guinea called Port Marobi. There was hardly any settlement there at all, and we were allowed to go ashore. We had maybe three hours, and I remember running as fast as I could away from Port Marobi into the jungle, going as far as I could so that I could see as much as possible before I knew I had to turn around and come back. I just wanted, you know, to see natives (*laughs*). I was so very naïve. And later I made friends with a young Melanesian boy. I taught him English, and he taught me songs, but I had a lot of trouble when I brought him back to the Quonset hut where I lived right by the airfield. Some of the guys in my outfit resented my dealing with this kid, who was so black, and my being his friend. And this had a big impact on me, too.

So this was me at that time. I was into social issues, but I was also wanting to see what was on the other side of the mountain. I was interested in what seemed to me exotic. I mean, I had read *Moby Dick* when I was 10 or 11, and I was fascinated by those kinds of stories, Melville and Kipling and *Bomba the Jungle Boy*. And when I had the chance, I wanted to explore remote places. I always wanted to be *someplace else*.

ETA: So World War II, in a sense, gave you this chance.

RY: Definitely. It's terrible to talk about the war in that way, I know. I don't want to diminish the war experience by making it my personal journey. I was very young. I did see combat. I remember screaming at the Japanese planes, daring them to shoot at me, to hit me. I was crazy, and an older sailor confronted me later and said he would throw me overboard if I ever did anything so stupid again. He had a family and I was not being sensitive. No one wanted those planes to come closer because it endangered everyone, you know, and I had to realize the *truth* of where I was. But, obviously, the war meant more to me than adventure alone. After all, I am Jewish. I was not terribly religious, and I had very little religious indoctrination, but I was aware of being a Jew, of being different, and I wanted to fight fascism and Nazism.

It's funny. While growing up, I often wished I was like everybody else, and I couldn't figure out why I wasn't. I'm sure that gave me an empathy with people who were outside the system, and so, from that point of view, it later became something that I felt good about. There's an advantage in not being in the mainstream and being in a position where you have to question some of the fundamental assumptions that people make in the society. If you are an outsider, you have to ask what makes you an outsider, what assumptions you operate under. It's not as if people *inside* the society don't do that, but they may not, because they don't have to. Maybe that helped Mike Roemer and me in writing the script of *Nothing But a Man*, or for me writing and making *¡Alambrista!* It's like de Tocqueville coming to America, or the Swedish sociologist Gunnar Myrdal observing and writing about life in the South. They were able to observe things that people in the system didn't talk about or didn't recognize. Obviously, there's no substitute on one level for living and experiencing something from the inside, but you can also sometimes artistically uncover the forms of things through the experiences and the situations that you observe from outside, and they can give you the insight into what someone might be feeling personally.

ETA: So all of these experiences contributed to your desire to make different kinds of films? Independent films?

RY: Well, I do think that's all tied in to my own aesthetic about filmmaking. I'm a little ashamed of the fact that I've never studied film. I think I could have learned a lot more and probably been a lot smarter about making movies, but I was in some way afraid of being derivative. Even today, it's very rare that I've seen a film more than once. And I've never gone to a film to see how to do something. Not that it's a bad idea. Writers do it all the time. You don't have to repeat what others did, and you can learn from what they did or didn't do. But I thought that I had to invent the wheel, and, you know, that isn't necessarily bad either.

But I felt that if I was going to make films, I had to be *involved* in all aspects of filmmaking. For example, I had always wanted to study acting, but I was too terrified to *be* an actor. I couldn't bear to have people looking at me. Still, I wanted to understand acting, so at one point during the 60s,

1966 or 1967, I signed up for Stella Adler's class. And I paid my money, and after the first class I never went back again. I was frightened. Later, I did the same thing with Jose Quintero. I mean, these were really good directors and teachers, but in both cases I went only once. It was by chance, really, that Marty Priest, a guy from the Actors Studio who was in *Nothing But a Man* and later had the lead role in *The Plot Against Harry*, spoke to Lee Strasberg about me and I was invited to come to his private class. So I went, as a complete novice actor and not as a director. Strasberg had classes in Carnegie Hall, and he was the guru at that particular point. It was really an honor even to be invited into his class, so I went, and I just loved it. I spent about six months. I stopped doing everything else. I just went to the class and I worked on the assignments.

And I found that the things that he was teaching were the things that I was already learning in a different way. For example, he kept talking about *situation*, and it made me think of Thomas Carlyle and his idea of the "blooming actual." I mean, everything is going on around you. And I was realizing that, in film, either you *tell about it* or you *experience it*. If you tell about it, then you become more of an essayist, which can be beautiful, and there are beautiful films that are essays, some that I love. But I didn't want to do that. I wanted to be more experiential, from the inside, and I wanted the story to tell itself. When I was in places where things were going on, I was always wondering, well, where would the camera go, what do you film, how do you tell the story?

ETA: Since your first films were documentaries, how did this aesthetic influence them?

RY: I think I first considered this while I was trying to make these documentaries about marine life. I learned that I had to find situations that connected things and gave the audience a basic understanding of what was going on. Then they would be positioned to watch and interpret behavior, and then I didn't have to *say* anything. The story told itself. Now, of course I *was saying*, because I was making the construct, manipulating what was seen, and I was very, very aware of that.

I never believed in twenty-four frames per second as truth — I thought all that was really a lot of malarkey. What I learned was that, in a sense, you had to *destroy* things in order to put them back together in some kind of analogical way, to make a model that was much more likelife. The reality that I filmed was anchored in time and space, and my job was to destroy it and put it back together in a way that made the connections that conveyed the psychological truth. My mind put certain things together, and then I realized that I was making certain connections that revealed situations, and that's really where the story was.

ETA: Let's back up a minute. How did you go from serving in the Navy to making these documentaries?

RY: Of course. I'm getting ahead of myself. Well, after the war I went back to school, but to Harvard, not M.I.T. And some of us started a film society there, maybe the first at Harvard, and later I formed a cooperative with two guys I knew at Harvard, Murray Learner and Lloyd Ritter. We came into this through a man named Al Butterfield, who had sold Marine Studios on the idea of making films about ocean life. I looked at some of the Marine films they had made, and it was obvious that they had been shot in a tank; there was a backdrop and they looked very phony. Moreover, they didn't work *kinesthetically*. I quickly realized that if you didn't have the right shots, cuts, then you couldn't put sequences together in that kind of analogical way, and then you had to *tell* about what you were seeing through external narrative, some ponderous voice and so on. So you had to film it differently to have the right cuts; otherwise, how did you edit it? I felt strongly: the eye must not be stopped.

I also realized that if you just filmed behavior, things that were going on, you *still* had problems. There had to be a point of view, a way of the camera being *inside* the experience, and then it would analogically become a correct sequence. But then, where would you go? Well, one way is a linear kind of structure, but that was kind of obvious and not very interesting to me. I began to recognize that, for me, the cuts had to be psychological, that what I needed to do was to take you *into* a situation, and to get *in* a situation you had to, in a sense, destroy it and then put it back together in an analogical way. Then you were really inside it and not simply talking about it and seeing it from the *outside*. When that reconstructed situation was created, then it would become experiential to the viewer.

OK, now I had this situation. The question then was, what should it go *against*? I began to understand the importance of triangulation in my own method. I didn't want to tell a linear story. It should be psychological as opposed to logical, something that played in some way *against* the scene but still in concert with it. It could be related to the previous scene, but very often it would be unexpected. And then I could follow that scene with another and then another, and then *life* was the story. The film would be much more like life in that things are seen in a more refracted way than they are directly. When you did see things directly, I thought, they were diminished. So I had all these ideas about how to make a different kind of documentary about the sea, very different from what Marine Studios was then doing. You can imagine how it sounded.

ETA: But you got the job.

RY: Yes. I talked the studio into giving us a contract, and for six years,

Murray and Lloyd and I had this cooperative. We had a communal fund, and we took money out as we needed it, and we worked on marine films. It was all very idealistic.

ETA: How did the cooperative end?

RY: In 1955, we did this film called *Wonders of the Sea*. In 1956, *Secrets of the Reef* came out and was very successful, but the partnership broke up around that time. It ended in a funny situation involving a whale. The three of us had done everything together, but Lloyd and I were both physical, more so than Murray. And I was very coordinated on water. I had been in the Navy and I could stand on a boat and I could hold the camera a lot steadier than somebody who hadn't experienced this could because I knew how to take it in with my knees. And here one day this whale was offshore of St. Augustine, Florida, with its young, and there was a chance to get shots of it. It should have been either Lloyd or me. I was the most experienced, but Lloyd was also a good cameraman. And Murray insisted that we flip a coin. We did and he went out and filmed it, and on the film you never saw the whale. It wasn't so much my frustration at that, but I realized then that my fate was being determined by flipping a coin. We had been very close, and this was six years later, but that was the final straw. There had been other things, obviously. For example, we all three put money in, and over time Murray took out $7000 more than we did. Then, when we were making a little bit more money, he didn't want to take less, and I thought that was wrong. That was another factor. But that was not *the* factor. That factor was the whales and flipping a coin. It's a crazy story.

ETA: So the cooperative broke up. What followed?

RY: *Secrets of the Reef* brought me to the attention of Merian C. Cooper, who had directed *King Kong* (with Ernest B. Schoedsack, 1933). I developed this close relationship with Cooper. I had written a script called *Children of the Sea* about a boy and a porpoise, and when he read it, he said, "This could be another *King Kong*." Well, *King Kong* had been a very important film to me as a child, full of exotic adventure and romance. So I went out to California to work with him. I did that for about six months, and we went to the Bahamas, looking for locations. And I loved him; he was a wonderful, wonderful man. At one point, he said to me, "You're another Merian Cooper," which was quite a compliment (*laughing*). He had made two great documentaries, *Grass* (1925) and *Chang* (1927), in his early life, and when I knew him he had recently sent some young man off to do a remake of *Grass*. *Grass* was filmed in the Hindu Kush mountains, and it was about these Iranian nomads making this long trek, crossing raging rivers and taking their flocks to the summer pastures. It was a difficult assignment, and the guy had failed. And Cooper had the sense that I wouldn't have come back without having done it. I think that's true. I might not have succeeded, but then I wouldn't have come back.

ETA: You did a series of other documentaries in the late 1950s, before you joined up with NBC.

RY: Right. I did a thing on molds (*Life of the Molds* [1958]), which again changed the way I thought. I wanted to film the growth of a strand of mold. It looked like a string of spaghetti. The outside is made of chitin — a substance like your fingernail. Inside is the protoplasm, the stuff of life. I set up my stop-motion camera and took one frame every second, so that when I would screen it I would see twenty-four seconds of time in one second, which would allow me to see the growth of the mold. I lit the mold from below, so it was transparent, and when I got the film and projected it, it was an amazing sight. The strand grew *across the screen*. It looked like a finger, and what was amazing was that the leading edge of the finger of mold was soft and thin and that was where all the protoplasm was — *pushing* the finger into the environment. It was such a striking image that I burst into tears. There, at the leading edge, where the mold grew, was Life. And behind, where the walls of chitin were hard, the mold dried up and was dead. Here was one of the most primitive forms of life *saying* by its own action that life and growth are at the leading edge, reaching into the environment. And behind, where things were static and settled, *there* was death. I also realized how boundaries keep shifting by *absorbing* what's around them. So Life was where we go into new territories and take chances. This is what the mold told me, growing across the screen, and it had an enormous effect on me. It made me look at life that way.

In addition to this film, I did a few films for the *High Adventure* series (*India* [1958]; *Danger Island* [1959]). But it was this film called *The Living End*, which was about death and dying, that brought me to the attention of Irv Gitlin, who was the head of creative projects at NBC. *The Living End* was a kind of documentary. We had used a real old man but I had partially dramatized it. That is, it was partly acted, but it was with all the real people, and it was quite a lovely film. It had a huge impact. Well, Gitlin saw this film, and he called me and said, "Look, we want you to come and be at *NBC White Paper*, which is this new thing we're starting." I knew it was in reaction to *The $64,000 Question* scandal, which had really embarrassed NBC. They needed to protect their reputation, so they decided to do this prestigious public affairs program, four shows a year, and here I was, the first person to be called to be a filmmaker there.

I'll never forget the interview. I was very excited at the idea that I might be involved in recording things of world importance. But it was a strange, strange interview because I never asked how much they paid; it just never entered my head. And I told them that I was not a journalist, and I asked if they were really sure they wanted me. I said, "Look, I've never worked for anyone in my life and I can't begin now, so if you really want me to come and work here, I would love the opportunity, but I cannot be assigned to anything." I had always been pretty much just a freelance person, and here I was telling NBC what I would accept. And I said, "I cannot do something unless I really believe in it, so if you really want me, it would have to be understood that I cannot be assigned anything and the topic has to be something that we mutually agree on. But the *quid pro quo* will be that I won't be on salary except when I am working. And I don't want any vacations or any perks. It's just that, when I'm working, I get paid. This seems to me a fair way of doing it. I'm not working for you except when you hire me, and then it's on something that we both want to do."

They had never heard of anything like that, I suppose. So I never had a contract for the two years I was at NBC. I met with a lawyer to discuss it, but nobody was going to put anything like this in writing. I don't think NBC would even have allowed it. But, in fact, they paid me very generously, and each year, for every new film, the salary went up, and they paid me in between, although I didn't want them to. It was altogether remarkable. And I was very successful making these *White Paper* documentaries, especially *Sit-In* (1960) and the Angola film (*Angola: Journey to a War* [1961]). I got the George Polk Award for Heroism two years in a row and the Overseas Press Club award and all that kind of stuff.

But other things developed. After I made the Angola film, I was approached by the C.I.A., and I was asked if I would go to Washington, D.C. for a meeting. There must have been 30 people there, people from the ambassador's office in Luanda, Angola, from Army and Navy intelligence, obviously members of the C.I.A., a whole bunch of people. They had seen the film and they questioned me very carefully about the morale of the rebels and the kinds of weapons they had, and I was very anxious to cooperate with them. I thought it was important that they understood the situation and not just listen to the Portuguese propaganda of the other side.

At the end of the session, three people in civilian clothes came up to me and said, "We could really use a guy like you." One of the things they were very interested in was how I had prepared for the trip, and how I had survived once I got behind the lines. The fact was that I had gone to the American Geographical Society, and I had more detailed maps on the ground of northern Angola than anyone else in Africa had. The border was about 120 miles from the capital, and Charles Dorkins and I — he was my cameraman — had to drive to the border and make contact with the rebels, the Congolese patrols. And the C.I.A. was very impressed that we had walked

400 miles behind the lines with the rebels and had made this movie and had even brought back nose cones from napalm bombs. Actually, I brought back two of them and had filmed a sequence of a village that had been napalmed, full of charred bodies, but that was later taken out of my film. Irv Gitlin told me not to talk about the sequence; he said it would be more exciting when the film was shown, and then they took it out.

When I think about it today, I think I should have quit at that point and gone to the *New York Times* and said, "Look, here are pictures of American napalm nose cones. We were providing them in Angola." I now think the United States was offering support to a policy that was killing people who might form an infrastructure for a new African government. The Congo, just the year before, had gotten its independence. And I had plenty of filmed evidence that the Portuguese were deliberately trying to eliminate people who could read, write, speak English. They were destroying the culture, trying to prevent any kind of national identity. I saw a lot of this firsthand. Although I was there only three weeks, it was a tremendously intensive three weeks. I saw places of massacres where they had been bombed. I still have the film.

Anyway, the C.I.A. was not supposed to recruit journalists, but they tried to recruit me. After the meeting, I went back to NBC and I called the head of the News Division and I said, "What do I do? I don't want to have any part of this." And he said, "Well, just don't do anything." There was no follow-up. I'm sure he said something, that I was not the right guy. I'm pretty sure some NBC people were in the C.I.A., although I don't have any way of knowing. I do know that some of them felt I was too sympathetic to the Congolese, and the Portuguese later had a hand in selecting another NBC journalist who went in to cover it from their side. This guy, Bob McCormack, wrote me a letter lambasting me and saying he was going to tell the other side since I had not done that.

But when I was in Angola, behind the lines, I had made it clear to the rebels we were with that nobody could exercise any control over me, that I was going to film whatever I saw. Now obviously, where I went was subject to where they would take me, and this was a 400-mile trip in the bush, hiding from the Portuguese. On the other hand, the soldiers I was with sometimes asked me military questions about the Portuguese that I could have answered, but I wouldn't. I wasn't going to be a party to killing any Portuguese, young men who didn't know what the hell they were doing there. Still, my sympathies were primarily with the Congolese. I saw the way they suffered. I treated some of their bullet wounds, which I'm not qualified to do, and I took back a person who had gangrene. I saw a lot of horrible things — a lot of great things, too, but many terrible things. I went to places where the rebels I was with had massacred Portuguese planters only weeks before, and here I was, the only white person, in the same places with them. The bodies were gone, but houses had been ransacked and there were still letters and personal things lying all around. And I asked these guys how they could do such things. But then they showed me the things that had happened to them, how they had also been brutalized and killed. You can never understand those things, really. They can be explained but not answered.

After three weeks, we came to a river, and there was a battle taking place on the other side. The rebels told me the river was full of crocodiles and very dangerous to cross, but I still wanted to go on. I was, you know, a little crazy in those days. In the background of anybody doing something like this is the heroic image of Lawrence of Arabia.

ETA: You soon ran afoul of NBC. Was it because the network was pretending to some sort of documentary objectivity that really wasn't there?

RY: Absolutely. Absolutely. There's a very interesting story that shows a lot of my own weaknesses, my not understanding that you've got to be operational sometimes.

ETA: What do you mean by "operational"?

RY: To be able to see what's going on politically, strategically, and to know that it is necessary to protect yourself, to be a little bit more like a poker player, not to expose yourself and your vulnerabilities.

ETA: OK, give me the specifics here.

RY: Well, this is about the Sicily film, *Cortile Cascino*, which I made with Mike Roemer the next year [1962]. After Angola, I began reading about the C.I.A. and I realized that tens of millions, if not hundreds of millions, of dollars were being poured into the Christian Democratic Party in Sicily to try to sustain it. It was the time that was called the "Opening to the Left," when the Christian Democrats were aligning with the Nenni Socialists, and Socialists were considered practically Communists at that time. So the United States was terrified that Italy was going Communist. In truth, it was very different from the Russian Communist Party, but still, any film that exposed the poverty and corruption in Italy was really the wrong program to put on at that moment when the United States was trying to shore up the existing Italian government. Now, the film itself said nothing directly against the government or what was happening, but it did show all this miserable poverty, and it showed that the government's attempts to bring the south of Italy up to the standards of the north were a miserable failure. And it also showed that the Church wasn't able to do anything about it. The priests would get beaten up if they went into the slums. So NBC felt it was a bad idea to put out this film at this point. They had to get rid of it, even if it meant taking Michael Roemer and me down with it.

ETA: Yes, but they had their professional reasons as well, didn't they? This goes back to your concept of documentary.

RY: This was their excuse. When Mike and I made the film, it was a very closely observed but also a very written film, and by that I mean a very structured film. Again, every work is a construct, and that construct says something. It's not just arbitrary. When we made the Sicily movie, we were observers there just for a short period of time. But there was a bigger picture going on, and that's what we were interested in getting. And there were ways of doing that by analogy, through scenes that suggested the larger truths. And this was what NBC got us on. What happened was that Angela, the central character in the film we gave NBC, gives birth but then loses her infant child, and at the end of the film they bury it. Now the *truth*, the *literal* truth, is that before we came to Sicily, she *had* lost a child, but when we were making the film she was pregnant again.

Now, I *do* believe that if you didn't have to make a construct, then there is nothing as powerful as the truth —*if* you can see it. I mean, the world is so very complex. But *if* you could really render all of that and be inside of it and begin to understand all of it as a great historian tries to understand, then it wouldn't be a movie. Some things movies can do are really extraordinary, and one thing movies can do is that they can position you, take you into experiences and cause you to have much more of an empathetic feeling about the people and about the place and offer some kind of insights. But solutions, no, they can't do that. You can have the *potential* for things that can happen, and there can be implications of other things that will happen, but you can only suggest them. As I've said, the negative space, the thing that's not there, is tremendously important to me.

But in the *finite* story of this film, the *actual truth* of what happened during this short period while we were filming wouldn't be the *real truth*. The film couldn't end with her pregnant, because to show that would have implied some hope. Mike and I both felt that to tell the story accurately — as a construct — we had to stage a scene where she's giving birth to a child. This had happened before we arrived, so we couldn't film it. So we brought in a practically newborn baby and we filmed the scene. Actually, you saw more of it in earlier versions of the film but they made me take it out as we had more arguments, before they got rid of the film altogether. I wanted the audience to witness the birth, to see that this woman loves her child, and then have it die. We found out that one out of five children died before they reached the age of five in these slums. I didn't want the audience to escape that reality. So, to reflect this truth, the film *had* to end with the mother losing a child, which had really happened. So we staged the birth, and then we staged the baby's funeral. We shot the undertaker carrying a little empty coffin down the street to the black van that would transport it to the cemetery. He *had* done this previously, you understand: there *was* a baby and it had died and been buried. But now she was pregnant again, and we couldn't end the film that way.

In another scene, the family is eating and one kid reaches across the table and the father slaps the kid and then he humiliates his mother-in-law. And Angela, his wife, laughs, to make him feel more the man, and he reacts accordingly. It's a powerful scene, but it was shot over three nights. It didn't happen all at once. We were present, of course, and the father was acting out. He knew the camera was there and he played to it, but at the same time this scene captures him, who he was. I'm not saying that's all of who he was, but that's a very strong aspect of him, and in this scene we captured him much better than if we had stayed back and pretended not to be there. I mean, if you *could* be there and still *not* be there and capture everything you wanted, that'd be great. But there's no way to do that yet.

This is the difference between life and art. It's so hard to do a biography, you know, because there is a central story, but you have to lop off so many of the branches to be able to see it. The experiential nature of one's life blurs the story, and you are part of the bigger story of a larger world. And I feel the urge to understand that, but also to make a dramatic form out of a life. I thought the *fictive* truth, which is the truth of the story I'm telling, reveals more about the society than if I had left it at the *literal* truth. And that was our decision, that was our choice, and that was the structure of the film.

So, yes, we structured the film; we *made* a narrative, even with the beginning and end of the film. Deliberately, the structure was that we came in on a train at the beginning, shooting as we enter this slum, and we knew all along that the last shot in the film *had* to be our going out on a train and these kids running along on the track after us, trying to keep up with us. So, the *form* of the film says, "We came, we saw, we left, and it's an unfinished story," and in the end, there's smoke as we go through a crossing, and the kids have been left behind. The form of the shooting is the content; you can't separate them.

ETA: OK, so parts of the film were staged and rearranged. By this time, NBC obviously had to know how documentaries are made, or, at the least, how you made documentaries. You didn't hide that from them, did you?

RY: Not at all. We had this confrontation with Irv Gitlin, who was looking for a reason not to show the film. And when I said that we had changed the birth, he acted as if he'd never heard about it. Now, my producer, a man named Al Wasserman, knew exactly what we had done because we had discussed it with him. And, OK, maybe Gitlin didn't know, but at this particular point I think he was simply frightened of the film.

This is probably bigger and more complex than I understand, because I see it from my point of view and there may be much more to it. This is my side of the story, and we look like good guys in the way I'm telling it because we're the Davids fighting Goliath. But when Gitlin made an issue of this, my honor was challenged, and I sat down at the typewriter and I wrote a confessional letter. I said that we had told everybody what we were doing and I was surprised that Gitlin didn't know, but if I had violated some kind of sacred tenet in journalism, I still thought that what I filmed was actually the deeper truth. I said, "Yes, I did change the *literal* reality of it, and if that is against the code, then you can consider this as my letter of resignation." I gave them that *proof*; he had that in his hand. I could have just said, "We told you," and left it that way. But that was a card that I shouldn't have played because I put myself in his hands, trusting to his honesty and his generosity. And he had neither. That's what I meant about not being operational.

So, when the Sicily film got challenged, we won every battle about why the structure should stay the way it was, but they whittled away at it. That's why we took out more of the baby, trying to satisfy them, until finally, they just came in and took possession of the film and that was it. Ultimately we quit, but we were really fired. They destroyed the film, but I later got a copy of it. It's remarkable that it survived. Someone at NBC, knowing the film was going to be destroyed, took the original film and sound elements out of the vault and copied them before they were destroyed. So we had the copies and put the film together, mixed it and finished it.

ETA: But in order to cancel the film without confronting the ulterior political motives, they had to discredit you and Roemer as well.

RY: Right. They announced the film "wasn't up to their standards." And I had won all of these awards by this time, which made it all the more difficult, for them as well as for me, because reporters were coming around asking what was wrong with this program. And that's why Mike and I left. We said, "OK, now we're going to make something that nobody can take away from us." And that film became *Nothing But a Man* (1964).

I had brought Mike in to NBC to do the Sicily film after I had made four films and was very successful there. So when we decided to do our own film, we both knew it had to be something that we could be involved in equally. And we knew we couldn't be doing something else for television; we had to do a story film.

Now, Mike is a much better writer than I am, and he already had some stories he was working on. But as we talked about them, I felt that they were his personal stories and we needed something that we could share. One of his stories later became the second film we did, *The Plot Against Harry*, but first we needed something more universal. In Sicily, we had made a film about the world, about poverty, about people. And I had been in the South making this film *Sit-In*, and we both were deeply concerned about what was happening in our country. I personally had a very strong feeling that if our country didn't solve its racial problems, if we couldn't learn to respect one another, then I didn't think the country would make it. And so we said, "OK, let's make a film about what it's like to be a black man trying to stand up for himself," just as we had tried to stand up for ourselves at NBC. I mean, that experience had a tremendous amount to do with it and gave us the energy.

So we raised $15,000—$5000 from my brother and $5000 from a friend of mine and $5000 from a lawyer friend of my friend, someone who believed in all this—and we set south in Mike's old car, the one that we used in the film. Five thousand dollars was for Mike, $5000 was for me, and $5000 was for our expenses, and that's all we ever took for a period of about two years during which time we traveled south, wrote the script and made the movie. We started in South Carolina, at the home of one of the students I had become friends with while making the *Sit-In* movie. Her father was a preacher. We started with her family, and we were passed on south through a kind of underground railroad going in the reverse direction, from one black family to another. We worked our way all the way down to New Orleans.

It was on that trip that we really began to write the story. Mike had also been working on another aspect of the story, because Mike had not known his father well, and that became an important element in our narrative—Duff Anderson's looking for his father who had abandoned him. I probably brought in more of the social concerns about race, and Mike put in the personal aspects. We were a good combination. We cared about one another, and we had dialogue during the course of *discovering* the film.

Anyway, we went south, we wrote the story, we came back, and we tried to raise the money to film it. The industry was clearly not interested: who's going to invest in a film about black people written by first-time directors? The only way we imagined we could make it was by raising money from our friends, and my brother, who ran DuArt, the family film laboratory, was the biggest contributor in money and in services. He was very brave about it. Our budget was $230,000 and we raised about $190,000, so we were $40,000 short. Since Mike and I were general partners, we had to come up with that money ourselves. My brother helped me on my side, and Mike did it on his own, but we each had to put in about $20,000 of our own money.

We had a very tiny crew, and in the course of shooting the film, which took about ten weeks, we had an investment from some friends of Mike who had an industrial company in Massachusetts. They supplied an assistant cameraman and one electrician and one grip for six weeks. These were really neat guys and they were very good, but they had really only done industrial kinds of films. After the six weeks, they left and we still had another four weeks to go. A friend of mine, Phil Clarkson, had a nursery and acted as our location manager. He knew southern New Jersey, and he helped us find all locations. He could do anything physical; he was just a brilliant guy at putting things together and he became our complete crew electrician. He learned how to tie in, and I placed all the lights myself. But that was the crew we had left — Phil Clarkson, myself, a young guy who did our clap sticks, another guy, a wonderful young black man, who was also like a general assistant, and the woman who did the costumes. But there was no production designer; there was no art director. We painted the walls ourselves, and essentially we used what we found. So it was just a crew of a few people, and we had to work very simply, but I'm very proud of that.

ETA: In *Nothing But a Man*, you were moving from documentary to narrative film. Did you have to learn how to shoot differently or did you adapt the techniques you already knew? For example, how did you work with professional actors?

RY: Well, Mike and I both had a very similar aesthetic, which, I think, had much to do with being in the moment, and we wrote it that way. But it was not an improvisational kind of film at all. The actors stuck to the script. And Mike directed the actors and I directed the camera. One of the limitations for me was that, because it was so written, I felt the camera work became more static. Still, I tried not to give you the images that would be expected. I tried to put the camera always where I thought the story was. For example, when Abbey Lincoln and Ivan Dixon meet in the bus station and he proposes to her, I put the camera right next to Abbey. Ivan is leaning in to her so that she's in profile and he's full face. I thought that's where the story was, this guy making this very, very personal request, "Will you marry me?" in this public place and playing it so intimately. But because it was so scripted and a lot of the decisions had been made before, I didn't have the potential for the kind of spontaneity that you can have in another kind of film. Later, making ¡*Alambrista!* (1978), which I wrote and shot and directed, I was able to leave much more story up in the air. So ¡*Alambrista!* is closer to me in terms of the stylistic way I work because I had more freedom. I didn't have to confer with another person about the script, and I think the camera work was more spontaneous.

But that doesn't mean that one is better than the other. *Nothing But a Man* was more thought out. Mike and I talked about things — the script and the performances and the camera work. I told Mike what I wanted to do, and he would make his comments and I listened. There never were any real differences. We would always arrive at the same place because we had the same vision. It was a satisfying kind of film for us to make and it spoke of how we felt about ourselves and what we felt black people were going through at that time. I remember one person criticizing the script, saying that Duff wouldn't go back and chop cotton. Maybe most people *wouldn't* have gone back; maybe they *would* have abandoned the kid and the marriage. But Mike and I felt that stories aren't about what the consensus would be, that the story should be about some kind of *new* sensibility. What was important to us was that Duff *did* go back and take his kid and says to the woman, "I'm going to *persist*, even if I have to chop cotton. They're not running me out of this place. This is my place, too." Just as Mike and I were saying, "They're not running us out of making films. We're going to make this *other* film that you can't take away from us. Yeah, we may have to hunker down and we're not going to make any money and it may be hard and maybe you won't like distributing it and maybe you won't put it in your theaters, but we're going to make it." And that was the attitude.

ETA: There was a long time, almost fifteen years, between *Nothing But a Man* and *¡Alambrista!*, your next feature film. What roads were you taking during that time?

RY: After *Nothing but a Man*, we had lots of offers to do big studio films. For example, we were offered *Goodbye, Columbus*. But when I say "we," it was essentially Mike because Mike was the director of *Nothing But a Man*. Now, this was something I had agreed to. I had said, "Mike, you're the director, it shouldn't be shared." It was not as if Mike were angling for it or anything like that. I felt that he was directing the actors and he really deserved the credit as the director, while I was the director of photography. We had written the story together; we had been on this journey together; we respected each other that way; and that was enough for me. But *tactically*, in terms of career, which is a way I had never thought about it, the fact that I wasn't also a director was devastating. People would come to Mike asking, "What do you guys want to do?" They weren't coming to me.

Actually, the next thing we did was option Elie Wiesel's book *Dawn* for about $15,000. It was a wonderful book. For some reason, we didn't do it, but that's when I became interested in reading the literature of the Holocaust, which led, ultimately, to my making *Triumph of the Spirit* (1989). If we had done *Dawn*, I don't know who would have directed it, or whether we could have done it together, which I'm not even sure is possible.

But Mike also had in his head a story called *The Plot Against Harry*, which was about this Jewish gangster. It was this comedic thing, and I thought it was terrific. We started writing it together but it wasn't working for lots of reasons, so I stepped out of the writing. I really did a lot of the producing in it, and I directed the camera. Like *Nothing But a Man*, it was shot in black and white, which I loved. Since I'm partially color-blind, I think I'm more sensitive to light than color.

After we finished shooting, Mike worked on the film while I supported the company financially. I must have put over $80,000 that I earned for the company into that film, money that I had earned so that we could support the process. I never resented that Mike's job was to make that film as good as he possibly could, and that my job was to keep the company going by earning the money. In fact, I felt very lucky because I fell into shooting a whole series of commercials for Exxon and Volvo and other people, and I was making a lot of money. I did that for a year and then I was asked to join one of the biggest commercial firms as a partner. I must have brought in $500,000 in one year, in the 1960s, and that was a tremendous amount of money then. I mean, I was making more than the President. I started thinking a lot about money. I started to feel arrogant, and it really frightened me. And so I quit, completely, because it scared me and I went back to just doing documentaries.

It was during this time that I made this film about sharks with Peter Gimbel (*In the World of Sharks*, 1966). For three weeks, we were swimming from 20 to 120 miles out off Montauk, along the edge of the Gulf Stream, chumming and looking for a great white shark. We brought up some major sharks, sometimes six, seven, twelve-foot sharks swimming around us. You had to learn to look not only from side to side, but also above and below when the sharks were about. Sometimes I had to hit them on the nose or push them away when they came at me. For one of the shots, they left me in the ocean—I had a cage with me, but I wasn't in it; I was free swimming—and I wanted to get a shot of the ship coming over the horizon. They didn't have to go all *that* far, but they had to go until I was out of sight. Then they turned around and came back to me, because I wanted to get that shot of the ship coming at me.

The captain with us was a famous shark hunter named Frank Munvees, who became the model for Quint in *Jaws*. Our film helped to inspire Peter Benchley's book. I know about the movie, but I've only seen little snippets when I've come upon it by accident on television. I've never watched the whole thing. I don't want to have those kinds of images in my head when I'm out at sea.

But then, eventually, I felt that I had to go my own way because *Harry* was still Mike's film. I mean, Mike and I remained very close. Our friendship never ended, but I felt that I had to move out on my own because Mike had his own ideas about what he wanted to do, and I was now a filmmaker myself and I couldn't just follow him as his cameraman. There was an incident in *The Plot Against Harry* where that became very clear to me. I was talking to this guy preparing to film a scene and Mike said, innocently and quite rightly, "Bob, let's go, we got to get this done." And I realized that I *needed* to be talking to this guy in order to know how to shoot it. I knew that I wasn't serving my own vision and that I was really losing some of myself. That led to the dissolution of the partnership, and I decided that I had to go off on my own.

But there were also things happening in my personal life during this time. I had left a marriage and was in love with somebody else. And I also made a film about the artist William Kurelek (*The Maze*, 1971) that further changed me. Kurelek was an extraordinary man who had tried to commit suicide three times. His father had rejected him as an artist, but that's who he was. Kurelek had converted to Catholicism to find a more perfect father in Jesus, and he did many things that were works of servitude. He made picture frames, for example. He didn't just do the things that were popular, that people wanted to buy. I mean, he was very, very successful, but he was also very modest. And I was in this tremendous personal struggle at that point in my life, asking if I weren't just serving myself and my own ego and my own needs. I was in a tremendous dilemma, and making this film was very hard on me because his example, in a sense, challenged where I was going in my own life.

But at the same time I could see in his work these *repressed* feelings; there was always something about to explode in the background. And I knew I had to go my own way. I couldn't just have this kind of denial of the forces that were operating in my own life. I had to give voice to them. So I embarked on this new life, both personally and professionally.

It was a rocky road, and I tried many things. I did the shark film and I did a series of films on Eskimos (*The Eskimo: Fight for Life*, 1970). I taught Milos Forman's class at Columbia one year, and I taught at the Yale Drama School along with Mike Roemer. We had these really great people in the class — Sam Shepard, John Guare, Megan Terry. It's where I met Eddie Pomerantz, whom I've worked with a lot over the years. He and I did *Caught* (1996) together, based on his novel. At one point a group of yogis, who had seen *Cortile Cascino* and the Eskimo film, came to me and said I had been selected, that I was a yogi or was going to be one (laughs) and they wanted me to make a film about Baba Ram Dass (Richard Alpert), which I did. For a while I went off to live in a yogi retreat of silence, and I sort of followed Yogi Sachadinanda, although I wasn't really a disciple or anything like that. I've never been able to be involved in any kind of movement that closely. But I was very influenced by the experience. And I also went off to live on an Indian reservation in Montana for three months, and I wrote a screenplay that I wish I had gotten to make. But I didn't know how to get to make anything at this time, so I spent almost a year just reading Native American literature. I even had an Indian name. Still, it wasn't as if I were walking around in robes or anything. I was very much the same guy. I even had a motorcycle for a while, but I gave it up when I realized I could get killed. I knew I had responsibilities since I had three children, so I gave the bike away. You can see I was never *really* a free spirit.

Then, in the late 1960s I met Mike Dann, the vice president of programming for CBS. This was in the days when CBS was the top network, and he was one of the most powerful people in the country. He had seen *Nothing But a Man* and loved it, and he offered me a film called *J. T.* (1971), which was about a little black boy in Harlem. Actually, it had been offered to Mike Roemer first, but Mike didn't want to make it. He didn't relate to it. So I made this film and it was a big success and won a Peabody award. The head of CBS saw it and I was really, like, hot, you know. It was first planned as a Saturday noon show for kids, an hour show, but then they preempted *Gunsmoke*, the number one show at the time, and played it at eight o'clock Monday night. They took full pages out in the *New York Times*, and it got all these raves. Actually, I thought it was a sweet film but derivative, although all the people involved in it were wonderful. The writer was Jane Wagner, a lovely, good woman, who later wrote *Signs of Intelligent Life in the Universe* for Lily Tomlin.

Anyway, Mike Dann wanted to see more of my work. CBS was in a ratings war with NBC, and so I told him about my Eskimo film and he looked at it and he loved it. He said, "Make an hour special out of this," and I did, and it won the Emmy for the best documentary of the year. So he said, "What do you want to do?" and I said, "Look, let's do a series of films on cultures that are threatened, that are becoming extinct. There's so much that's being lost in the world!" I was enthusiastic and excited because *this* was the direction that I wanted to go in my life. It was the idea of making films, telling stories from *inside* cultures. You would go into the culture, and you wouldn't know what the heck it's all about, really, and then you'd begin to learn about it. I live on a pretty narrow spectrum, and some of the things that came to me took me into areas that were very valuable in helping me to learn more about other people and to learn more about the world. So I took — and still take — these opportunities when they came. In the next few years I went to the Serengeti (*Man of the Serengeti*, 1972) and lived with Indians (*Navajo Girl*, 1972) and crossed part of the Kalahari Desert with some Bushmen (*Bushmen of the Kalahari*, 1974) and tracked these great apes through the jungle (*The Great Apes*, 1975). I was always going into some new territory, and my life was expanded with each trip. I almost died tracking the apes. I got very sick and was in the hospital with a very high fever, and I had all these hallucinations that were very, very strange. Even now I'm being asked to go to places, like to China to film the pandas (*China: The Panda Adventure*, 2002). But I'll do it only if I think it's interesting or worth doing. No matter what the financial rewards are, I won't do it if I'm not interested or if I don't think I might make a contribution.

Anyway, during these experiences I was learning more and more about the power of situation in film. Because you'd talk to one person and this informant would tell you something, and then you'd talk to another informant and you'd ask about some of the same things and he'd have a completely different point of view. And I continued to ask myself, how do you deal with these contradictory points of view and include both people in the film? And I saw that the answer was *situation*, that in situations people could have completely different attitudes and behavior, but if the audience understood the situation, the audience would be positioned so that they could appreciate the behavior. And then I didn't have to be *telling*. Now you could look at the behavior and draw your own conclusions. And that was for me a huge, huge discovery that I was always looking for, how to tell a story without imposing on the story.

ETA: You were making the viewer take an active part in telling the story.

RY: Yes, that's what I wanted to do in these films. I wanted it to be just like in life. And, you know, most documentaries weren't being made that way. The Eskimo films are a good example. Asen Balickci, who was the anthropologist in charge of them, saw the Sicily movie and asked me to critique the films they had done so far. The other filmmakers involved in the project were anthropologists, and they had had their cameras on tripods and were staying back so that they wouldn't interfere with their subjects. I looked at the films and thought they were very interesting and exciting. I loved the Inuit and I loved seeing them and the textures and the faces, but everything was being filmed from *outside*. And I said, "No, you can't stay at a distance. To think that you're capturing it because you're not interfering is malarkey." I felt it was telling more about the filmmakers than about what they were trying to observe. It was the other end of the telescope. What they saw is what they were *able to see*, but what they avoided and how they put it together told more about them than the ostensible subject.

I wanted the films to be much more experiential. I came in at the end of the series. I did, I think, the last four films, in the winter camp. And in my films, I wanted to be *with* the Eskimos. I filmed inside their dwellings. I traded punches with them in their games. I wanted to *be* an Eskimo. I thought, "My God, the other filmmakers never get to see the look in the husband's face when his wife has something in her eye and he puts his mouth over her eye and sucks, licks her eye to clean it. I want to see his face and her face! I wanted to be *inside* the situation, not standing at a distance with the camera on a tripod." But you also have to be willing to take *responsibility* for being inside, for destroying literal truth in order to present the deeper truth of the people you're filming. That's what I was talking about earlier.

Look, I don't claim to be an artist, but I am passionate about what I do. I have to stand up for that, because otherwise I'm not true to myself. This is what I was learning at this point in my career.

ETA: It sounds like by the time you did *¡Alambrista!* (1978), which was another feature film, although with strong documentary overtones, you had reached a crisis point both in your personal and artistic life. In this film, you were beginning to put into practice a lot of these ideas that had long been fermenting.

RY: Yes. In *¡Alambrista!*, I would set up real situations and then I'd move inside with my camera. And I'd shoot very quickly. And then I would do it again and would see what I had missed the first time. I might even say to somebody, "Look, stay longer, do that other job. Instead of picking this many tomatoes, do twice as many." Because I knew then the timing would be better when they came back. I've sometimes used the analogy of a surfer: you're riding a wave and feel the exhilaration of being in the moment and of having things moving under your feet. And when you film, the ground is *literally* moving under your feet, so there's no safe place to stay. You have to be balanced in the moment because if you lose your balance, you're finished. So you must be internally connected, always. It can't be what somebody else said or a consensus of ideas. Of course, I do listen to suggestions and criticisms, and I say, "Ah, I have to make this adjustment. OK, let's do it again," but now the wave starts and I'm on it again.

I think I'm more in touch because not knowing exactly what's going to happen and being allowed to incorporate that into the living moment is what, to me, filmmaking is all about. The story, what happens, is the ultimate truth, and that's the structure you're presenting, but the way you get there is what's so exciting and exhilarating. I like to be going for the moment when everything is trembling and nothing is really set but you're going with it and you're making the choices. And that's the way it was shooting *¡Alambrista!*. Some scenes didn't work, and they're not in the movie. And some scenes could be better, but this is what I did. I was an active participant; I was shooting it myself.

ETA: Is this the way you still work today? For example, you have a cameraman now on your films. You're not directing and doing the camera work at the same time.

RY: It depends. Mike Barrow, my cameraman, will give me the camera on certain situations — "Bob, you do it." — because I can't be saying what to do when it's happening. But he's such a sensitive guy and we shoot very much alike so that when the things are more set up, Mike can do it. There's the scene in *Caught* where Eddie Olmos dies, I shot that, or when the son is in the fish store blowing bubbles and everything is moving around. That would have been such a complex scene to do with dollies and everything like that and trying to tell Mike what I wanted. So I took the camera hand-held and I shot it in about five different takes. I knew how I was going to be able to cut it, so that I could say to Maria [Conchita Alonzo], "Maria, take a little bit longer with cutting that fish before you turn," and I knew how it was going to piece together. The cameraman would never have known how I wanted it.

Another example: I remember driving in to the set, and we were going to do this scene where Arie Verveen was going to make love to the wife for the first time, as it was written in the script, on the bed. And I had had this idea that something was going to fall over and a parrot was going to say something and scare them, and I was so excited about that, that I was not thinking deeply enough about the scene. And I find that very often you don't think deeply enough about the scene until you're doing it, because part of it has to come out of the moment of seeing the actors and seeing physically what you can really do. So I don't storyboard in that way, because I don't want it to be set. I want to be open and free to the potentials of what could happen.

ETA: Is this true of the actors as well?

RY: Oh, yes. I want them always exploring the scene. Sure, they think about how they're going to do it, but I want them to dismiss it, play it funny, play it sad, try all kinds of things in their exploration, and then forget about it all and not have any idea about what they're going to do, because you don't know what's going to happen. Then, as things happen, they react to them.

But to complete the example: So we're filming *Caught* and we're driving in the car on the way to shoot this scene I just described, and on the way Arie, who's very sensitive, says to me, "Bob, I don't know. Somehow the bed seems sort of *public*, you know, even though they're in the privacy of the bedroom." As soon as he says the word "public," I *know*. When we get to the set, I explore the room, and they have a big closet. The closet! At that moment, I *knew* that's the way I was going to do the scene. It was just like that, and I shot it. I stationed myself in the closet, and they start embracing and kissing and I said, "Look, just push yourselves into the closet and go for it." Everybody knows at that point what we're doing. It's not a big mystery, and I don't want to say anything explicit. I've stationed myself where

I know I'm going to be right for when they come in, and they're going to come into the clothing and knock things over and I'm going to be shooting. I shot it in one take, and that was it. And at a certain moment, she knocks something over in the closet and there's a bang and the parrot says something. I made a motion and somebody banged something. I didn't know at which moment I was going to do it. But that's riding the wave, and it takes a kind of boldness like that, and, OK, if you don't get it, then you do it again. Maybe you get it better, or sometimes maybe you don't get it as good, but I'm prepared to do it the first time.

ETA: After ¡*Alambrista!*, you turned almost completely to feature films, and you did quite a variety of subjects, from prison drama in *Short Eyes* (1979) to a comedy about the upper crust in New York (*Rich Kids*, 1980) to Paul Simon's film *One Trick Pony* (1981). It must have been an exciting time for you.

RY: Oh, sure. You know, I don't get asked to do any Hollywood films any more. I used to be asked all the time to do major — I should say, expensive — films, and I would criticize the script and that usually was the end of it. I was asked to do *Never Cry Wolf* (1983), and I met with the writer, who was the producer's wife. I loved the book and I wanted to make the film because I love the Arctic, and they were actually using some of the Eskimos from my Eskimo films. All that would have been great. But they really didn't have very much about Eskimos in it, and I thought there were some other things that should be done to get deeper into it. But when I talked to the writer, I felt she would be resistant to some of the things that I was thinking, and so I backed away when I was asked to do it.

ETA: Who ended up directing that? Carroll Ballard.

RY: Yes, Carroll Ballard, who also did *The Black Stallion*. I don't know him but I think he's a very talented guy. But I never went to see *Never Cry Wolf*. It would have been too hard for me to see it. It still is.

It's odd, because I'm a very mild, inoffensive person who wants to be liked; that's one of my biggest faults. I'm not confrontational. As a result, some of my experiences have turned out not to be enjoyable experiences. The Paul Simon movie, *One Trick Pony*, is an example. I had just done *Rich Kids* with John Lithgow and Trini Alvarado, which was a pleasure. My agent liked that picture and brought me Paul Simon's script. I should have known better, but Paul is a very interesting, talented guy, and I was flattered that he wanted me to do it. I think ego partly betrayed me in this case: I don't know what work of mine he had seen, and later he spoke very critically of something I had done that he didn't like, maybe *Short Eyes* (1979). Why did Paul turn to me? I don't know.

Anyway, we talked. I had a lot of ideas about what I wanted to do with the music. He had written all these songs, and I thought we ought to rehearse to the music: the actors could have little ear wigs and they could hear the songs as we were filming and we could shoot to the rhythm. And sometimes the song would stop and a line would come and then it would syncopate. Some of it would have been a little bit more like MTV, which didn't exist in those days. I wanted to liberate some of the story from where it was rooted and have the camera moving around the room while the song is going on and then catch pieces of the conversation. I had a whole bunch of ideas, and at first Paul was very interested. And then summer came and I thought we were going to be working and rehearsing, and I wanted to go more on location with the band. He had written the script and knew what was in it, but I wanted him to be open to rewriting it and making it much more unexpected. So I would say things to Paul, and he would listen and then maybe walk away. He was so strange. He would be affectionate one day and the next day he'd walk by me and wouldn't say hello.

But at least I didn't get fired. I think I'm the only director who ever worked with him on anything through a whole project. At first, he told me that he liked very much the way I was directing him. But then he got an acting coach when he should have been coming to me. And there were always so many people, sycophants, people who wanted to be involved, hanging around. There were times when we got along great, but he had written the script and he didn't want to explore a lot of things I did. He didn't want to be very demanding on himself, and that's what my job was, so it didn't work out.

ETA: You've made movies developed from your own ideas, and you've made films for hire, where you don't have the final say. How far are you willing to push it, to keep the film as close to your intention as possible?

RY: Quite honestly, I take myself on the one hand very seriously, and on the other hand I really don't. I always have this other eye that goes away from me and looks down and says, "Who do you think you are? Have some sense of proportion about your life and about what you're doing." And I need to make money, of course, but, still, it's too painful to do something that you don't really care about, or, just as bad, something that you think is not serving the truth. I don't think that I ever wanted to be a success. Maybe there's something lacking in me. But it's too important to me, it's too connected to things that I believe in, to make films just as a journeyman.

Extremities (1986) is a film that I turned down at first because it was being financed by Atlantic Pictures and I didn't trust them, and there were a lot of things I didn't like in the script. It is about a brutal rape, and I didn't want to be involved until my daughter encouraged me to do it because she felt it could make an important statement about the subject if it were done honestly. So I did it. But quite often when you're doing a movie that's not a studio film, there's a bond company involved. And the director has to sign off on the budget, saying that you really think you can do it for that amount of money. I was nervous about it because the schedule was so tight, but somehow I figured that I could do it. So I agreed, and we had to shoot the film in something like thirty days. And then, somehow, they never asked me to sign the bond, so we started the movie without it. By the middle of the second week, I was several days behind. Farrah Fawcett, the star, was not the easiest person to work with, and there were a lot of technical things that were difficult on this film. We were shooting in one room and it's all happening in one afternoon and we had to control the lighting as the time kept advancing and all that was very complicated

Anyway, we started shooting, and finally they remembered, and they came to me and said, "Bob, sign the bond." Well, when I looked at it, the first thing I saw was that they'd taken a week out of the shooting schedule. It was going to be difficult to do it as scheduled without going over, and if we did go over, the bond company had the right to come in and take over the production and tell us what to do because it's now their money. And here they were taking out a week. So, I said, "I'm not signing it." And again, here's me, I'm a nice guy and I'm not confrontational and want everybody to like me, but I'm saying, "I'm not signing it." And it continues. "If you don't sign it by the end of the day, we don't come to work tomorrow." "I'm not signing it." "You're a journeyman director. When we tell you to do scenes in a certain way, you do them!" "I'm not signing it."

The next day I talk to the producers. Now, producers hate to hear the director tell them something about production, which is their responsibility, but I said, "You don't need a bond. We're going to finish this film; there's nothing to worry about." And they had seen and loved the dailies, for I really had some very powerful performances, beyond what they had expected, so they had to treat me with a little bit of respect, although they probably thought I was very arrogant. But I said, "You don't need a bond. You'll save a quarter of a million dollars without it, which will pay for one week's shooting, and then you'll need only another week to keep on schedule." They didn't want to do it, but they did, and they ended up making something like $35 million on the film. So, yeah, I'm willing to push it for the sake of making a good film. You've got to be willing to do that, or you shouldn't be making films.

ETA: You've had films like *¡Alambrista!* and *Short Eyes* and others that have had a second life. They get rediscovered later, as is happening now with *¡Alambrista!*. How do you react to that?

RY: Well, you're right, that is happening to me. There have been retrospectives of my films at the National Museum of Art and the National Gallery in Washington, and in other places. I certainly appreciate it. I am almost 80, you know.

ETA: Sure, although I don't get the sense that you're running out of time. But of the films you've done, are there others that you would love to see rediscovered?

RY: Well, I think the Sicily film, *Cortile Cascino*, is a really good film. It may be the best thing I've done. And I'm very proud of the film my son and daughter-in-law made, *Children of Fate* (1992), where they revisited this family years later. But you can learn something from any of the films, I think, even the ones that weren't that personal to me. *Roosters* (1995), for example, was not my film, not my story. I was brought in to replace the first director after shooting had already begun and it just wasn't working. But I can still show you what I did because the film represents found opportunities to make something that's not yours but to which you still bring parts of yourself, your life and your experiences, your theory, your aesthetics.

And, you know, it's never that clear cut anyway, what belongs to whom. I always honor the writers of my films; I am very respectful of their work. The most extreme example of this relationship was on *Short Eyes*. Miguel Piñero had written the play, but other guys, real prisoners, had also worked on adding to the script. And the first director wasn't honoring their work. I replaced him when the actors, ex Sing-Sing prisoners, said he would be killed if he came back the next week. And something *would* have happened to him. We shot it in the Tombs in New York City, and maybe he wouldn't have been killed, but he would have fallen off a gallery or something. When these guys had finally found some kind of meaning in their lives, they were not going to let it be destroyed by somebody who didn't care and was going to do his own movie and make money off of them, not when they had finally earned respect for the first time in their lives. And from that point of view they were right. Maybe a little extreme, but right. He couldn't come in and take over their work like that. But I respected their work, and I respected Piñero, although he was in terrible condition at this time. He was a sad guy, but he was also an amazing guy.

You see, in all my films I make a clear distinction: there's the writer and I'm the director. But things happen on the set. In *Caught*, for example, Eddie Pomerantz did the writing. It's an adaptation of his novel. But some of the things in *Caught* are mine. Ideas, lines, the foot thing in the film was completely my idea. I created that moment. That wasn't in the script.

ETA: That's a great scene.

RY: Yes, and I came up with that. And the ending came really from the cameraman, Mike Barrow. He said there had to be a blood sacrifice. Originally, there was a knife fight and then they throw the knife in the water and walk away from each other. But there were no consequences. And Mike said that there had to be consequences, and he was right. But, in the end, Eddie was the writer and deserved the credit. The story originated with Eddie.

ETA: It's clear that you're always open to collaboration.

RY: Absolutely. It's essential. You know, films don't have to solve the questions, but they do have to take the audience to the leading edge, to the place where we, in our own lives, have to face the challenge of who we are. It doesn't have to solve this question, because the next moment is never really known anyway, is it? And I honestly don't care about the solution. I don't think there ever *needs* to be a solution. What's important is the taking you to the point where you make the brave decision and you do the thing that is going to make you confront who you are as a human. Then whatever happens, happens, because solving something is almost reductive. I'm not saying that things don't get solved, but there's still the life that goes on, and it's ultimately not about solving, it's about facing.

It's like in the movie I'm now making, *Below the Belt* (2004), which is based on the play by Rick Dresser. There's this scene where Hanrahan had just said to the other character, Dobbit, "Well, you've been a perfect little gentleman," and then Dobbit says, "Why don't you like me?" And Hanrahan says, "Does it matter?" And Dobbit says, "Yes, because I don't want to be alone." And Hanrahan replies, "We're all alone." And then Dobbit says, "Can you at least meet me halfway?" And Hanrahan says, "I'll meet you a third of the way," and Dobbit says, "Well, that's a start, but there will be no more gutter talk about my wife." End of the scene.

Now, I've been working with this scene, and I've taken out, I think, maybe too much. I took out "Because I don't want to be alone." I left in "Why don't you like me?" and "Does it matter?" I think that's good, but then the other line—"Because I don't want to be alone"—I think is weak. And then Hanrahan says, "We're all alone." I liked the performance immensely, and the line works, but right now I don't think it's necessary. It fills in the space, but I think that when you take out the line, there's more reverberation because you're jumping off at a more interesting place from "Why don't you like me?"/"Does it matter?" than from "I don't want to be alone."/"We're all alone." Those last lines are more reductive; it takes the scene to this "We're all alone" kind of statement, which everybody knows anyway. But "Why don't you like me?"/"Does it matter?" Wow! That's a much bolder kind of place to leave someone. There's more to think about. It's a much more gripping kind of question, because we're all asking that question at different points in relationships, and "Does it matter?"—what a remark! Because in a way, it *doesn't* matter in terms of who I am. I have to be who I am and I have to do what I have to do whether you like it or not, or whether you like *me* or not. That's a much bigger question, and a much more important place to leave the audience than "We're all alone."

OK. Now, here's the thing. I love all of the dialogue, and I definitely run all this by Rick, the writer, because it *is* his work. It took me a while to think about it and say, "Rick, let's take this out." But you know what? When you do it, the acting becomes more powerful! The actors are doing the same performances, of course — it's already on film — and this is the intersection where you see what the writing does and how it gives the actors the opportunity to perform. But the editing can *also* make the difference between the performance being a *good* performance or one that takes you into some other kind of place where the performance is even greater. And this is what I love about making film.

ETA: So the editing actually changes the quality of the performances?

RY: Yes, and this is what makes editing so fascinating. You change the reality from this to that. The actors are long gone. Their performances are on film, but they continue to change. And in this case, I think they get stronger.

ETA: You're finishing up *Below the Belt* now. What's next?

RY: I often get asked to look at other people's scripts and projects. For example, I'm very close to Edward James Olmos — we've worked together on a lot of films — and I help him a lot with his writing, although he's a good writer without me. So I actually end up spending a lot of time on other people's things without pay, but that's how I meet people and sometimes become involved. That's one of my weaknesses, but as I've said, there's a lot you learn by lending yourself to different experiences. Otherwise I'd just be narrowly in my own little box. I don't have to, but I'm *inclined* to go for any bait where I think there's potentially something very good or unexpected or interesting. You never know how things will connect.

I've also got this script I wrote years ago that I keep coming back to, an adventure story called "Bird of Paradise." This script is very important to me, because I have spent a lot of time in New Guinea, and I learned a lot about the indigenous people there. As I told you, I was there during World War II, and I went back in 1968 for about four months, on patrols, and I've read a lot of books about the mind-set of tribal people. I love the idea of going off into the jungles and not knowing what's going to happen. It's scary! It's not as if I like being scared, but I loved the idea of seeing new things. That's why I had this close relationship with Merian Cooper.

But "Bird of Paradise" even now is very, very important to me. At one point, I thought that if I didn't finish it, I would die, literally. I had this vision. Things were happening in my life and I was not well, and I had this

Edward James Olmos, director and star of *American Me*, with Sean Daniel, and Robert Young, who produced the film for his friend.

dream that I was washing my plate, a white plate so really it's the mandala, and I was washing it in a sink like a laundry room sink, but I was in a kitchen somehow. And the sink was here and the door was here and the door was pushed opened part of the way. And I heard a voice calling me to come, and I knew it was Death. I was terrified. I just wanted to run. But somehow, and I don't know how I did it, but somehow in the dream I *jumped out* through the door and went "RAAAA!" you know, and I saw this cowled figure in the hood standing there, and then it disappeared, and I woke up. I had shouted and woke up, but it was in a context where I knew I had to finish the screenplay, because I had been working on the script for fifteen years. I knew I had to finish the script; otherwise, I wasn't going to make it. And I went back to work on it and actually I finished it.

"Bird of Paradise" is almost completely mine, but I brought in Eddie Pomerantz near the end because I was having trouble with some scenes and he really helped me. But all the characters and the action and all of the situations, I created and wrote by myself. I've come close to making it several times. Right now we're trying to get the financing for it, at a modest level,

1. Interview with Robert M. Young (Arnold)

Robert Young with Arie Verveen on the set of *Caught*.

like $8 million or something like that. But then it depends on the actors, whether you get more or not. So I don't know if it's going to really happen. People are interested, so maybe next summer. We'll see.

    The other thing I'm up for — I don't think I'll get it — is the biography of Cesar Chavez. I have a great idea of how to do it, and I told them about it, and I said they could use it if they wanted to whether I directed or not.

I would love to see the movie made properly. But, I'm not Latino, so I think it's not going to happen, but that's OK. It would be a lovely thing to do, and a very worthwhile film because his life was so interesting. The whole thrust of the film is that, when you see his life, you have to think, "My God, anyone can be a saint. The power that was in Chavez, the power that can transform the world, is in everybody. All they have to do is just make a simple little decision to give up something and serve others. All you have to do is do that, and you could be Mother Teresa or Cesar Chavez."

That's what my story is about. It takes you into what his childhood was like and how he was a migrant worker and how he didn't get to go to school. But later, he didn't allow bodyguards, and the power came to him because of that kind of simplicity and that sense of abnegation. He never made more than $6000 a year, and he never owned his own house, really. It's the idea of the potential, the possibility, in every human.

ETA: Well, we've been at this a long time, but I want to get to at least one other big question. I want you to talk about the morality of filmmaking, your sense of your own moral responsibilities as a filmmaker as opposed to your artistic obligations, or in connection with those artistic obligations.

RY: Yes. Well, I think they are very strongly connected. One of the things that I often think about is that if you make a film and it's two hours long and a million people see it, that's *two million hours* taken up. I think about lifetimes wasted or lost just by watching something that I make. So if all I'm doing is *diverting* people, I'm using up their lives for something that really is not doing them any good. This seems to me to be something you have to be concerned about. I'm putting more stuff out into the world. I think it has to serve some kind of purpose.

ETA: Are there stories that you just wouldn't tell?

RY: Yes. It's not as if I want to be thought of as a prude. I've been offered many things that I've turned down because I thought that they didn't go *far enough*. And it's not as if I won't tell a story that deals with sex or sexual nature, because this is a tremendously important part of our lives. *Caught*, for example, is intensely erotic, and that's one of the reasons I did it. The young man coming in and getting caught up between his lust for this beautiful woman and his sense of loyalty and love for Joe, her husband, I think is a real dilemma. One of the things that Eddie Pomerantz and I explored is that it's just not all black and white. She becomes in a sense a younger woman and more alive, and in some ways the family is happier with him there.

ETA: And the young man becomes a better son to Joe than the son he already has.

RY: Absolutely. And I thought all those things were interesting, because so much in life is paradoxical, and part of the problem we have in living is that we expect some kind of simplicity. Stories, it seems to me, should be clear, but they've got to be obscure too. By that I mean that when they're *too* clear, they become simplistic, and when they're too obscure, you don't sometimes see them. Just as I think everybody's life always has these moments where you feel like God is testing you, and even if you are strong and face it and finally think, "Now I've mastered this," it comes back in another way to challenge you again. So that the things that happen to you in life — the births, the deaths, the divorces, the rebellious children — all of these things are testing you. Our interest in stories has to do with the fact that they are all relevant to all of us. We're all being tested.

I also believe that, in an existentialist way of thinking, you give meaning to who you are by how you act. You give a meaning to what it is to be a human. And so, the stories that I want to tell are stories that give this meaning to what it is to be a human, and that puts a demand on the stories. That means that the story can't be frivolous. It can be funny, because I think humor gives a sense of proportion. But it has to have some essential meaning.

Look, I'm not some kind of a moralist. I'm not on some kind of platform. But there are these things that I just *know*. I won't make a film if I think that it's doing harm to people, or if I think that it's not going to take them to some kind of understanding of their lives. I also can't make something that I don't think I can bring something to, that — and I hope this doesn't sound arrogant — that somebody else could do just as easily. I know I've been very privileged in my life, and I'm grateful for the circumstances that have opened up so many opportunities to me. But I lament that there aren't more things done that relate to our lives, because I think the whole purpose of art is to help ground us, and a good story or painting is all about helping us to understand more deeply and experientially the way things really are. Serious art grounds you. It shows you life, both the beauty and the terror of it. It awakens in you the awareness of the mystery of existence.

I don't really understand life, but films are to me are about trying to restore the power to experience, to make experience new again. That's the core of what I believe and feel and think. It's what I fall back on to restore my faith in trying to make a movie.

ETA: There's no way for you to retire from making movies, is there?

RY: No. I couldn't stop trying to tell stories. I'm so poorly organized and the moment can capture me so intensely that I often lose my sense of direction, but there are so many things that I continue to be interested in that I would fail myself if I didn't follow them. As I say, everything in life is a story, and there is always in any story the inevitability of life. Time is inexorable, and we all are approaching an end. That's the power and mystery of any story.

So I'm not interested in doing the formulaic kind of film, and I don't want to do things that are just done for the surfaces. I think that's a betrayal. I get in trouble that way in this industry, not serious trouble because I'm not important enough and I'm not a challenge to the way things are done, but in my own little world I have to go in my own direction. But I wouldn't trade places with anyone in the world. Nobody could buy me with millions of dollars. You may be misguided, but who's to say that this guy who has this dream of El Dorado and is wandering out into the wilderness with his donkey and his shovel isn't doing a hell of a lot better than the guy who found the gold? I think it's the journey, it's the quest that's really what it's about. I don't know what the *logic* is in living, but the *act* of living is always fascinating.

Not that I've ever experienced real success, you know, except in minor ways. Some of the films that I've made have been praised and I've been treated with great respect as if I had really done something. It's certainly nice to have that happen, but it's hard to take it that seriously. I don't make a connection with it. As a matter of fact, I get to be embarrassed.

But the thing that *really* is great is having an idea and getting to do a scene. It doesn't even have to be your idea. It's the "How about this?" and the "Ah, that's it," and the "How are we going to do it?" and then the doing of it. That is what I love. It's the scene. You imagine it and work at it and then maybe it comes together. *That's* why I make movies.

2. NBC White Paper, Cortile Cascino, and the Assault on the Familiar
Craig Fischer

One of the finest achievements of Robert Young's early career is *Cortile Cascino* (1962), a documentary Young made with collaborator Michael Roemer for the NBC Network's anthology documentary series, *NBC White Paper*. *Cortile Cascino* explores in painful detail the lives of the inhabitants of a Sicilian slum, focusing particularly on the day-to-day experiences of members of an extended family, and became controversial when NBC refused to air it. The history of *Cortile Cascino* intersects with many important issues — the rise in television documentary in the early 1960s, the birth of cinéma vérité, the role of repetition and flow in television spectatorship — because the film functions as a perfect example of subversion. The form of *Cortile Cascino* is accessible and elegant, even as its content focuses on downtrodden people in brutal circumstances, but beneath the structure of the film are pointed challenges to televisual codes of storytelling. In the end, *Cortile Cascino*'s experimental *cri du coeur* violated too many of television's rules, even in an era when the networks were committed to documentary and social relevance.

Media critics call the early 1960s the "Golden Age of Television Documentary" for various reasons. As Young notes in his interview with Edwin Arnold, NBC began to make documentaries "to protect their reputation" after the quiz show scandals of the late 1950s. As Robert Redford's 1994 film *Quiz Show* dramatized, NBC's popular *Twenty-One* was one of the first shows investigated and revealed to the public as rigged, yet the quiz show disclosures were just one reason why the networks needed to improve their image during this period. There were other ethical lapses. As William Boddy writes,

Hal Roach Jr., flush with his studio's telefilm profits, acquired the Mutual Broadcasting System in 1958, and in January 1959 he and his partners negotiated an agreement — that became public by spring — with Dominican Republic dictator Rafael Trujillo: in exchange for $750,000, Mutual guaranteed 425 minutes a month of favorable news and commentary for the dictator. Later that year, national attention was captured by charges of payola and conflicts of interest in the radio and television industry, and of promotional "tie-ins," cases in which uncredited sponsors paid to have their products displayed on network programs.[1]

Such suspicious practices were, for some critics, a violation of television's responsibility to act in the public interest. Jack Gould of the *New York Times* saw TV as a symptom of the "spreading virus of materialism" in American culture, while esteemed broadcaster Edward R. Murrow accused television executives of sugarcoating the American *Zeitgeist*, of using "every instrument at their command to empty the minds of their subjects, and fill those minds with slogans, determination, and faith in the future."[2] Criticisms like Murrow's led the heads of ABC, CBS and NBC to reach an agreement in 1959 with FCC chairman John Doerfer to increase their documentary and public service programming.[3]

Despite this agreement, the vast majority of network shows were cookie-cutter action-adventure series. In the mid-1950s, the Warner Bros. studio signed an exclusive deal with the flagging ABC network to provide adventure programs, and scored their first hit with *Cheyenne* (1955–1963), a show whose enormous popularity established the western as the dominant genre on TV for the next ten years. Warners/ABC followed *Cheyenne* with *77 Sunset Strip* (1958–1964), *Hawaiian Eye* (1959–1963), *Bourbon Street Beat* (1959–1960) and *Surfside Six* (1960–62), shows which adhered to the same narrative formula — an exotic locale, a private eye or two, a wacky sidekick, a pretty girl — and which were produced in such a relentlessly Tayloristic fashion that many scripts originally produced for *77 Sunset Strip* were given only a cursory re-write before being used for one of the other programs.[4] Also, ABC aired the first season of the Desilu-produced The Untouchables (1959–1963) during the 1959–1960 season, and the show was quickly denounced by social scientists and government officials for its violence.[5] Shows like *77 Sunset Strip* and *The Untouchables*— and events like the quiz show scandal — led President Kennedy's FCC chair Newton Minow to famously proclaim television a "vast wasteland. You will see a procession of game shows, violence, audience participation shows, formula comedies about totally unbelievable families, blood and thunder, mayhem, violence, sadism, murder, Western badmen, Western goodmen, private eyes, gangsters, more violence and cartoons. And, endlessly, commercials — many screaming, cajoling, and offending. And, most of all, boredom."⁶ For the networks, then, documentary programming was an important public relations move; in the face of criticism from Murrow and Minow, the networks could point to documentary and news shows as evidence of civic service.

Sometimes, these programs were popular and financially wise, too. One obvious example was the four debates between Kennedy and Nixon televised on September 26, October 6, 13 and 21, 1960. As Erik Barnouw notes, "all the debates held vast audiences," with ratings never dipping below 61 million viewers.⁷ In 1962, the documentary *A Tour of the White House with Mrs. John F. Kennedy* aired on three of the four networks and pulled in the biggest audience of the season. Television historian Michael Curtin estimates that these high ratings, combined with extensive syndication of the program to other countries, boosted the viewership of *A Tour* to several hundred million.⁸ Curtin further argues that the subjects of the various television documentaries helped the networks earn formidable profits. By focusing primarily on international issues—the danger of the Communist "Other" and the importance of the Free World that comprised the middle ground between the U.S. and U.S.S.R.'s Cold War struggle—the documentaries served as implicit propaganda for the Kennedy administration's policies of Communist containment and neocolonization of Western Europe and Third World countries. And the networks, of course, had a stake in such neocolonization. In the early 1960s, all three of the major networks invested vigorously in international television, in what Curtin calls an attempt to overcome "geographical and cultural differences in an effort to forge national audiences and national consumer markets."⁹ The documentaries, then, mirrored and justified a vision of neocolonialism shared by Kennedy, ABC, CBS and NBC, a neocolonialism destined to reap enormous profits for the United States (generated by the United States' position as the central producer of the world's popular culture) and enormous tragedy for both Americans and non-Americans alike in such neocolonial manifestations as the Vietnam War.

An influential aesthetic of the early 1960s television documentary was cinéma vérité. The vérité goal—to present unmediated reality to spectators—manifests itself in various ways in the films of Robert Flaherty and John Grierson, in the Italian neorealist movement of the mid–1940s, and in the English "Angry Young Man" movies of the 1950s. Breakthroughs in 16mm filmmaking and transistor sound recording, however, made vérité more viable for full-scale television documentary. Robert Drew, a *Life* magazine reporter and editor, was the pioneer who brought both the vérité aesthetic and portable technology to television documentary. In 1955, Drew convinced

Life to establish a film division, and made a series of short documentaries that aired on *The Tonight Show* and *The Ed Sullivan Show*. Based on the success of these short films, the Time/Life Corporation gave Drew the resources to create his own documentary unit, and Drew immediately hired a crew that reads like a who's who of future vérité filmmakers: Richard Leacock, Donn Pennebaker, Albert and David Maysles, and others. The unit's first film was *Primary* (1960), a vérité chronicle of John F. Kennedy and Hubert Humphrey as they campaigned for the Democratic Presidential nomination in Wisconsin. *Primary* was never aired on network television, but its innovative technique persuaded ABC to hire the Drew unit to contribute to their anthology news show, *CloseUp*.[10] As Barnouw notes, this hiring gave vérité "a foothold in prime time" (270), and the vérité style began to influence the filmmakers who contributed to the news programs on the other networks, *CBS Reports* and *NBC White Paper*.[11]

NBC White Paper premiered in 1960, and was helmed by Irving Gitlin, who began his career in radio news at CBS. By 1956, Gitlin had worked his way up to the position of Director of Public Affairs Programming at CBS Television, and in 1959, when the network launched its CBS Reports series, Gitlin assumed that he was the logical choice for *Reports*' executive producer. When veteran broadcaster and Gitlin rival Fred Friendly was instead chosen for the position, Gitlin was ready for a new job at another network, and NBC President Robert Kintner hired him as the Executive Producer of Creative Projects for NBC News and Public Affairs. In that capacity, Gitlin began *NBC White Paper*, a news show closely modeled on *CBS Reports*' anthology format. Other key *White Paper* personnel included producers Al Wasserman and Fred Freed, both members of Gitlin's CBS "Golden Shop" who had been lured to NBC by Kintner.[12] Freed, in particular, was interested in cinéma vérité techniques; some of his earliest work at CBS, on Gitlin-produced daytime specials titled *Woman!*, adhered to an unobtrusive, vérité-like style. As Freed writes:

> We were using this technique with thirty-five-millimeter cameras on *Woman!* and nobody made any comment at all about it, favorable or unfavorable. I guess the network executives didn't watch daytime television. In the first of the two shows, "Raise Children," we went to New Haven and filmed a real family, and even with all of the heavy thirty-five-millimeter gear we followed them around the house, kids and all, and it came out fine. The technique worked. I think that technically we broke new ground in television with those two shows.[13]

Robert Young was one of the central contributors to *NBC White Paper* during its first two seasons. In the Arnold interview, Young describes his extensive experience making documentaries — a six-year stint making films about life in the sea, his photomicrographic work on *Life of the Molds* (1958), his contributions to the television show *High Adventure with Lowell Thomas* (1958–59) — before his film *The Living End* (a report on aging that focused on the life of a retired garment worker) was aired as part of NBC's *World Wide '60* series and earned him an invitation from Irving Gitlin to direct and produce a documentary for *NBC White Paper*. Below is a list of Young's first three *White Paper* assignments:

Sit-In (aired 12/20/60) is a documentary on African-American struggles for civil rights, focusing on lunch counter sit-ins in Nashville. Irving Gitlin was the executive producer and Al Wasserman, the producer; Young directed *Sit-In* and co-wrote the program with Wasserman.

Anatomy of a Hospital (4/16/61) chronicles medical personnel as they do research and treat patients in Cambridge, Massachusetts' City Hospital. Again, Gitlin was the executive producer, Wasserman the producer, and Young the director.

Angola: Journey to a War (9/19/61) is Young and cameraman Charles Dorkins' document of rebels in strife-torn Angola. Executive producer: Gitlin. Producer: Wasserman. Director and director of photography: Young. As Young points out in the interview, Gitlin censored footage of a napalm bomb nose cone with English-language instructions out of the broadcast version of *Angola*.[14]

Despite aesthetic and political differences with Gitlin, Young carried on with his next *White Paper*, a study of how poverty affects the inhabitants of Cortile Cascino, a slum neighborhood in Palermo, Sicily. Young invited Harvard classmate and fellow filmmaker Michael Roemer to collaborate with him on the project. Roemer was born in Berlin in 1928, and he and his family left Germany in 1939, on the eve of World War II. After spending most of the war in England, Roemer moved to the United States in 1945 and attended Harvard, where both he and Young were English majors. Together, Young, Roemer and other students (including Murray Lerner, later to be a member of Young's Marine Studios films collective) founded Harvard's first film production club. After graduating in 1949, Roemer worked for eight years for Louis de Rochemont, the founder of the *March of Time* newsreel series, who by the later 1940s had shifted into independent feature film production. (Even as Roemer began his job, de Rochemont's most famous independent film, the race drama *Lost Boundaries* [1949], was playing in theaters.) Between 1949 and 1957, Roemer worked as a writer, editor and location scout at de Rochemont Associates, working on such films as *Cinerama Holiday* (1955), the second showcase for the three-screen Cinerama process. In 1957, Roemer left de Rochemont and made over 100 educational films, while writing plays and movie scripts, including one that would later morph into the script for the Young/Roemer feature film *Nothing but a Man* (1964). When Young asked Roemer to join him on Cortile Cascino, Roemer was on the verge of accepting a two-year, lucrative job making educational films in Paris. As Roemer tells it, however, a specific moment persuaded him to travel to Sicily with Young instead:

> I went over to NBC the second of January [1962], and I still hadn't made up my mind. The people who wanted me to go to Paris were waiting for me to go. We were up in Bob's office, and he was getting ready to fly over to Rome, to go to Sicily. He looked at me in the elevator, and he said, "Mike, I don't think you're coming." And that was it ... he wanted me, and he was *really* disappointed. And he was sad. I put him in a taxi, and I went to my office, and I said, "I'm not going to Paris." It was a big leap, as far as I was concerned.[15]

Young and Roemer shot in Palermo for six weeks. The collaboration was harmonious, with the biggest disagreement regarding living quarters: Young wanted to live in the poor quarter to fully immerse himself in the lives of Cortile Cascino's inhabitants, while Roemer balked at doing without running water and hygienic living conditions.

Young and Roemer were united, however, in their deviation from vérité protocols of production. A vérité documentarian would run the camera first and arrange the footage later, but Young and Roemer first conducted interviews, developing a web of voice-over commentaries they could use to structure *Cortile Cascino*. Most of their filming came after the structure was written, and the filmmakers employed two editors to cut the dailies according to the overall design of *Cortile Cascino*. After returning to the States, Roemer, with Young's blessing, cut ten minutes out of the documentary to make it fit in one hour of television time, and removed a great deal of voice-over narration, since both filmmakers discovered that the pictures and sync sound were often sufficient to make the point intended in their "script."

The constructed nature of *Cortile Cascino* is by design readily apparent to any viewer; however, because many haven't seen it, the following paragraphs describe it in detail.[16] The documentary begins with a train driving through the Palermo slum, and shots of children playing near the tracks. Mothers are shown supervising the kids, and doing chores like washing dishes; the men are a group apart, playing cards. Then we meet Adriana, the matriarch that anchors *Cortile Cascino*, hearing her speak (through an English translation on the soundtrack) as she describes her children: Beatrice, her youngest, who gives Adriana "some hope" because she's still young enough to marry outside of the slum quarter; 23-year-old Angela, who has been married six years, has three children with another on the way, and who lives in a small apartment with her children and husband, Luigi; and Gildo, an unemployed son living off his half-blind wife's disability pension and the money his aged mother-in-law makes working as a cleaning lady. We are also introduced to Santina — Angela's closest friend, and a bride-to-be — and Salvatore, the man Adriana married after her first husband died. This segment of *Cortile Cascino* ends with a fade-out after Angela puts her kids to bed.

The next section examines the lives of men and boys in the poor quarter. We are told that the men in the slum get jobs "no one else wants," like digging through the city dump. Many work as street vendors in richer neighborhoods, and some have inherited occupations from their fathers. (The family business specifically shown is the weaving of rope from the human hair clippings collected on barber shop floors.) Scenes of children sorting rags are juxtaposed with voice-over commentary that points out that children are the most common laborers in Cortile Cascino, because employers can pay them less. (The voice-over commentary falls into two types: a female voice that represents Adriana's words, and a male voice that repeats observations that Young and Roemer collected during their preliminary interviews. Direct sound is usually left untranslated.) Boys collect metals, polish furniture, barber, and perform other tasks while the narrator points out that these boys will lose their jobs when they become older and qualify for higher wages. The narrator notes that the children of the neighborhood learn about life and death "very early"; the images elaborate on this claim by showing boys butchering a hog, and scraping the pig's hair off its skin with a large knife.

The next section of Young and Roemer's documentary examines what happens when the boys become unemployed men. Adriana points out that Gildo has given up trying to find a job, and *Cortile Cascino* charts the endless diversions men use to fill their days, particularly games of bocce, pool and Foosball. Voice-over commentary makes it clear that the men go to political headquarters just for the free pool tables, and that the political affiliations are resolutely monarchist — a position that their fathers and grandfathers held before them, no doubt because they, too, held out a fascist hope for a *deus ex machina* figure to straighten out Italy. Then a band plays outdoors, and Young's camera performs a vérité prowl around the group of listless men who congregate to listen to the music. Adriana says that the men put up a strong front (although many of the close-ups Young captures are of very sad and bored men), but "inside they feel as if they are nothing."

The film then ironically juxtaposes these nowhere men with a scene of people — mostly women — screaming in a crowd and battling to receive free food. While the women argue uncontrollably with each other, Adriana looks sad and lost in the melee and declares in voice-over that "the only ones who can make order among us is the Mafia." *Cortile Cascino* then explores the various "industries" the Mafia controls: gambling houses where, for an hourly fee, men and boys can go to play cards; prostitution (with footage of Luigi's sister working the street); illegal slaughterhouses and meat markets; and even the death trade, where the Mob controls concessions for funerals. After a baby coffin is loaded into a truck, *Cortile Cascino* cuts to gravediggers carving out burial trenches and removing previously interred remains. (The male narrator observes that "for those unable to pay, there is no resting place," as after eight years, bodies from underfunded funerals are dug up and discarded, to make room for new cadavers.) This tour of Mafia activity ends with almost too-symbolic shots of a funeral carriage driven by a man in a black cloak that makes him identical to the Grim Reaper. The male narrator underlines the link between death and the Mafia by intoning, "The Mafia is very old. They claim us for their own."

Cortile Cascino's construction informally zigzags between the men and the women of the slum, so the male-centered activities of the Mafia are followed by a look at the women of Cortile Cascino and their dependence on the rituals of the Catholic Church. Women visit the home of a disreputable faith healer, praying for miracles to alleviate their suffering. We see shots of altar boys in a choir and an opulent church (obscenely opulent, given the poverty of the parishioners) while Adriana observes that "we are religious, but only a few of us go to mass." The film then zeroes in on a specific instance of a religious ceremony, as Adriana morosely sews Santina's wedding veil, musing in voice-over that "God has abandoned us because we are sinners." Santina smiles as women from the neighborhood (including Angela) adjust her wedding dress to hide her pregnancy. We see Santina and her husband married at the altar, and we watch as an impeccably dressed bride and groom, in long shot and with their wedding party, navigate through the mud puddles and industrial debris of the Palermo slum.

Clearly, however, a wedding day is one of the few "glamorous" events in the life of a neighborhood woman. The images that began the documentary reappear — women doing chores in unimaginable poverty, Angela taking care of her children in her Dickensian apartment — before Angela gives birth to a new child, assisted by Santina and other female friends. Young and Roemer then switch to the only talking-head interview in *Cortile Cascino*, as Angela explains how one of her daughters came down with a high fever, refused to eat, and then died. As Angela speaks, the image track alternates between a somber close-up on Angela's face and scenes that replicate the images that illustrated the Mafia's control of the funeral business: a man carries a child's coffin to a crowded hearse, the hearse drives to the graveyard, and the gravediggers pitch old bones out of the trenches and put the new coffins in. *Cortile Cascino* ends in an exact reversal of its beginning, as Young and Roemer ride the train out of the neighborhood, filming children running after them and waving to the train.

NBC had originally intended to air *Cortile Cascino* on May 18, 1962, as part of the *White Paper* series, but as Young points out in the interview in this volume, the network announced a few days before the scheduled airing that the film failed to meet their standards. Young further points out that Irving Gitlin raised vérité-based objections to Young and Roemer's documentary practice, particularly with chronological manipulations that allowed them to end *Cortile Cascino* with the death of Angela's child. Roemer also notes that several other scenes are loosely "staged," including the birth of Angela's child and the procession following Santina's wedding — which appears on screen in long shot and actually features another couple rather than Santina and her new husband.[17] Both Young and Roemer argue, however, that these stagings and chronological liberties allowed them to capture the *truth* about life in the neighborhood more faithfully than blind fidelity to the actual order and unfolding of events.

Young speculates that Gitlin's complaints were motivated by political reasons — the Kennedy Administration was in the process of economically propping up the Democratic Italian government (in order to prevent Italy from going Communist), and these efforts would be undermined by *Cortile Cascino*'s devastating portrait of Sicilian poverty. For Roemer, the true cause was the intense personal animosity between Young and Gitlin, following in the wake of Gitlin's censorship of *Angola: Journey to a War*. As Roemer says, "I felt that there was a father-son issue involved.... I thought that Bob was rebelling against somebody who had already castrated an earlier film of his."[18]

In addition, perhaps another reason for the censorship of *Cortile Cascino* was its depressing tone. Nothing is resolved at the end of the documentary; the train pulls away, leaving the characters mired in poverty and despair, and this despair is magnified by *Cortile Cascino*'s form. The most influential program of the "Golden Age of Television Documentary" was *CBS Reports'* "Harvest of Shame," aired the day after Thanksgiving in 1960, which portrayed the atrocious jobs and living conditions of migrant agricultural workers in terms as brutal as the lives of Adriana and her family in *Cortile Cascino*. "Harvest of Shame," however, was narrated by Edward R. Murrow, who directly addresses the camera at the end of the program to advocate for reform. As Michael Curtin makes clear, "Harvest of Shame" tries to mobilize public opinion to alleviate the plight of the migrant workers.[19] But in *Cortile Cascino*, there is no erudite narrator to tell us how to put the situation right; there is only Angela's face after the death of her baby.

Further, one might argue that the structure of *Cortile Cascino* violates central ideas of televisual flow and character familiarity. In his seminal 1975 book, *Television: Technology and Cultural Form,* Raymond Williams argued that we experience television not as a sequence of discrete programs, but "as a planned flow," a cascade of attractions designed to retain viewers for an evening's lineup or some other large block of time. As Williams writes,

> Most of us say, in describing the experience, that we have been "watching television," rather than that we have watched "the news" or "a play" or "the football" "on television." Certainly we sometimes say both, but the fact that we say the former at all is already significant. Then again, it is a widely if often ruefully admitted experience that many of us find television very difficult to switch off; that again and again, even when we have switched on for a particular "programme," we find ourselves watching the one after it and the one after that. The way in which the flow is now organized, without definite intervals, in any case encourages this. We can be "into" something else before we have summoned the energy to get out of the chair, and many programmes are made with this situation in mind: the grabbing of attention in the early moments; the reiterated promise of exciting things to come, if we stay.[20]

Of course, flow can have pernicious consequences. If the distinctions between televised segments constantly blur, then everything runs into everything else: the news programs start to look like entertainment shows, the commercials crossbreed with the hour-long dramas, and television becomes, at best, a meaningless jumble and at worst, a medium that implicitly equates coverage of the war in Iraq with a commercial for Alpo dog food. Also, Williams' notion of flow has been modified and augmented by various critics; John Ellis, for instance, argues that flow is achieved by planes of passage, short segments that seamlessly carry viewers from one program to another, while Todd Gitlin and Mark Crispin Miller have identified the strategies (product placement, quick editing, etc.) used by television producers to make commercials more like programs and programs more like commercials.[21] The Williams quote comes from a time when it was necessary to "get out of the chair" to change channels, but TV's almost Heraclitean flow becomes even more frenzied when we pick up our remote and channel surf.

Williams' theory usefully explains how TV works to keep spectators interested from moment to moment, but as we move beyond an evening's worth of programming, the situation becomes more complex. One major counterforce to flow, for instance, is the serial nature of television shows.

Unlike most novels and movies, which tell self-contained narratives, TV programs are predominately *serial narratives*, defined by Robert C. Allen as

> not merely a narrative that has been segmented, but one whose segmentation produces an interruption in the reading, listening, or viewing process. Furthermore, that interruption is controlled by the producer or distributor of the narrative, not by the reader. In other words, the producer of the narrative determines not only how and when the narration of the story stops and starts, but also how and when the reader's engagement with the text stops and starts.[22]

The quintessential example of the TV serial narrative, Allen points out, is the soap opera, where "to be continued" plotlines dangle so often at the end of Friday's show that they become a part of viewers' expectations. But various TV strategies work to minimize the possible interruptions to flow that seriality represents. One is simple repetition; as Sarah Kozloff points out, "Television texts are played again and again; ongoing series repeat themselves each spring and summer season; older series are played endlessly in syndication; once 'live' programs reappear as 'canned'; cable and PBS networks play the same program or film over and over again in different time slots."[23] This repetition allows viewers to dip into the flow at random and still access the same narrative; it is not uncommon for a viewer to watch the last half of a movie on HBO and then catch up with the first half a few days later.

Flow is further supported by genre familiarity, by our previous knowledge of the types of programs typically broadcast. When we turn on the TV and see three seconds from an episode of *Frasier*, we enact a series of quick mental calculations: we recognize *Frasier* if we've seen the show before, but if not, we can still use our awareness of the traits of the sitcom genre (laugh track, half-hour format, plots driven by misunderstandings, etc.) to identify this unknown show as an example of a sitcom.

In contrast, *Cortile Cascino* is a critique on the televisual strategies of repetition and familiarity. Instead of providing viewers with an easy transition into image flow, Young and Roemer's documentary uses instances of repetition to represent captivity, powerlessness and death. The film begins, for example, with footage of a train as it enters the Palermo neighborhood — perhaps chronicling the filmmakers as they arrive to begin filming — and ends as the train (and Young and Roemer) pulls out of Cortile Cascino, leaving behind Adriana's family and all the children running across the tracks behind the train. The beginning and the end create "bookends" that frame the film, but "bookending" like this in visual narratives typically highlights some sort of character growth. In his commentary on film criticism, David Bordwell notes that repeated moments or objects in a film "translate semantic structures into architectonic unfolding," mostly through a journey that precipitates a shift in a character's personality and/or the audience's response to that character.[24] Robin Wood posits, for instance, that several Hitchcock films are structured around a "therapeutic theme," where a character is introduced with some sort of flaw, and over the course of the narrative changes enough to overcome the flaw.[25] The bookends in the therapeutic narrative dramatize the character's improvement. *Rear Window* (1954) begins with photographer L.B. Jeffries (James Stewart) alone in his apartment, laid up in a cast; it ends with him in two casts, with his girlfriend Lisa (Grace Kelly) present, a reminder of how over the course of the narrative Jeffries has learned to commit himself fully to Lisa. *Vertigo* begins with Detective "Scottie" Ferguson (James Stewart) paralyzed by a fear of heights, and ends with him overcoming this fear in order to drag Madeline/Judy up a bell tower. The repetitive bookends in *Cortile Cascino*, however, signal no such change; we see Angela's face in bereaved, resigned close-up, and then the train rolls out. Nothing changes. Angela, Adriana and their families continue to suffer.

Young and Roemer also use verbal repetition to capture the futility of living in Cortile Cascino. The early scenes involving street vendors, for instance, are comprised almost entirely of close-ups which allow us to see the desperation on their faces while we hear the panicked edge in their loud, persistent sales pitches. The most heartbreaking repetition of words, however, occurs early in the film, as Angela serves up a meal of pasta to her children, who are sitting and playing on the bed that dominates Angela and Luigi's apartment. Angela's daughter Finnucia refuses to eat, and Angela says, over and over again to the little girl, "Eat!" ("Mangiare!"). Of course, Finnucia is the child who dies after becoming sick and refusing to eat, and Angela's almost mechanical commands are ineffectual, emblematic of both her inability to control Finnucia's behavior and to improve her circumstances. Young and Roemer further dramatize Finnucia's death by making her a specific example of systemic problems. During *Cortile Cascino*'s catalog of industries controlled by the Mafia, we see baby coffins loaded onto a hearse, and trenches dug for these coffins at the graveyard. We see shots of exactly the same activities intercut with Angela's closing interview, where she discusses Finnucia's death. In essence, Young and Roemer repeat the footage, metaphorically placing Finnucia in the coffin and giving us a personal example (and a more emotional connection) to the piles of baby coffins we saw in the footage the first time. Angela sputters commands like a robot in a vain attempt to save her daughter's life, but the dominant symbol of *Cortile Cascino* is a child's casket.

In the late 1980s, Britain's Channel 4 asked Young and Roemer for permission to air *Cortile Cascino*, but Young instead suggested that a crew be sent back to Italy to film what has happened to Adriana's children. In 1991, Young's son Andrew and daughter-in-law Susan Todd directed the documentary *Children of Fate: Life and Death in a Sicilian Family*. Inspired by Michael Apted's *7 Up* series of documentaries — where Apted returns every seven years to interview the same men and women about their lives — *Children of Fate* juxtaposes footage from *Cortile Cascino* with material shot in 1991 that centers on Angela, now fifty-three years old and still living a hard life. She has become a house cleaner in Ragusa, a more forgiving region of Sicily than Cortile Cascino, but history repeats itself: she is present at the death of another daughter (her eldest, Anna, from lung cancer), and, like her mother, Adriana, sees her children fall into poverty and crime. Angela, however, has made one lasting improvement in her life: she has left her husband Luigi after twenty-eight years of marriage, and for good reason. Luigi reveals on camera that he has been physically abusive to both Angela and himself.

Film reviewer Rita Kempley succinctly defines the message of *Children of Fate* as "one avoided in Hollywood fiction: we don't find it easy to change."[26] As we have seen, *Cortile Cascino* is an even more complete portrait of inertia and desolation. Such a piercing strain of hopelessness was suppressed by NBC because it was so out of sync with the can-do optimism of Kennedy's Camelot era, but nowadays, despair gets more attention and praise: *Children of Fate* won the Cinematography Award and Grand Jury Prize (shared with *Silverlake Life: The View from Here* [Peter Friedman and Tom Joslin, 1993]) at the 1993 Sundance Film Festival, and was nominated for a 1994 Academy Award for Best Documentary. And history continues to repeat itself, more children die, more adults languish in unemployment and ignorance, and Fate — or societal engines so arbitrary and impersonal that they seem like Fate — stutters on.

Notes

1. William Boddy, *Fifties Television: The Industry and its Critics* (Chicago: University of Illinois Press), 219.
2. Michael Curtin, *Redeeming the Wasteland: Television Documentary and Cold War Politics* (New Brunswick, N.J.: Rutgers University Press, 1995), 22–23.
3. Ibid., 23–24.
4. For a definitive survey of Warner Bros.' television production in the 1950s, see Christopher Anderson, *Hollywood TV: The Studio System in the Fifties* (Austin: University of Texas press, 1995), 156–255. A good reference work on shows like *77 Sunset Strip* is Lynn Woolley, Robert W. Malsbary and Robert G. Strange Jr., *Warner Bros. Television: Every Show of the Fifties and Sixties Episode-By-Episode* (Jefferson, NC: McFarland, 1985).

5. For more on *The Untouchables* controversy, see William Boddy, "Approaching *The Untouchables*: Social Science and Moral Panics in Early Sixties Television," *Cinema Journal* 35.4 (1996), 70–87.

6. Minow delivered his "vast wasteland" speech to the National Association of Broadcasters on May 9, 1961. The entire text of the speech is available in Newton Minow, *Equal Time* (New York: Atheneum, 1964), 52.

7. Erik Barnouw, *Tube of Plenty: The Evolution of American Television* (New York: Oxford University Press, 1990), 274.

8. Curtin, *Redeeming the Wasteland*, 86.

9. Ibid., 76.

10. The best concise information on Drew and cinéma vérité is in a textbook, Robert C. Allen and Douglas Gomery's *Film History: Theory and Practice* (New York: Alfred A. Knopf, 1985), 215–241. For a more in-depth history of the movement, see Stephen Mamber, *Cinema Verite in America* (Cambridge, Mass.: M.I.T. Press, 1974). Incidentally, the complete name of the ABC documentary show was *Bell and Howell CloseUp*, an amazingly appropriate name since the Bell and Howell company pioneered many of the technical innovations that made Drew's work and cinéma vérité in general possible.

11. Barnouw, *Tube of Plenty*, 270. There were, of course, other news and documentary television shows before this early 1960s proliferation of programs. For an in-depth analysis of the most important of these earlier programs, Edward R. Murrow's *See It Now*, consult Thomas Rosteck, See It Now *Confronts McCarthyism: Television Documentary and the Politics of Representation* (Tuscaloosa: University of Alabama Press, 1994).

12. A. William Bluem, *Documentary in American Television: Form, Function, Method* (New York: Hastings House Publishers, 1979), 111–120; David G. Yellin, *Special: Fred Freed and the Television Documentary* (New York: Macmillan, 1973), 101–105.

13. Yellin, *Special*, 92.

14. Information about *White Paper* credits and broadcast dates is from Daniel Einstein, *Special Edition: A Guide to Network Television Documentary Series and Special News Reports, 1955–1979* (Metchuen, N.J.: Scarecrow Press, 1987), 346–348.

15. This quote and the information about Roemer's career in the preceding paragraph are taken from an interview I conducted with Roemer on January 5, 2004.

16. *Cortile Cascino* is available for rental or sale on DVD from Filmakers Library, 124 East 40th Street, New York, NY 10016; (212) 808–4980; info@filmakers.com; www.filmakers.com. The DVD of *Cortile Cascino* also features Michael Roemer's 1976 PBS documentary *Dying*.

17. Interview with Roemer, January 5, 2004.

18. Interview with Roemer, January 5, 2004.

19. Curtin, *Redeeming the Wasteland*, 168.

20. Raymond Williams, *Television: Technology and Cultural Form* (New York: Schocken, 1975), 94.

21. John Ellis, *Visible Fictions: Cinema, Television, Video* (New York: Routledge, 1982), 160–171; Todd Gitlin, "Car Commercials and *Miami Vice*: 'We Build Excitement,'" in Todd Gitlin, ed., *Watching Television* (New York: Pantheon, 1987), 136–161; Mark Crispin Miller, "Prime Time: Deride and Conquer," in *Watching Television*, 181–228.

22. Robert C. Allen, "Introduction," in Robert C. Allen, ed., *To Be Continued: Soap Operas Around the World* (New York: Routledge, 1995), 1.

23. Sarah Ruth Kozloff, "Narrative Theory and Television," in Robert C. Allen, ed., *Channels of Discourse: Television and Contemporary Criticism* (Chapel Hill: University of North Carolina Press, 1987), 69.

24. David Bordwell, *Making Meaning: Inference and Rhetoric in the Interpretation of Cinema* (Cambridge: Harvard University Press, 1989), 187–188.
25. Robin Wood, *Hitchcock's Films Revisited*, Revised Edition (New York: Columbia University Press, 2002), 71–72.
26. Rita Kempley, "Poverty's Relentless Grip: 'Children' Traces a Family in the Throes of Despair." *Washington Post* 30 July 1993: G7.

3. Demanding Dignity: *Nothing but a Man*
Bruce Dick and Mark Vogel

> *John Henry said to his captain,*
> *"A man, he ain't nothing but a man,*
> *Before I'd let that steam drill beat me down,*
> *Oh, I'd die with the hammer in my hand."*
>
> —"John Henry, Steel Driving Man"

In his January 1963 inaugural address as governor of Alabama, George C. Wallace proclaimed, "I draw the line in the dust and toss the gauntlet before the feet of tyranny, and I say segregation now, segregation tomorrow, segregation forever" (Woodward 175–176). Within days of Wallace's declaration, disturbances broke out in towns and cities across the state, including Birmingham, where, according to an earlier newspaper report, authorities had used "the whip, the razor, the gun, the bomb, the torch, the club, the knife, the mob, the police and many branches of the state's apparatus" to ensure racial separation (175). By April, Birmingham police had arrested Martin Luther King, Jr., and other prominent ministers for staging sit-ins against discrimination. Riots by local racists broke out and federal troops were sent in to restore order. In spite of military assistance, recalcitrant whites managed to dynamite the basement of the 16th Street Baptist Church. When it was all over, four black youth lay dead — one was 11 years old.

Released in 1964, *Nothing but a Man* is set in a rural town near Birmingham during this time of explosive racial tension. The film stars Ivan Dixon as Duff Anderson, a young, independent-minded black man searching for dignity in an oppressive environment. White bigots enter Duff's world at leisure, demanding that he live by the demeaning strictures of Jim Crow. But while the threat of violence serves as an ominous backdrop, at the story's center is the fragile relationship between Duff and Josie (played by Abbey Lincoln). Duff's daily concerns, including his search for meaningful employment and his newfound desire to connect with his alcoholic father, help shape and define his destiny.

This focus on the daily lives of "average" African-Americans at the height of the civil rights movement makes *Nothing but a Man* a unique and important film. Folklorist William E. Lightfoot suggests the "film is clearly inspired by the John Henry legend's universal theme of an ordinary man behaving heroically against seemingly unbeatable odds" (273). Robert Young, who co-wrote the script with Michael Roemer, the film's director, speaks to this universality in a recent interview: "We wanted to get away from the issues and what people were listening to on the radio. We felt that the most important thing that we could do would not be to talk about Duff's situation from the civil rights point of view, but to make a film that would take everyone into the fabric of the life of a black man — and subsequently the black woman he marries, and their eventual family. So that anyone viewing the film could understand and empathize with this character, could feel with him, yet come up against what he had come up against."

The evolution of *Nothing but a Man* stands as a testament to how far Young and Roemer were willing to go to make their film. In 1961, two years before the picture's release, Young and Roemer shot a controversial documentary, *Cortile Cascino,* depicting families struggling against poverty in Sicily. The film includes stark images of dying babies, deplorable living conditions, and rampant crime in the street. Three days before the documentary's scheduled release on *NBC White Paper,* the film was shelved. NBC argued that the film contained images too graphic for the American public. The cancellation both enraged and humiliated the filmmakers, who between them already had won prestigious Polk Awards and other honors for earlier work. The failed project and the pressure to compromise their principles also strengthened the bond between the two men. Further, according to Young, this adversity gave them "character." He stated in the same interview, "When we lost the Sicily battle, we lost the most precious work we had ever done -- a film that had come from the deepest place within. To reclaim ourselves, to redeem ourselves, we needed to stand up as men. We took those feelings and said, 'Look, we're going to make something nobody can take away from us. We're going to make something that is ours.'" That "something" became *Nothing but a Man.*

For subject matter, the filmmakers turned to the ongoing racial problem in the American South, a topic Young had explored earlier in *Sit-In* (1960), a documentary illustrating the complex emotions surrounding the integration of public facilities in Nashville, Tennessee. Using Roemer's semi-autobiographical screenplay about a man searching for his estranged father to structure their drama, the two men ventured through the Deep South to gather material for their script. Beginning in Columbia, South Carolina, at the home of a minister whose daughter Young had met while filming *Sit-In*, the filmmakers drove through territory unseen by most whites — talking and eating with blacks, and even staying in their homes. They saw firsthand not only the difficulties for black men in the workforce, but they also witnessed black men and women in love, as functioning members of a nurturing and healthy black community. "It wasn't just about what was happening in the news," Young argued in his interview. "We wanted to make a film that exposed the basic kind of social structure and human relations that really did exist in the South, and that still do exist in some places." Four months after their journey began, Young and Roemer had the framework for a film that would capture both the strengths and frailties of black Americans in the 1960s segregated South.

In *Nothing but a Man*, Duff is a Korean War veteran who has returned home to rural Alabama after discovering that conditions for African-Americans in the North are no better than they are in the Deep South. Duff is seen in the opening sequence of scenes with his all-male friends, working as a section hand laying ties on the railroad. The strenuous labor offers a steady $80-a-week paycheck, as well as social stability, but both come at the expense of the community. Working for the railroad means constant travel and the unlikelihood of putting down roots. The railroad section hands are on the outside of civilized communities, looking in, far removed from their birthplace, their family, and any children they might have fostered. The conflict between making attachments and living in a community versus living alone without significant attachments continues throughout the film. Later in the film, Duff's derelict father tells him: "Ya gotta stay light on your feet or you won't make it." Yet, from the beginning, the sense of freedom provided by the transient railroad life is not satisfying for Duff. His military experiences in Korea and Japan have provided glimpses of a better life with respect and dignity.

This inability to settle for something less, and his staunch individualism is seen whenever Duff interacts with others. In an early scene, when Duff and his male "family" visit a seedy juke joint, the contrasting outlooks of Duff and his fellow workers become evident. Duff isn't as coarse as others on the crew. When Frankie, an outspoken crew member, verbally abuses the local prostitute at the bar, it is Duff who helps her maintain dignity. He tells Frankie, "Quit ridin' her," and buys her a beer. Then Duff, alone, leaves the juke joint. As he walks the dark streets, the popular music from the jukebox fades, and the strains of gospel singing from a nearby church emerge.

Duff is drawn to this church revival, where he sees "righteous" members of the community singing and praying. As Duff witnesses the inspired congregation from the church door, the sharp contrast with the harsh bar scene suggests the gulf between these worlds. When Duff is introduced to Josie Dawson, who is preparing food for the worshippers, he quickly learns Josie is a college-educated teacher with an extended family, who lives in a community of church members who know her well. Josie talks freely about her minister father and her life in the town; in contrast, all talk of Duff's family and his past is fragmented and hidden. When Josie asks, "Your folks live there [in Birmingham]?" Duff replies starkly, "No. My mother's dead." Their differences are further reinforced when Duff tells Josie that he never "had much use for hell-howlers."

The contrast in how Josie and Duff are viewed by the outside world is also made evident in this scene. She has a profession, an education, a respectable family, and a place in the community. His freewheeling, working-class existence differs from Josie's middle-class, professional life set within the conventions of family and community. To the white community in this small town, Duff, as an unattached "outsider" male with a job, is a potential troublemaker. Knowing how others might see his independent status, Duff bluntly confronts Josie: "Look, I don't know what you been told 'bout section gangs, but how 'bout seein' me sometime?" Although their first encounter is brief and inconclusive, as if these disparate worlds could never come together, a connection between the less sophisticated Duff and a more educated Josie has occurred. They agree to meet again. As the scene fades, Josie moves toward the church service; Duff remains on the outside, in the darkness.

The contrast of Duff's long-term romantic goals and those of his coworkers is made starkly evident in the next scene in the bunk car when the men talk about Duff's new acquaintance. The section crew reacts as if the only reason to be with a woman is to have quick sex. One says, "Man, why you messin' around with a gal like that? You won't get no place." Another quickly responds, "Just get her drunk." A third worker says, "Hell, they're all the same." The oldest crewmember, Pop, revealing that he has been married and has a sixteen-year-old daughter, joins the chorus of skepticism, claiming, "All a colored woman wants is your money." The crew sees any attempt to "settle" into a family life as largely a futile enterprise. The conversation in the bunk car is juxtaposed with a view of Josie's living arrangements in her father's home. Dressed in a tie at the dining room table, Reverend Dawson is reading the newspaper. Later, during the meal, Josie's stepmother talks bluntly about Josie's tentative relationship with Duff. She states, "Well, there's just one thing you can be looking for in a man like that."

Yaphe and Kotto (Jocko), center, playing cards with his workmates in the converted railroad car where the laborers live, in *Nothing but a Man*.

Her father reinforces this point of view, suggesting the relationship has no future. At this stage, the relationship seems to have little chance of growing. If Duff and Josie wish to bridge the gulf between their worlds, they will have to do so without the help of others.

When the film returns to the roadhouse juke joint and the smoke-hung floor, a "different" Josie is enjoying herself with Duff. Clearly, despite her staid appearance, Josie is a complex character, able to thrive in diverse environments. Recognizing her many sides, Duff comments on her dancing: "That's pretty good for a preacher's daughter." He then asks in his outspoken fashion, "So what you doin' with a cat like me in a joint like this?" Josie responds to his question by saying, "Most of the men I know — they're kind of sad." Something at the core of the black men Josie has met has been wounded or destroyed; she knows from firsthand experience how black men trying to function in a segregated world with few economic opportunities can be hurt in the process. She has seen how oppression affects all aspects of their lives, including romantic relationships. For Duff and Josie, this brief exchange foreshadows an ominous future.

When the scene shifts to an ongoing conversation in his borrowed car, Duff explains the benefits of his "cut-off" life on the section crew. The job "[keeps] me out of trouble ... I don't get on so well most places." When Josie states that she would like to continue to see him, he says, "Well, either we're gonna hit the hay or get married. Now, you don't want to hit the hay, and I don't want to get married." Duff's harsh response only reaffirms the gulf between their worlds. Josie responds by commenting on his "primitive ways." As Duff and Josie struggle to make sense of their newfound attraction, two young white men approach the car. They shine flashlights in the car and comment on the lack of overt signs of sexuality — as if that is all they could expect from a black couple. They exhibit their ownership over the couple by shining the flashlight deliberately across Josie's breasts. After the men drive off screeching and hollering, Duff says about whites, "Don't sound human, do they?" The scene with the two young white men reinforces that any relationship between Duff and Josie must take into consideration a white world that undermines their sense of dignity. Duff and Josie don't have the option of simply falling in rapturous love, oblivious to the viewpoints of others.

Knowing the history of black-white relationships in this town is essential to understanding these characters. On the way home, Josie reveals a history of violence perpetuated by the white community, including a lynching of a black man only eight years before. Josie notes quietly that her father was aware of who was responsible for the murder, but he did nothing about it. In this scene the contrast between father and daughter is reinforced. Though she loves her father, Josie doesn't approve of his failure to confront the evils of the community — or to even admit these evils are still alive and well. She cannot accept that her father is simply content if the evils remain relatively hidden from public discussion. For Josie, Duff's willingness to talk about black-white relations suggests a willingness to honestly confront evils. Nothing in this scene suggests that Josie and Duff can stop the racism in this town. Both aim for a less ambitious goal — simply being allowed to maintain dignity amidst oppression.

When Duff and Josie part after their first date, their future together is uncertain. The scenes up to this point reveal the gulfs between this independent and thoughtful black man and the intelligent and beautiful preacher's daughter Duff falls for. They also vividly show the dangers. The white racism Duff and Josie experience in this less-than-ideal town is a backdrop that helps the narrative unfold. In this community, where young white men openly harass black couples at night, where potential violence is more than a memory of a recent lynching, the threat posed by the white community seems to make any attempt to construct a healthy relationship nearly impossible.

Yet, at this point, Duff has made no commitment to settling in a community. He still freely travels from town to town with black crew members who choose to settle nowhere. The view of the unencumbered black man as uncultivated is reinforced in the next brief scene as the section crew is shown hunting rabbits in the tall grass, killing them with large clubs. The men aren't portrayed as brute killers here, but rather as resourceful and adept survivors who have learned how to use available resources. The ability of these men — who live outside the confines of towns and cities — to make do, contrasts with the previous church social scene where food was abundant and carefully supervised by women. The rabbit-hunting scene suggests these men live outside the community of comfort.

Despite his differences with Josie's lifestyle, Duff quickly moves to keep his budding relationship growing. Visiting Josie at work, he explains that having been in the military and having experienced Asian culture, he briefly escaped the clutches of systematic racism. Duff states that he almost "didn't come back." He reveals that he has also lived in the North, although he tells Josie that "it ain't that good up there neither." In this same visit, Duff sees firsthand the difference in attitudes between himself (the unencumbered traveler),

Ivan Dixon (Duff Anderson), Gloria Foster (Lee) and Julius Harris (Will Anderson) in *Nothing but a Man*.

3. Demanding Dignity: *Nothing but a Man* (Dick & Vogel) 65

and the reverend, who has spent his life cultivating a community under the cloud of oppressive racism. Inside Josie's home, Duff watches Josie's father interacting with the white superintendent of schools. While the superintendent conveys the impression that blacks and whites live in equality, Duff senses the compromises that both Reverend Dawson and Josie have been forced to make under the direction of white leaders. Duff, at this point, does not feel that coerced compromise need ever occur. When the superintendent leaves, Dawson tells Duff, "I think if you tried livin' in a town like this, instead of running free and easy, you'd soon change your tune." After Duff disagrees, Reverend Dawson says, "And since we're talking, my wife and I don't want you hanging around our daughter." Walking out to the porch, Duff tells Josie, "Hell, I don't belong here. I don't know what I been thinking." Despite this adversity, Duff leaves the Dawson home determined to deal with his young, illegitimate son, who lives in nearby Birmingham. Though Duff hasn't seen his son in several years, his growing relationship with Josie has reinforced his desire to deal with his past.

The love story grows when Josie arranges to accompany Duff on the bus to Birmingham. When Duff visits his son and sees the squalor his child is living in, he feels guilty, and the audience knows that his guilt hurts. His son, distant and emotionally withdrawn, obviously does not know him. The boy has been left with a stranger, his mother having abandoned him and moved to Detroit. Observing his son, Duff sees him growing up unwanted, neglected, without a mother or father, and recognizes that he too has grown up in a similar environment. Ironically, as Duff confronts his failures as a father, he is reintroduced to his own father, who is played with emotional intensity by Julius Harris. His father is an alcoholic who is abusive to his girlfriend, Lee (Gloria Foster). Though his father is clearly dependent upon Lee, he is disdainful when Duff suggests he may marry Josie. "Is she good in the hay?" he asks. "No point marryin' her just to find out." In this scene Duff sees the "history" etched into his father's persona: his father has been mangled, literally, by his work and wounded inside by a grasping white power structure. His father tells him, "You ain't got a chance without dough. They take it all away from you." Maintaining pride and self-confidence, Duff realizes, will be difficult as the litany of events takes its toll. His father tells him more than Duff wishes to know: "Your mother used to lay for her boss, boy. Did you know that? ... I'm tellin' you, boy, keep away from marriage." Like Josie's father, Duff's father — left arm hanging limp, his spirit consumed in alcohol, and broken — is only "half a man." Duff's father concludes the exchange by shouting, "Okay, boy, beat it." Duff leaves, knowing he will get no help from his father. He is left on his own to salvage a life.

Duff's visit helps him measure himself against these two father figures.

Seeing his own son makes Duff's role as a bad father even more self-evident. Duff's encounters with his son and father convince him to ask Josie to marry him. When he returns, he asks her upfront, without the benefit of small talk. "Look, baby, I don't know 'bout you, but it's the right thing for me. I just know it is. So, what d'you say?" Josie accepts by saying she wants a "small scene." Though Josie's acceptance is heartening to Duff, his news is not embraced by his fellow workers. Their reaction to his dream of marrying and settling down is shocking. They react like adolescents: "Musta knocked her up." They ask incredulously, "What're you gonna get out of it, huh?" Earlier, Duff wouldn't have known how to respond. But having seen his own father and the future of his son, Duff has an answer for them: "A whole lot.... Like a home." But their conception of home life is paltry, and the scene fades with one of the men asking, "You're gonna sit at home the rest of your life?"

This mundane vision of married life as a crippling attachment isn't easy to shake. In Duff and Josie's first home, the rooms are rundown, full of discarded furniture and dilapidated ceilings. Outside the window, they view a woman toiling over laundry, surrounded by three children and her husband, who is stretched out on the porch steps. Duff and Josie are framed inside the window, its broken shards of glass a suggestion of what may be the future of their own family. Noting the neighbors' kids playing in the junk-filled yard, Duff says to Josie, "Guess you want a house full of pickaninnies, too, huh?" When Josie asks about his boy, Duff is defensive and unsure. Although he has made the first steps, Duff has no illusions about the potential difficulties of creating a healthy, productive family. He knows that simply getting married will not ensure happiness and economic success. If what he sees of his neighbors' plight is indicative of their future, their marriage may lead to poverty and frustration. Yet, Duff embraces Josie's vision of a nurturing marriage. He has a powerful ally in Josie, who smiles at the obstacles, already planning how to remake their dilapidated home. She has a vision for what their marriage can produce. We are less sure of Duff's staying power.

In the workplace (that facet of Southern culture most rigidly controlled by whites), Duff faces difficulties that threaten his newfound happiness. In his first days on the job, when Duff refuses to smile at a white man's condescending humor, his stance is the beginning of his troubles. A black coworker tells Duff, "You want to get along, act the nigger." Duff answers, "Like hell," and says, "You know, if you fellows stuck together 'stead of letting them walk all over you, they might not try it." Another worker responds with pessimism: "They been doing it all my life." Though Duff will eventually be fired from this job, he is no in-your-face radical of a civil rights movement. Yet, as Desson Howe suggests, "[Duff's] powerful self-restraint speaks volumes to these [white] men [who confront him and try to put him in his place]; they recognize a spirit that won't be broken. Without realizing it, Duff is heralding the coming decade of black power and self-determination. He's also learning about himself" (*Washington Post* 2).

Though the loving sense of play between Josie and Duff sets an intimate tone, their love is tested constantly. The film suggests that even love, that most essential emotion, is affected by the economic and social racism in their community. In a childlike and sensuous outdoor scene soon after their wedding, Josie and Duff seem secure in future planning. As they playfully shadowbox on their lawn, the good time and music is interrupted when their neighbor's wife — the same woman seen earlier washing laundry — berates her husband for being worthless. Knowing all too well how his neighbor could be beaten into depression sobers Duff, who fears he could end up in similar straits. He says to Josie: "It sure scares you, a guy like that — settin' out on his porch, doin' nothing. I seen hundreds of them all my life." These scenes provide an edge that tempers their heartfelt love.

Despite his difficulties with work-related racism, Duff is bolstered by his newfound love. Duff and Josie's quiet intimacy in their modest home contrasts with the "bad town" outside, where potentially violent racism is a daily reality. Though nothing is easy for this young couple, they aren't defeated by this adversity. Nurtured by his new family life, Duff invites his friends — the railroad section hands — over for dinner. Duff tells the men about his new in-town co-workers: "Those guys are scared. Guess they've never known nothin' but takin' it." He sees a world where steady workers can support their families without harassment. He does not seek friendship with his white co-workers, or equal status. What he seeks is more basic: respect and dignity. This dinner scene demonstrates how far Duff has moved from the lifestyle and values of the section hands. He has taken on responsibility for another, and in the process, has gained support and love. He has moved from a rootless railroad existence to the complexity of family life. When the men prepare to leave, Frankie (who has belittled Duff the most about his new relationship) says, "You got a good thing, man."

Duff knows well that threats against success remain. His role models — including his father — have shown him how strong men can be devoured by adversity. When Josie talks to Duff about having babies, she sees the fear in his eyes. Although Duff is unsure he can maintain dignity within the confines of small-town life, Josie, the optimist and rock of strength, pushes for more. Josie confronts him with the same words Duff speaks when he asks her to marry him: "Don't look so scared." With confidence they will survive, Josie says, "We'll be all right." Despite the gains Duff makes by marrying Josie, he has more ground to cover. When Josie inquires once again about his boy,

Duff is irritated, for he knows he has failed as a father. But Josie's optimism and determination control the scene, and Duff tells her, "Baby, we're going to put a whole lot of little kids into this world. Hell, we'll swamp 'em."

If Duff and Josie could live removed from the world, their love would surely grow each day. But the outside world threatens the relationship daily. When Duff loses his job because he won't bow to his supervisor's humiliating coercion, Duff takes his frustration out on Josie. When she responds sympathetically, he brushes her off, telling her: "I don't like bein' mothered ... Jesus, baby, leave me alone, will ya?" In another moment of foreshadowing, Duff tries to tell Josie of his fears: "I'm telling you, baby, maybe we better get out of here." His frustrations threaten to undermine their newfound stability. Yet, now, Duff is no longer alone, and his wife counters his rising tide of hysteria, refusing to let him go. On this occasion, Duff and Josie are able to laugh their way out of the despair. At this moment, his love (with or without a job) is enough. Duff laughs, vowing to fight on. With bravado he states that he will stay; he won't give the whites the privilege of seeing him leave town.

Despite the strength Duff and Josie give each other, the bleakness of Duff's choices close around him. Having left the comparative freedom of the railroad, he must live within the brutal rules of the racist small town. The next scenes show Duff looking in vain for work—at the restaurant, at the other mill, at the grocer's. He continues to apply for nearly any available employment. He even considers the slavelike conditions of picking cotton. On his job hunt, he meets a former co-worker, who explains that his fellow black workers at the sawmill were at fault for not sticking by Duff because they weren't used to "seein' anyone stand up." Duff's quiet restraint and his determination to withstand humiliation mark him as a mentor for those who have sacrificed dignity to maintain their jobs. Duff, however, has no desire to be the leader of a movement.

As Duff's job possibilities grow bleaker, his frustration and fear grow. When he must ask Josie for money to fix the car in front of women in the beauty parlor, he is embarrassed that he cannot be the husband he wants to be. It doesn't help that Josie understands the difficulties faced by black men seeking work. The fact that black women find it easier to maintain employment does not bolster Duff's self-esteem. Josie explains to Duff: "It's not as hard on a girl. They're not afraid of us." When Josie offers to support the family, Duff responds bitterly. "Sure baby," he answers sarcastically. "Fact, I don't ever have to work no more. When that baby comes, I can just stay home and send you back to school." As reviewer Chris Norton notes, Duff's attempts to deal with futility are the controlling force in the film. "Duff equates his masculinity with being able to work and support his family.

Without work, he feels he is nothing, not even a man. His frustration arises out of his inability to hold a job in a white-controlled environment and still assert his right as an equal human being" (*Black Independent Cinema* 2).

Knowing that other black men have long been denied economic opportunity doesn't help Duff adjust to his frustration. He has seen the world, and he cannot passively accept the chains of the past. The image of his neighbor, beaten and depressed on his porch, haunts Duff. Living with his futility leaves Duff with his self-esteem shattered. As a result, he lashes out at the one person trying to keep him strong. He says to Josie, "Stop being so damn understanding."

With self-esteem intimately connected with work and the ability to support a family, failure at work affected all aspects of family life. Robert Young states: "We were looking for the absolute center of what you need to be a man.... You can't be a man if you can't look the other guy in the eye ... and you can't live as a family man if your wife is the only one footing the bill." Young explains the irony of the film: "So love traps him; love traps the black man. Sometimes fathers leave because they don't think they have the capacity to live up to being a father" (Interview).

Fighting white racists is difficult enough, but Duff must also deal with his father-in-law and the black community. Rather than supporting Duff, their words and actions suggest to Duff that dignity and respect may not be attainable. Reverend Dawson openly tells Duff to "make 'em think you're going along and get what you want." But Duff is not an actor. He tells his father-in-law, "It ain't in me." When Dawson persists, insinuating that Duff's lack of social skills may be the real problem, Duff lashes out: "Well, at least [Josie] ain't married to no white man's nigger! You just half a man!" Duff can only exist as a whole man; his worst fear is that his efforts may leave him as damaged as his father-in-law and his own father. The reverend knows there is truth in Duff's assertion and walks out of Duff and Josie's home, head bowed.

Both men know that in a small town, white domination and the threat of violence can control a black man's public persona. Hatred for the oppressor can be damaging, even if the hatred is justified. Duff asks Josie, "How come you don't hate their guts?" Josie replies: "I guess I'm not afraid of them ... just of getting hurt. They can't touch me inside." But Duff knows too well how thoughts and fears are connected to white oppression. He responds, "You ain't never really been a nigger, have you?" Duff has a limit to which he will stoop, and he knows that his inability to find steady work is destroying his marriage. At this point, it is far from clear whether the conflicts faced by Duff will be resolved. As viewers, we're not sure whether the racism and lack of opportunity will destroy the marriage and leave Duff rootless once again, or whether Duff will find the inner strength to accept the love offered by Josie.

The next scenes suggest that Duff's overwhelming difficulties will only produce violence and chaos. When his father-in-law helps Duff land a job at a gas station, Duff is determined to quietly do his work. But trouble follows Duff, and when he engages in a verbal scuffle with a white man, the man returns with reinforcements to harass him and ultimately threaten the station owner. "You keep him workin' here and this place won't be around." That night, Duff, in his frustration at being fired, pushes Josie violently to the floor. He tells her, "You'll be better off without me. I ain't fit to live with no more. It's just like a lynchin'. Maybe they don't use a knife on you, but they got other ways." When he storms out of the house, bound for Birmingham, it is unclear whether he will ever return.

In Birmingham, Duff unearths more of his past, and in the process confronts his own possible future. Duff arrives in Birmingham just in time to see his father's last pathetic moments. On the way to the hospital, Duff is lost in thought — perhaps over his son, perhaps over his father and how he, Duff, is becoming like him. Later, as Duff and Lee make funeral arrangements, the undertaker asks the most fundamental questions about Duff's father's age and place of birth. Duff cannot provide any answers, nor can he identify his father's profession. Duff responds, "Well, he worked around." When asked if there are other family members, Duff responds, "No, just me." His father's rootless and hedonistic life has left but a thin connection between father and son.

After the funeral, attended only by Duff and Lee, Duff has found new determination. He tells Lee that he will return to Josie and even pick cotton if he has to. He will endure what he must endure. He hasn't conquered the outside problems, but he has reached an understanding. He has also found strength to face other unfinished problems. When Lee says that Duff's father wasn't much of a father, Duff answers, "Who is?" Refusing to relive his father's aimless lifestyle, he drives directly to his son's caretaker and picks him up. He will work to create a family, to be what his father wasn't. Together, he and his son return to Josie, where they have a tearful reunion. Looking to the future, Duff says to Josie with determination, "Ain't gonna be easy, but it's gonna be all right." The film ends with Duff telling Josie, "Baby, I feel so free inside." He has found a new freedom more permanent than the absence of commitment he experienced on the section gang. He has traded in one kind of freedom for another.

In his "I Have a Dream" speech delivered at the March on Washington, Martin Luther King declared: "America has defaulted on this promissory note insofar as her citizens of color are concerned. Instead of honoring this sacred obligation, America has given the Negro people a bad check which has come back marked 'insufficient funds'" (28 Aug. 1963). *Nothing but a Man* was released late in 1964, a year and a half after the March on Washington. In conducting the research for *Nothing but a Man,* Young and Roemer had seen first hand the truth of Dr. King's statement. To realize the significance of the film, one must see *Nothing but a Man* as one of the first full-length civil rights films, released in small movie theaters in the midst of the maelstrom. But the fact that no overt references to the burgeoning civil rights movement appeared in the movie was a deliberate choice by the filmmakers. Both Young and Roemer were well informed about the burgeoning movement, the confrontations and the potential for violence. Young had already made *Sit-In* and *Angola*, which documented the guerilla war in Angola in the early sixties. Young and Roemer weren't evading the legal and political realities of the civil rights struggle. In fact, the very racial tensions depicted in the film forced the filmmakers to shoot most of *Nothing but a Man* in the Northeast rather than the South.

Young and Roemer were searching to convey what other forums couldn't show — how racism and lack of economic opportunity affected *all* aspects of black lives. They knew that simply showing the humanity of the black community was revolutionary for the times. They sought to show a complex black community where, as Judith Crist noted in 1965, "no one is a hero, a villain or a cause but every one is human" (29). They wanted to show how love and dedication could exist despite the harshness of adversity. Thus, as Hal Hinson declared in the *Washington Post* after the film's re-release in 1993, "[The] movie isn't about racism or prejudice per se. Though it deals with such issues as the shortage of jobs for blacks and the roots of poverty, its focus is not political or sociological. *Nothing but a Man* is a compassionate film about human problems that's careful to anchor its story not in rhetoric but in the lives of real people.... It's an early portrait of black pride, presented long before showing pride in being black was accepted" (2).

Significant also is the fact that the movie's action takes place largely in a small town world and not in urban centers of power. Thomas Cripps notes that rural and small-town heroes in film and literature face a different world than the powerful black urban outlaws that first appeared nearly a decade after *Nothing but a Man* was released. In the years after the heyday of the civil rights movement, filmmakers began to move away from the pastoral rural and small-town protagonists like Duff. As Cripps suggests, "[To] be on the side of the pastoral hero was somehow to acquiesce in his plight" (*Black Film as Genre* 115). Yet, the very anonymous independence achieved by later urban outlaws hides the daily struggles of those forced to live intimately with their oppressors. The small victories achieved by rural and small-town protagonists who know that ultimate success will elude them is a different, less obvious, form of heroism. Cripps explains that "[unlike] the outlaw picaresque hero, the pastoral hero succeeds by keeping faith with himself, by remaining the same rather than changing, and by acquiring self-knowledge that eventually reinforces his preference for the small victory of survival with dignity" (118).

When Duff moves from running to staying, from living outside the community to joining the community, he joins others struggling to find ways to survive with dignity. The depth and complexity of this struggle are shown from the moment Duff stumbles upon the nighttime church service. He is torn between worlds. Cripps notes that in the brightness of the revival, the "opposing life styles at last confront each other: black male celibacy versus the warm circle of black institutional life in which respectable women have a place" (120). For much of the movie, it is uncertain which lifestyle will help him best find self-respect, and which will provide a future. The fact that the love story in *Nothing but a Man* transcends any overt political message reflects the desire of the filmmakers to show the daily struggles of black Americans. Donald Bogle, writing in his 1988 encyclopedia, *Blacks in American Film and Television*, declares that "no other American film has yet treated the black male/female relationship with as much sensitivity" (157). In 1963, simply portraying the common humanity of these inherently decent characters was revolutionary. As Joseph Gelmes suggests, *Nothing but a Man* showed "images of a viable, whole community existing and thriving amidst the pervasive racism of the time.... The very fact [the protagonists] remain nonviolent, they don't explode in ferocious violence, shows they are powerful survivors interested more in dignity than in ultimate justice" (*Newsday*). Because white Americans, as a whole, knew so little of the daily struggles of black characters, Gelmis suggests, "this vivid look at one African-American community is as fascinating as a documentary as it is moving as a drama" (*Newsday*).

Confronted with the realities Duff faces, the viewer leaves the film knowing, as Sylvester Leaks notes, that no one "with the will to fight the system, will survive the ordeal of being black in America. One cannot run, or hide, or compromise. One must face it. One must fight it. Duff chose to be nothing but a man" (*Muhammad Speaks* 15). The filmmakers' refusal to simplify the difficulties or to give the protagonists superhuman abilities make *Nothing But a Man* an extraordinary film.

Works Cited

Bogle, Donald. *Blacks in American Film and Television*. New York: Garland Publishing, Inc., 1988.

Cripps, Thomas. *Black Film as Genre.*
Crist, Judith. "Pointing a Pinky at the Negro." *New York Herald Tribune* 17 Jan. 1965: 29.
Gelmis, Joseph. "New Filmmakers Are Anything But Typical." *Newsday* 25 Jan. 1965.
Hinson, Hal. "Nothing But a Man." <http://www.washingtonpost.com.../videos/ nothingbutamannrhinson_a0a832.htm> (10 July 1993).
Howe, Desson. "Nothing But a Man." <http://www.washingtonpost.com...es/ videos/nothingbutamannrhowe_a0afd8.htm> (9 July 1993).
King, Martin Luther. "I Have a Dream." Speech delivered in Washington, D.C. 28 Aug. 1963.
Leaks, Sylvester. "Film 'Nothing But A Man' Hailed as Honest Negro Saga." *Muhammad Speaks* 29 Jan. 1965: 15.
Lightfoot, William E. Review of *John Henry: A Bio-Bibliography*, by Brett Williams. *Western Folklore* 4 1984: 272–274.
Norton, Chris. "Black Independent Cinema and the Influence of Neo-Realism: Nothing But a Man." <http://www.imagesjournal.com/issue05/features/black3. htm.>
Woodward, C. Vann. *The Strange Career of Jim Crow.* 2nd ed. New York: Oxford University Press, 1966.
Young, Robert M. Interview. By Dick, Bruce A., and Mark Vogel. Boone, N.C., 22 July 2003.

4. ¡Alambrista!
Walking the Illegal Tightrope
Melissa E. Barth

When asked about his 1977 film, *¡Alambrista! The Illegal*,[1] writer-director Robert M. Young told an American Film Institute Harold Lloyd Master Seminar that "with its faults, I sort of like [*¡Alambrista!*] a lot because there was a lot of passion and love. I love the people. I didn't and I still don't really speak Spanish. How I had the nerve ... I sat down at the typewriter and I actually remember going like, 'I don't speak Spanish, what am I trying to do?'"[2] *Alambrista* not only means "illegal" but also "tightrope walker," and Young's film captures the precarious lives of these Mexican workers who came illegally to America seeking a better life and money to send home to their families left behind in Mexico.

Young attributes his inspiration for *¡Alambrista!* to the six weeks that he and his wife had spent making a documentary about the lives of an Hispanic family in Arizona:

> The two of us traveled for about six weeks with a Chicano family out of a little town near Phoenix. They were terrific people and we got very close to them.... I picked onions the first day and so did my wife ... we worked as hard as we could but ... we couldn't compare ... the way we worked with the way they worked. They actually attacked the onions and it was just fantastic. So I did one day of work. I had this idea I'd work for a couple of weeks and really get into it and understand them but one day was enough. I understood it all. And then we got to be very close friends with them. And in the course of making this [documentary] I saw these people living in junkyards and I heard stories about people who were here without papers and I just determined that I was going to make a film about them. And then at some point someone told me ... of an incident ... that has been repeated, of a woman who gave birth in the customs shed and her kid had

the right, therefore ... would have papers and would have the right to work. And having that image in my head helped me enormously. I knew I was going to make [¡*Alambrista!*] no matter what.³

¡*Alambrista!*, the film that grew out of that six-week experience, graphically brings to life these people's attempts to work their way to a better life on the American side of the chain-link, razor-wire-topped border fence. Despite Young's diffidence about his film's import or impact, ¡*Alambrista!* is a strong film that explores the black-market enterprise that trades in human energy, in human workers, an industry that is as far-reaching in its effects as the drug trade, another exploitative business that receives far more attention in fiction films. Like the drug trade, trafficking in human beings generally benefits a very small, already wealthy, white American elite class, at the expense of minorities. For it is the coyotes — underclass or unclassed people — who do the dirty work of recruiting and supplying the human workhorses to the factories and fields of America. But, as with the drug "problem," the popular media places the blame for the "problems" of illegal workers not on the true profiteers, but on the exploited *alambristas* and the coyotes who "run" them. Young's film quietly but insistently captures the realities of this form of exploitation, a business that annually victimizes countless thousands of *alambrista* hopefuls who find their way across the Mexican-American border to the fields and factories of America, the Land of the Free. But, Young asks, free for whom and at what price?

¡*Alambrista!* reveals Young's deep commitment to and respect for these undocumented workers, which he states directly in the film's 2001 Director's Cut release dedication: "'ALAMBRISTA — THE DIRECTOR'S CUT' IS DEDICATED to the Spirit of TRINIDAD SILVA AND the UNDOCUMENTED WORKERS who labor in our fields." The film layers scene after scene of *alambristas* working tirelessly in seemingly endless fields of food — onions, tomatoes, avocados, strawberries, grapes, melons, lettuce. But ¡*Alambrista!* makes us realize that, no matter how long an *alambrista* stays in *Zona Norte* [the northern zone], those lushly green farms offer an illegal worker nothing more than an empty promise of unattainable economic freedom. None of the food, except for the little the *alambristas* steal while picking, will feed the workers or their families. Even more demoralizing, little actual pay is forthcoming for their hard work. Young repeatedly shows Roberto Ramirez, the film's protagonist (played by Domingo Ambriz), being denied or tricked out of the wages he has rightfully earned. Neither the American fields nor the profit derived from their produce will ever belong to the *alambristas*.

In contrast, the Mexican farms that *alambristas* like Roberto abandon when they go to America in search of money *are* theirs and, in most cases, have been in their families for generations. But America seduces these people, drawing them north, away from what little they have at home to the next-to-nothing they will soon discover they earn by working hard in America. It is this belief that he can succeed that motivates Roberto to leave his family and farm in the southwestern Mexican state of Michoacan and travel by bus about fifteen hundred miles to the Mexican-American border, where he is convinced that economic emancipation lies on the American side of the fence.

Young stipulates that his goal in making ¡*Alambrista!* was wanting "to humanize the statistics that I had read about in the papers of the people who crossed the border and the people didn't know who they really were.... Here Roberto was in Mexico, he actually came from a valley where he did have a life and it was fertile but economically he needed something more and what I wanted to express was that I don't think you can live with your stomach in one place and your heart in another place."[4]

"I wanted to honor these kinds of people," Young says, "...there was something powerful to me in the idea that in California, particularly, where there are ... hardly ... any family farms, but the people who pass through the fields and pick. And the wind ... like the ballad ... about the dust, there's not even a footprint left of them.... They spend their lives picking the things that are growing for us, and they don't have the chance to grow themselves was the feeling ... I had."[5] As ¡*Alambrista!* demonstrates, everyone except the anonymous, unseen American farm owners loses with the current system: *alambristas* who cross to America to work in the fields — often for wages only promised but somehow never delivered; the American poor farm workers whose jobs the *alambristas* unwittingly "steal" while being stolen from themselves; and, ultimately, the consumers of this *alambrista*-harvested produce, since the cost they will pay at the checkout line for their "American-grown" food will include the hidden costs of hiring this "cheap" illegal labor: the fees paid to the coyote/middleman who delivers working bodies to the farms willing to hire and exploit them, and the per-head price paid by this middleman to the other coyotes and various intermediaries who transport this human cargo from Mexico, across the border, and to the work site. Young's film was made in 1977, yet the hiring and exploitation of undocumented workers in the United States continues apace in 2004. Obviously, this system works to the economic advantage of *someone*, just not the *alambristas*.

As well as honoring the *alambrista* tightrope walkers, ¡*Alambrista!* also pays subtextual homage to Hispanic-American activist and union organizer Cesar Chávez, himself the grandson of a Mexican immigrant. Founded in 1962 by Chávez, the National Farm Workers Union (which changed its name to the United Farm Workers of America in 1973) has actively fought to better conditions for exploited farm workers — legal and *alambrista* alike. For decades, Chávez took *La Causa* (The Cause) to the streets and to the fields, including the well-publicized grape pickers' strike in 1965 when 300 workers refused to harvest the fruit and it rotted on the vines — until the owners brought in illegal workers to conduct the harvest. Naturally, violence ensued, principally injuring or otherwise disadvantaging these same exploited people, scabs and strikers alike. By 1970, as the farm labor movement grew, lettuce was added to the list of produce to boycott, but it was not until 1978, a year after *¡Alambrista!* was released, that the United Farm Workers of America and the growers reached a partial agreement and the boycotts ended.[6]

Oddly, given *¡Alambrista!*'s depiction of violence towards and exploitation of the *alambristas* — not to mention the negative portrayal of American authority figures such as border patrolmen and other police officers — Young said that although "I've dealt with people and situations that I think were very unjust ... I think sometimes my failing has been wanting to be liked and wanting to be nice and therefore not standing up enough."[7] However, anyone attentive to the tone and content of *¡Alambrista!* cannot help but see the injustice of a system that exploits these largely nameless Mexican men, women and children. Young and his film do "stand up enough," but no one film can force a culture to end its exploitation of *alambristas* when it seemingly intends to do nothing. In fact, Young makes a point of explaining that he "shows" rather than "tells"; that, in effect, his films are there to be "understood" and acted upon if the audience so desires. Young states that, as a filmmaker,

> I had to find situations and it was situations that really revealed ... the dynamics of things, whether they were social or economic or psychological.... And I began to see that, from my perspective, that to try to get at what the truth was, ... it wasn't that I wanted to be saying something, but [that] I wanted to be taking people into certain experiences ... I didn't want to be "telling" anything.[8]

Moreover, Young recalls explaining to his then-agent, David Begelman, why he had moved from making documentaries to making fiction films — the former of which would seem, at first glance, to be the stronger weapon against tyranny, yet Young "[told Begelman] that I come from documentaries ... and I'm interested in fiction because I can't go as far in documentary as I want and I want to rub fiction's nose in the dirt ... and then I start telling him the story of ... farm workers."[9] Young emphasizes that he did not turn to fiction film to grow rich himself:

> There's gold out there! I don't mean gold like it's taken thirty years and now we're going to finally make some money, maybe. I don't mean that kind of gold, although there's that too, I'm sure. But there's gold in terms of stories, you know.... Jack London said he went west 'cause that's where the gold was. Well, I'm telling you, it's all around you — the stories that are out of our own lives. The things that nobody else is touching.... That's the way I felt when we did *Nothing but a Man*, when we did *¡Alambrista!* Now, on the other side, you might say ... who is going to see it?... There are going to be a lot of other people who are going to say, "He's not commercial," and there are a lot of people who have written me off that way. That's their right. Part of the thing about growing up is ... your own personal aesthetics. At a certain point you find out ... I mean, I'm not on the A list, I'm never going to be and there's no reason why I have to care about it. That's their list. I have my own list, you know, and as long as I'm true to that and my kids are proud of me as their father, ... then you know, what the hell. I mean, here I am here [addressing the American Film Institute's Harold Lloyd Master Seminar], you know. This is pretty nice.[10]

Young forces his audience to bond strongly with the *alambristas* through his choice of Spanish as the film's principal language. With the exception of dialogue involving Anglo-Americans, the entire film is in Spanish with very incomplete or even nonexistent English subtitles. If a viewer does not know at least some Spanish, she or he will be as confused about what the *alambristas* actually say and feel as Roberto is about what the English spoken to him means. Both this technique and Young's use of the hand-held camera both serve to disorient, to make outsiders of, those viewers who ordinarily assume English-speaking white class privilege, people who are used to operating from the arrogant premise that "everyone" speaks English, at least everyone worth listening to. *¡Alambrista!* gives such an audience a taste of what it feels like to be the uncomprehending illegal outsider,[11] like Roberto, who knew no English when he illegally entered the U.S. and takes precious little English back with him when he is deported, except for compatriots' Joe and Berto's "*primeo*" lesson on how to "pass" as a Chicano-American.

At the end of his first full day working illegally in America, Roberto has just dressed after his metaphorically baptismal shower that washed away the external signs of his journey. With the help of Joe and Berto, two "veteran" *alambristas*, Roberto begins to learn how to walk the *alambrista*'s tightrope. Joe (played by Trinidad Silva) — who has adopted the Anglo version of his name, José — remarks to Berto (played by Paul Berrones), "We've gotta teach him or he ain't gonna make it." As a confused Roberto looks on, Joe demonstrates how to walk into a café: Open the door "with confidence. Smile. Look at people," and sit down correctly. "Cross your legs. The gringos they always cross their legs, eh," says Joe. Then smile some more. "You are going to drive the girls crazy. But you've got a lot to learn.... You've gotta be nice. You've got to smile. But not too much.... A little, with confidence," instructs Joe. Berto demonstrates then says, "Show 'em the teeth. So you'll be like the gringos." Although the scene has comic elements, the first English that Joe and Berto teach Roberto has a utilitarian value: to begin passing for Hispanic-American. Joe cautions Roberto, "What you really want is tortillas and beans. But here [in America if you want to pass for American] you must order ham, eggs, coffee. No beans." Captivated, Roberto later tells Joe, "Before I go back, I'd like to speak English like you." To which Joe replies, "I'll make a gringo out of you." Some days later, after Joe has died while the two of them rode the rails to "Stockton," it will be the waitress, Sharon (played by Linda Gillin)—herself a member of the poorly spoken blue-collar-but-white-and-blonde caste—who takes him in, becomes his lover, and teaches him to ask for that most–American dish, "apple pie with ice cream." If he can say it "correctly," Sharon teases him, she will give him some.

The way the *alambristas* must live reflects anything but the American dream: sleeping hidden under plastic sheeting among the desert scrub and living in a made-over chicken coop ("Well, sure," Joe tells Roberto, "they call us illegals, *pollos* [chickens], don't they? It's OK. It's gotta be."), in bunks crowding both sides of the aisle of converted school buses, and in the smashed cars in junkyards. There are no "fancy" migrant trailers for these men, no possessions to speak of, no change of clothing, no place, and no language to connect them to the world they entered via the slit in the Mexican-American border fence: a perverted, repeated birthing image that mocks the actual births at the beginning and end of this film.

Strong visual and musical threads add emotional and political depth and resonance to Roberto's journey. For instance, in *¡Alambrista!*'s opening scene, native flute music plays softly as a small trickle of water slowly runs into an irrigation ditch beside the lush, green bean plants growing in an otherwise dry field. As the camera slowly pulls back, the flow of muddy water increases to fill the ditch, and we see the main character, Roberto, working his horse and plow between the bean rows. Here, in this dry landscape, things are growing. It is in the middle of this fertile, small field that Roberto gets called to come home quickly because the baby has arrived. Roberto drops the reins, whistles up his dog, and easily leaps across a low one-strand barbed wire fence encircling the bean field. The fences along the American border will not be so easily surmounted nor so innocent.

A Mexican guitar ballad softly plays when Roberto enters his home to be greeted by a tableaux composed of his wife (played by Ludevina Mendez Salazar) being comforted by his mother (played by Maria Guadalupe Chavez) while a midwife (played by Rafaela Cervantes de Gomez) bathes his newborn daughter in a small basin of water. In these first, simple, intercut scenes, water promises life: for the crops, in the amniotic fluid that contained the baby, and as signaled by the "baptismal" washing and welcoming of this new daughter into the world. Shortly thereafter, the camera angle widens, revealing the lush green bean field among similarly verdant fields all nestled amidst the dry hills of the west-central Mexican state of Michoacan, whose name means "fishermen's place." Ironically, this name brings to mind the saying, "Give a man a fish; you have fed him for a day. Teach a man to fish; and you have fed him for a lifetime." Indeed, as Young observed, on his family's home farmland, Roberto has the dependable means by which to feed his family, more so than he will ever find on the American side of the border. And this family land is certainly where his heart remains no matter how far north he travels, even when he has become sexually involved with the blonde Anglo, Sharon. Despite this transgression, and with Sharon's unwitting help, Roberto determinedly sends a fifty-dollar money order to his *esposa* [wife] back in Michoacan.

Some weeks later (the passage of time marked by the much taller bean plants), Roberto prepares to leave for America, much to his mother's obvious distress. Roberto's mother laments, "[You are leaving us] just like Alberto, your father. He never returned." But Roberto bids her goodbye as she stands in the door of the small village chapel looking down on him, telling her to "relax. In the United States I'll make lots of money." When he turns to walk to the bus with his wife and baby, they are accompanied by the guitar ballad that also played during the earlier scenes inside their home. As sad as this farewell seems to be for Roberto's wife, like Roberto's mother before her, all this nameless woman can do is watch the bus disappear into the distance. In light of seeming insurmountable problems at home — food and other necessities of life in short supply and an infant daughter who never seems to get enough to eat — what could Roberto see as a solution but to make the more than 1500-mile trip north to America and its promise of "good money?"

Emphasizing the motifs of entrapment and estrangement, the bus on which Roberto rides north has partial grills on its windows, a Virgin of Guadalupe *santos* hanging behind the driver, and a black Star of David on the rear window, an image that partially obscures Roberto's last view of his home, farm, and family. On the outside of the bus, painted on either side of its destination sign reading "*Zona Norte,*" are white crosses. Iconographically, the bus resembles the trains that transported the Jews away from all they knew to a place of "work," a place of spiritual aridity, physical danger, and death. All that is missing is the sign at the Mexican-American border crossing proclaiming, "*Arbeit macht frei* [Work makes one free]." A lie then; a lie now. The film's music also reminds us that Roberto is leaving home for unfamiliar places. As the bus pulls away from his wife, the quaint, soft guitar ballad plays again, but as it nears the Mexican border town from which Roberto will make his bid for America, festive Norteña music begins to play, letting us know that Roberto is now far from home. Then, when Roberto faces the actual border fence, the music stops altogether and does not resume for some time.

The north country is also conspicuously more visually arid than Roberto's home valley far to the south. The narrow path moving to, through, and away from the border fence is dry, featureless dirt. And the spot where Roberto first enters the United States is anonymous: a dusty border crossing that could be almost anywhere along the more than one thousand miles of border fence running between Tijuana, Mexico, in extreme northwestern Mexico to Ciudad Juárez, Mexico (near El Paso, Texas), in the east. Here, in this dry border limbo, all physically separating Roberto and the other *alambristas*-to-be from their dream — America is a high, chain-link and barbed-wire fence topped with razor wire. As Roberto moves up to and through the man-sized slit, birthing himself as a true *alambrista*, the camera focuses on a tight shot of a small kite bouncing in the air of Mexico, framed and contained on all sides by the chain-link fence that also now separates Roberto from his homeland. The only moving "stream" in this dry, hopeless place is the desperate, thin line formed by the *alambristas* pushing their way through the fence and traveling on along the snaking dirt track into America. No one carries belongings with them; no one has water or food. All they bear are their hopes and dreams.

Ironically, perhaps even mockingly, the landscape grows gradually greener as Roberto leaves his hiding place in the desert to find work, moving closer and closer to the American farms that Roberto believes promise him and his family a better life. But America is still bone dry when it comes to sharing its wealth with hard-working Roberto. The only real water that Roberto finds on his first day as an *alambrista* is in the cistern where he hides from the border patrol during their raid on the dusty but lushly green tomato farm where he has picked fruit. The cistern and the dusty rows Roberto has just crawled through to outwit the border patrolmen serve as his baptismal entry into the Land of the Free, particularly because the lesson he learns there is that he can be easily cheated out of his rightful wages by unscrupulous *mayordomos* (field bosses). Moreover, in his time as an *alambrista*, with regard to real water, Roberto rarely has the luxury of available water to drink, bathe in, or even see. And generally, when moisture of one kind or another is available or offered to him, Roberto spills or spits it out. In one scene, he is shown drinking Coors beer with other illegals, a cash cow of a conservative Colorado family. In another, he must flee the cantina where he had been drinking when U.S. Immigration officers raid it, catch him, and deport him to Mexico. In a third, the beer he is given is the gift of the coyote who has conned him into returning to the United States as a strike breaker. Water — or any liquid — has its consequences in America.

No matter where in America Roberto goes, he finds derision, danger, or both. In a sterile and thus metaphorically arid nighttime scene on an anonymous skid-row street, two drunken, abusive men — one an African-American, the other an Hispanic-American (played by Julius Harris and James Edward Olmos — respectively) — harass Roberto and the other *alambristas* who, in the pre-dawn neon glare, await the arrival of the *mayordomo* who will bring his truck to collect the morning's "load" of *alambristas*. According to the drunken African-American, how these *alambristas* live "...ain't the American way of life." "Think about it!" he shouts at Roberto and the other illegals, and sneers, "Tote that fruit. Put it in the bucket. Bendin' over like a mule ... or somethin' else." His Hispanic-American companion also scorns these silent men, shouting drunkenly, "You *hombres* are *loco* ... rent-a-slaves. Even a whore's got her money, got to get her bread, man!" The irony is that two members of American minority groups nevertheless feel empowered by their status *as Americans* to abuse those whom they see as being even lesser than themselves, drunken Americans on a seedy side street in nowhere America. However, in contrast to the cowering, shamed *alambristas* who sit passively taking this abuse, these two American citizens feel able to exercise a right afforded them by their citizenship, a privilege out of reach for the *alambristas*: the "right" to live on the street and behave violently towards frightened people.

The America of Robert Young's *¡Alambrista!* offers no place for a hopeful Mexican illegal. And the film chronicles Roberto's shift from a fearfully hopeful husband, son and father leaving for America to a beaten-down deportee walking back into the arid uncertainty of Mexico. Although a less-determined man might have left sooner, Roberto persists until he learns that the man who has just died of heart failure in the melon field where they are both working as strike breakers was his father, Alberto Ramirez. Finally, Roberto gains the most crucial knowledge that an *alambrista* must have, something far more central the *primeo lección* (premium lesson) of "ham-eggs-coffee" taught him early on by Joe and Berto. The lesson that Roberto must now learn is the one stated on the dilapidated, ancient fast-food sign standing at the entrance of Dick's Auto, the junkyard where the Colorado strike-breaking *alambristas* live: "Fried chicken.... Ready to go!" As Joe earlier explained to Roberto at the strawberry farm, the chicken coop was a fitting "home" for *alambristas* like them because, "Well, sure, they call us illegals *'pollos'* [chickens], don't they?"

The sign at Dick's Auto bluntly reveals the true meaning of the word "*pollo*": "Fast food" equals cheap or free labor. Chicken equals alambrista ... undocumented worker ... illegal alien. All this cheap Mexican *alambrista* labor is "ready to go" thanks to the Anglo and Hispanic coyotes, men who recruit and pack up loads of human *pollos* in Mexico, shipping them north like livestock being driven to a slaughterhouse. For Roberto and the other *alambrista* deportees rounded up on the Mexican side of the border fence by an Anglo-American and an Hispanic, possibly Mexican, coyote (played by Ned Beatty and Salvador Martinez, respectively), their journey will be a 36-hour trip to Colorado melon fields in the back of a canvas-covered truck, enduring the blazing desert sun and cold night air, without food, water, or rest stops. Their job will be to work as strike breakers in fields under siege by Cesar Chávez's United Farm Workers of America Union. Cries of "*Huelga! Huelga!* [Strike! Strike!]" greet them as they leave the truck to enter the melon fields. "*Huelga!*" shouted by other Hispanics whose jobs and income they do not even realize they are taking.

Alambristas, as cheap and easy to come by as fast food ... as memorable and as disposable: "Get rid of her!" shouts the Anglo coyote to the Hispanic one, after discovering a woman and crying child among the *alambristas* waiting in a crowded trailer in the middle of nowhere to make the long trip to Colorado. When the Hispanic coyote asks, "What am I gonna do with her?" the Anglo replies, "I don't care what you do with her. You can take her back with you [to Mexico] or you can turn her loose on the road. It's your problem." As the Anglo had earlier reminded the Hispanic coyote when they recruited this load of illegals, "I want the labor. We're gettin' paid for every one we deliver. That's the important thing. You've got to remember we're making it on the number of bodies—that's where you make your money. The number of bodies. You don't know what's gonna happen to them once the job is over.... Remember, amigo, bodies ... about 10 or 15 more."

The life Roberto leads as an *alambrista* parallels that of the Chicano people with whom Young and his wife had worked near Phoenix, Arizona, the source of his inspiration to create ¡*Alambrista!* Young recounts, "In the course of making this [documentary] I saw these people living in junkyards and I heard stories about people who were here without papers and I just determined that I was going to make a film about them."[12] However, unlike the other *alambristas* who keep re-entering the United States after being deported, Roberto soon gives up. What appears to push him to abandon his dream occurs while he is laboring as a scab in the melon field. Rushing to the side of an older man who has just died of heart failure, Roberto discovers Alberto, the father (played by John Sandoval) who abandoned Roberto and his family in Michoacan so many years ago.

But his father's lengthy absence and silence are not what breaks Roberto's spirit and makes him cry out to go home; rather, it is the discovery that Roberto makes while going through his father's few possessions, which include a comb, a hotel-sized bar of soap, a book in English ("He spoke good English," observes the *mayordomo*), a few letters, a picture, and a money order. The woman in the picture with a dark-haired child is blonde. "This is not my mother," remarks a confused Roberto. "He was married," the *mayordomo* replies. When Roberto then shows him the money order, the *mayordomo* explains its contents to Roberto: "*Un* money order *por* fifty dollars, Alberto Ramirez to Mrs. Grace Ramirez. Grace, that's her name. They don't live too far from here.... I can take you there if you want. It's only a few hours away." This "wife," Grace, the blonde Anglo woman in the photo, is the only other woman in this film whose name is revealed — the other being Roberto's lover, the blonde waitress Sharon, who filled the same role as Grace had for Roberto's father, albeit for a much shorter time. Alberto's fifty-dollar money order for Grace is in the same amount as the one that Roberto had earlier sent home to his wife and daughter when he lived with Sharon. Roberto seems to recognize that he has unwittingly started down a path similar to that of his father; he, too, has become involved with a blonde Anglo. Ironically, early in the film, when Joe and Berto were teaching Roberto to pass as an Hispanic-American, they told him, "You are going to drive the girls crazy. But you've got a lot to learn.... If the waitress is pretty, talk to her." Roberto protested: "But I'm married." To which Joe scoffingly replies, "That's in Mexico. Act like an American.... Here everyone is free." Roberto again denies that he would ever betray his wife, telling Joe that "[Berto's] crazy. I'm married." Yet now, after discovering his father's double life, Roberto flies into a rage at what he has become since crossing into America, and, in a very real sense, denying his culture, family, and core identity. He has become, in *fact*, a "true" *alambrista*: of neither Mexico nor America. Only now Roberto realizes it. While the other men in the junkyard migrant camp sit in their car "rooms" eating their beans and tortillas, Roberto spits out his coffee, throws away his food, and attacks car after car with a crowbar, breaking glass and denting metal.

A progressively more shaky and discordant accordion version of the *Star-Spangled Banner* begins playing in the background as an exhausted Roberto, dirty, and close to tears, repeats, "I want to leave, I want to leave, I want to leave, I want to leave." The *mayordomo* asks him, "What about the money you're going to make?" To which Roberto does not reply. The American national anthem, by now almost unrecognizable, continues to unravel as, shortly thereafter, Roberto is picked up by a border patrolman who returns him to the border to once again be deported to Mexico.

Young says that he drew on his own experience with Chicanos in Arizona to create the film's concluding sequences.[13] Standing outside the American checkpoint building, Roberto's attention is riveted on a young, nameless Mexican woman (played by Lily Alvarez) who cries out and wraps her arms and hands tightly around a metal pole supporting the entry port's roof: "My baby is coming!" We know that she is married because the camera calls attention to the wedding band on her left hand, a reminder that Roberto's wife has also given birth — to a daughter who will be a Mexican citizen. The camera cuts back and forth between the birth, a tired and disheveled Roberto watching from behind a throng of foot traffic, and a parade of gawking Americans expressing varying degrees of lewd curiosity as they slowly drive past the laboring woman on their way back into the United States from Mexico.

Never letting go of the post, the young woman quickly delivers her baby with the help of two older, nameless Hispanic women (played by Virginia Bachicha and Armandina Ramirez)— mirroring the birthing tableaux in the film's opening sequence. Hearing her son's first cry, this young woman repeatedly exclaims ecstatically, "He was born here! My son won't need papers!" This young mother has realized her greatest dream, a son who is a true American, a son who will never need a fake green card such as the one Joe told Roberto he had paid forty dollars to obtain. However, instead of the water images that were associated with the birth of Roberto's daughter in Michoacan, this time the camera moves in to show a close-up of the pool of blood growing beneath the young woman who just gave birth. While not exceptional given the physical realities of childbirth, the moving pool of blood, the stream, is remarkable in that this Mexican mother is paying with her blood to ensure her son's future as a "real" American. The camera cuts away to catch Roberto's reaction to this young mother's joy at having given birth to a "real" American citizen, and he briefly smiles wistfully before turning to join the small stream of men walking back into Mexico.

Roberto's reality is not that of the newborn baby boy: Roberto's life, his past and potential future — his wife, mother, and daughter — wait on the family farm 1500 miles away in Michoacan. Roberto can never give them the gift that this young mother's persistence affords her son. Having seen what he cannot have nor provide, Roberto walks as if on a tightrope — the *alambrista*—joining the other dusty, dispirited Hispanic men who move slowly and carefully down the chain-link-fence-lined sidewalk back into Mexico. Roberto leaves America, presumably acting on his expressed desire to go home. In the background, a lively Norteña-style song plays, describing Roberto's horrible experiences during his brief time as an *alambrista* in America. But perhaps a different kind of despair will again overtake him, and Roberto will return to the high wire, as an illegal farm worker, as an *alambrista* — as do so many other deportees. The film leaves viewers with the same doubts and uncertainties that must be plaguing Roberto's wife and mother on the family farm in Michoacan: "Will he come home? Will he send money? Where is he? Will we ever know?" *¡Alambrista!* provides no answers, perhaps to emphasize that no one "over there" in America who would be powerful enough to make a difference would care enough to make the effort to find out, much less help.

On the other side — on the Mexican side of the border — a dusty, bleak and dilapidated scene greets Roberto. He and the other men walk off-screen leaving only a shot framed by the border fence on the left and foregrounding five empty shopping carts that surround a large trash barrel. In the middle distance, in front of what appears to be a closed business, stands a large sign proclaiming, "Fiesta." But nobody's celebrating.

Notes

1. Robert M. Young. *¡Alambrista! The Illegal.* 110 min.; 132 min. (New York: Bowin-Filmhaus, 1977; Director's Cut, 2001), videorecording.
2. Center for Advanced Film and Television Studies, transcript of the American Film Institute's *Harold Lloyd Master Seminar: Robert Young* (©1993 American Film Institute), 9 September 1993, 1.
3. Ibid, 1–2.
4. Ibid.
5. Ibid, 9.
6. César E. Chávez Institute, "César E. Chavez's Biography," n.d., <http://www.sfsu.edu/~cecipp/cesar_chavez/cesarbio5-12.htm> (26 December 2003).
7. Center for Advanced Film and Television Studies, 19.
8. Ibid, 4–5.
9. Ibid, 18.
10. Ibid, 23.
11. The first book-length study related to Young's 2001 Director's Cut version of *¡Alambrista!* issues associated with immigration and the Mexico-U.S. border is in press at this time and not yet released: David Carrasco and Nicholas J. Cull, eds., *Alambrista and the U.S.-Mexico Border: Film, Music, and Stories of Undocumented Immigrants* (Albuquerque: University of New Mexico Press, forthcoming). The University of New Mexico Press's web site (28 January 2003) lists the book as also including a CD of the newly scored film soundtrack by Dr. Loco and Los Tiburones del Norte [northern sharks] and a DVD of the 110 minute version of the film *http://www.unmpress.com/Book.php?id=10427374676741* (5 January 2004).
12. Center for Advanced Film and Television Studies, 2.
13. Ibid, 2.

5. From Cell to Celluloid: A Dramaturgical Note on Miguel Piñero's *Short Eyes*

John Crutchfield

It is said that American film director Robert Young got the job of directing *Short Eyes*, based upon the late Miguel Piñero's award-winning play of the same name, because the cast had kicked the original director off the set and threatened to kill him if he returned. Though the rationality (not to mention morality) of this threat may be questionable, its sincerity is probably not. Many of the people involved with the film, including Piñero himself, were ex-cons with histories of criminal violence, and some of them would return to prison not long after the filming was completed. Moreover, the script itself is structured around the prison murder of a rather mild-mannered, middle-class white man. This is the situation into which Young, to all appearances a rather mild-mannered, middle-class white man, stepped in 1977, when he agreed — against union rules — to take over the directing of the film.

One imagines this set of circumstances may have lent the project a certain existential urgency, for lack of a better term. One also imagines it may have been precisely this that drew Young to the project, and enabled him to work successfully with his cast. Young was by that time already fairly well known as a documentary filmmaker, with all the requisite sensitivity for working with people who were personally — in more ways than one — invested in the material. Legend has it, in fact, that it was largely Young's skills as a documentarian, which Piñero saw exemplified in *¡Alambrista!*, at that time still a work-in-progress, that convinced Piñero to bring Young on board as director.[1] Young seems to have been not only willing but eager to embrace the fraught circumstances of the project, including Piñero's insistence on control of the casting. ("He wouldn't let it lose its integrity," Young has said, by way of explaining Piñero's insistence on a Puerto Rican actor to play Juan, the lead.[2]) But when Young took over the project, it was in a shambles. On the one hand, many of the actors had spent months developing and then performing, under Marvin Felix Camillo's direction, the highly successful stage version, and were, as its originators, emotionally attached to the theatrical form of the material. It was, after all, on some level, *their own* experience of prison that they were portraying. On the other hand, however, a play cannot simply be filmed and called a movie. As he remembers in a recent interview, Young first spent a week "feeding Miguel cherry brandy so he wouldn't get a fix," and then, "together we restructured the movie."[3] The result is edgy, and bears a number of marks (or, one is tempted to say, scars) of its volatile, collaborative origin.

The same could certainly be said of the play. *Short Eyes* originated not only in the penal system, and particularly in Sing-Sing, where Piñero was incarcerated in 1972 at the time he began writing the play, but also in the improvisational, ensemble work begun there by Camillo, in the form of basic acting classes for the inmates, and later continued with "The Family," a working ensemble of actors and writers recently released from Sing-Sing and Bedford Hills. As Camillo tells it, he literally met the ex-cons at the prison gate as they were released, "and brought them from a prison slave system to a Manhattan workshop that they themselves created.... Instead of going back to the block or a kind of situation that could lead them back to jail, they went to a workshop to rehearse."[4] It was at the Theatre of the Riverside Church, where "The Family" eventually came to be in residence, that *Short Eyes* was born as a play — through a workshopping process that emphasized collaboration and improvisation. It is no surprise, then, that the play hovers somewhere between straight drama and personal testimony, and in this sense might be seen to foreshadow certain more recent dramatic trends, such as Anna Deveare Smith's "Theatre of Testimony," Touchstone Theatre's *Steelbound*, or even the popular *Laramie Project*, in which the text is woven from a variety of documentary materials, including personal interviews, TV reports, newspaper articles and court records, and in which either the actors play real historical people, or real historical people have a shot at acting. In either case, what the audience sees on stage, regardless of production values and quality of execution, is often scary in a way only real things can be: not because the story *in the play* is frightening (it might, after all, be quite humorous), but because the story *of the play* is. Looking at a work of art of this kind induces a certain double-vision: one person's entertainment is someone else's life.

5. From Cell to Celluloid: *Short Eyes* (Crutchfield)

On the surface, the original *Short Eyes* tells the story of what happens when Clark Davis, a young, white, middle class man accused of raping a little girl, is placed on a cellblock populated primarily by black and Puerto Rican criminals from the inner city. Not surprisingly, though with a good deal of encouragement from a corrupt prison guard named Mr. Nett, the other inmates view Clark as a victim's victim, as the absolute bottom of the food chain, and they project upon him all of their own unacknowledged animality. He becomes, in effect, the emblem of all they must deny in themselves in order to maintain even the most truncated sense of human dignity. Once the scapegoating logic of projection is set in motion, it is only a matter of time before it reaches its conclusion with Clark's murder.

But this is really only the structural framework or *occasion* of the story. Within that framework is the more important story of a younger Puerto Rican, a character the stage directions describe as a "pretty boy of twenty-one who looks younger," nicknamed Cupcakes, and his mentor, an older Puerto Rican named Juan. At the beginning of the play, before Clark's appearance, Cupcakes is the obvious victim, and Juan his only protector. Though he has only been on the cellblock a short time, Cupcakes' body has already become the site of amorous contention among the other inmates, and it seems only too probable that the delicate balance of competing forces will eventually tip in one direction or another, and he will become someone's "stuff." When Clark enters the scene, however, Cupcakes seizes the opportunity to deflect the other prisoners' aggression onto the clueless newcomer, and to position himself as an aggressor along with them. Once Clark has

Competing for cigarettes in *Short Eyes*.

been sacrificed in his place, Cupcakes is free, but at the cost of going against his mentor's teaching. Juan pronounces upon this failure: "[Y]our fear of this place stole your spirit.... And this is no pawn shop." Despite Juan's best efforts, Cupcakes has forfeited his humanity and surrendered himself to the brutal, Darwinian ethos of the prison. At this level, then, the play is really about the failure of an initiation into moral responsibility.

But Juan is more than just Cupcakes' failed mentor and the deliverer of wise but ineffectual aphorisms. He is also the one man to whom Clark tells the history of his sickness. Though Clark's story tests Juan's understanding and compassion to the limit, Juan nevertheless sticks his neck out to protect Clark from the escalating animosity of the other inmates. And apparently, Juan's moral authority is grudgingly recognized on the block. Nicknamed "The Poet" by the others, Juan's voice is everywhere the voice of humane reason, and he alone decries the animal logic of projection. While the other characters are motivated chiefly by their most basic instincts (for physical gratification, revenge, or mere physical survival), Juan seems motivated by the higher ideal of moral responsibility, of surviving prison with his humanity intact. He offers a glimmer of moral hope in the play's otherwise bleak moral landscape. The play is certainly a tragedy — Juan, despite the clarity of his moral vision and his courage in acting in accordance with it, fails to prevent a murder in which his own protégé participates — but it is no study in sadism or nihilism. Though far from perfect (he is, after all, a convicted criminal, and one who seems perfectly free of remorse for his unnamed crime — as are most of his colleagues in the play), Juan is still a recognizably good human being.[5] Given that his goodness runs so disproportionately contrary to the world he lives in, Juan might even be seen as an heroic figure.

This is the basic story that emerged in "The Family's" ensemble workshops during their residency at the Theatre of the Riverside Church, where *Short Eyes* was first produced in early 1974. The run was a success, and attracted the attention of Joseph Papp, who eventually brought it to the Lincoln Center. There, in the Vivian Beaumont Theatre, on May 9, 1974, *Short Eyes* opened as part of the New York Shakespeare Festival. It went on to win two Obies and a New York Drama Critics Circle Award for the Best American Play of 1973–74. In the aftermath, Piñero himself seems to have become somewhat of a celebrity — there were dozens of interviews in a variety of newspapers and journals, and reviews of the show (mostly laudatory) were legion. Moreover, the reach of the play's significance beyond merely documenting prison life was immediately apparent. In the words of one reviewer, *Short Eyes* was "significant not only as a theatrical event, but also as an act of social redemption."[6]

5. From Cell to Celluloid: *Short Eyes* (Crutchfield)   91

There are many things that enable a play to effect its audience powerfully. Certainly not least of these is the level of commitment and communal genius with which cast, director, and designers address themselves to the project. Given that several of the cast members were acquainted with prison life through personal experience, and furthermore, that their work in theatre, if Camillo's testimony is to be believed,[7] was virtually the only thing keeping them from landing in prison again, it is very easy to imagine that the show carried with it an edginess, intensity, and authenticity not frequently found on Broadway. The actors on stage were playing characters of whom they had more than theoretical knowledge, and the drama they were enacting was one ultimately based upon their own experiences, albeit transformed through the alembic of the ensemble workshop. The director, as well, had spent many hours visiting prisons as teacher-in-residence, and seems to have possessed a fairly detailed knowledge of prison life, a knowledge brought to bear in his vision for the production.

One reason it is so tempting to mention these "extrinsic" factors, and to speculate upon the contributions they may have made to the success of the original production, is that the play itself seems not entirely to justify that success. Considered "intrinsically," in terms of its dramatic structure, characterization, etc., *Short Eyes* is at best uneven — which is exactly the sort of showing one would expect from a beginning playwright, even one of unusual gifts.

Before taking a closer look at some of these intrinsic elements, however, it needs to be said that considering the play in this "dramaturgical" light — i.e., as an example of the playwright's craft — is somewhat different from the approach most often taken by scholars of literature to this (or, for that matter, any other) dramatic work. That approach might broadly be called "interpretive."[8] But while the play's interpreters have made some valuable and compelling discoveries, and will hopefully make many more, they have tended to do so at the expense of a certain theoretical obscurity, if not to say carelessness.

The enabling presupposition of interpretation, and it is apparently an unconscious one, is that the play is a "literary text." But plays, by their very nature, trouble any traditional notions of literature and textuality. This is because plays are fragmentary in a very radical sense. What the playwright has made — the "script" — is deliberately partial, incomplete, and provisional. It is in fact like nothing so much as an architectural blueprint. Just as the architect cannot hope to specify every detail of the eventual building he envisions, so the playwright, no matter how obsessive, cannot script the precise shape of every gesture, the minute tilt of every inflection, the exact duration of every pause, for the characters he imagines. Likewise, just as the architect knows full well that many other people, and many practical contingencies to boot, will determine the final product of his efforts, so the playwright must constantly keep in mind the collaborative reality of his art form. The play's the thing only if by "play" we mean *performance*. To be sure, a performance can be "read," analyzed and interpreted. But the *script* itself, which in most cases represents the extent of the playwright's contribution, is not, strictly speaking, a work of art, because it is not yet whole.[9] It lies somewhere among the discarded scaffolding used to construct the performance. Any engagement with the "play" which forgets or ignores this fundamental distinction between script and performance, is doomed to reify the script as a literary text like any other, without reference to its provisionality — and ephemerality — as a vehicle for performance. This is not to say that it is simply wrong to look at playscripts from a purely interpretive or textual point of view, for the best scripts (*Hamlet* comes to mind) certainly hold their own against the best literature in the language — and on literature's own terms. But that is not the essence of what they do. The essential quality of a play can only be perceived in the light of its ultimate purpose: to be performed.

Reading with an eye to performance (i.e. from what one might call a "dramaturgical" perspective) brings a different, and in a sense, much more practical set of questions into view. We are not interested so much in "what the play *means*" (a question that too often becomes, "to what *political use* can we put the play"), but rather "how (or to what degree) the play *works*." Here again, though, one must be careful with such terms. A playscript can be said to *work* in two senses: when it tells a coherent story, and when it tells the story in a way that is suitable for (and conducive to) live performance. Milton's *Samson Agonistes*, for example, is certainly a structurally coherent work of drama; but it consists almost entirely of talk rather than action, or language that *says* far more than it *does*; and this renders the work (as far as anyone can tell) unperformable as is. The same goes for Goethe's *Faust*, though for different reasons. Anyone who wished to perform one of these plays would need to make some fairly radical changes, to come up with a script whose language is dramatic, i.e. not *informative* (expressive) so much as *performative*.[10]

To complicate matters, both structural "coherence" of this kind, and dramatic "suitability" are understood differently on the avant garde than on Broadway. Generally speaking, however, the dramaturgical perspective will keep one basic question in mind: *Does the script give the actor, director, and designer a structure that is sufficiently well-imagined to occasion a compelling performance (in whatever genre or style)?* We want to know whether the plot-structure supports the characters and their journeys; whether the language, when spoken by an actor, is a suitable medium for the action; in short, whether the script is something the other artists can *work with* to create a coherent experience for an audience.

Why is the dramaturgical perspective important? For the purposes of this essay, its importance lies in the fact that it is the perspective from which any director, but particularly a film director given the task of turning the playscript into a screenplay and the screenplay into a motion picture, would be obliged to consider the material. Hence, if we want to understand Robert Young's art as a film director, we will have to do more than simply track the differences between the film and the play. We need to see those differences as *choices*, as deliberate changes he made to Piñero's play during that mysterious, brandy-soaked week of script-work. Only by looking at the script dramaturgically, as he might have looked at it, will we be able to understand the artistic reasons why Young might have made those choices.

The dramaturgical questions a film director asks are similar in certain basic ways to the theatre director's questions. Both want to know what the *spine* of the story is. Whose journey is the central one here? How do the other characters and their stories depend upon and influence the central story? Moreover, through whose eyes does the audience see the world in which these stories take place? Whose world is this, and what are the rules of that world? What are its architecture and its governing principles? Also, what clues, in the form of salient images, gestures, or verbal figures, has the writer given about the kind of experience he imagines for the audience? The film director, like his theatrical counterpart, has a myriad of more specific questions in mind as well, however questions that are more or less native to his art form. Since film, as commonly understood, is a visual rather than a verbal medium, a film director looking at a playscript will first ask himself which parts of the story can be *shown*, through images, rather than *told*, through character dialogue. The most urgent concern for the film director is to compress, to economize language even more radically than the playwright has already done with his play. This also generally means streamlining the story, zeroing in on its essence and distilling it yet further. The bottom line in film is not the embodiment of poetic eloquence, but the structuring of *what happens next*.

As noted earlier, Piñero's play is uneven in ways that reveal the playwright's "youth" as a theatre artist. The most obvious of these is the inclusion of material that, while well-written in itself, nevertheless unbalances the play structurally. The character Ice's monologue about Jane Fonda, and the pages of dialogue surrounding it, might be cited as a particularly egregious example of this. More often, though, what occurs is a bit subtler, when something is said not out of any dramatic necessity,[11] but out of the playwright's desire to tell the audience something he thinks they should know. We might refer to this as "megaphoning"—the tell-tale sign is when a character seems to speak *as if for the audience's benefit*, rather than in order to achieve a particular end in the scene. One rather brief example in *Short Eyes* occurs at the top of Act II—a prominent position. Again, the perpetrator (or victim?) is Ice. Act I ends with a brutal scene in which the verbal abuse and taunting of Clark finally erupts into physical violence, as the other inmates first beat him, then ram his head into a filthy toilet. Now ("half an hour later," the stage directions tell us), Juan and Ice are playing chess.

> ICE: You know, it's kinda like a shame what these dudes did to that poor ugly misbegotten son of a bitch. I feel almost sorry for the slob ... [p. 57].

It is as if Piñero feared the audience might forget Act I over the course of intermission. Unfortunately, this bit survives into the film, where there is no intermission, and hence little chance of the audience forgetting anything. In any case, it certainly isn't *Juan* who needs reminding here. Not only does he *know* what happened on the floor half an hour earlier, he's probably *thinking about it right now* (as evidenced by the fact that he loses the chess game to Ice—for the first time ever.) But even something apparently so minute and harmless as having Ice say, "these dudes" instead of "they," or "that poor ugly misbegotten son of a bitch" instead of "him," tips the balance into megaphoning, since Juan wouldn't require such specificity in order to understand Ice's meaning here. No, Ice is speaking for the audience's benefit, and the effect is to remind the audience that they are an audience. Such reminders are never welcome, unless of course the aesthetic world of the play is founded upon self-consciousness toward its own action—as one finds, for example, in Brechtian theatre, or in "camp." Otherwise, no matter how bizarre and fanciful the world of the play may be, the audience wants to believe in that world, to participate in it. When characters megaphone, however, they come across as fake, and the play as amateurish and clunky.

But megaphoning is not to be confused with the kind of "role-playing" that characters in plays, like people in real life, do for each other continually. In this case, the actor has the double task of playing a character who is himself playing one or more characters. While this may sound unnecessarily complex, the truth is that what gives a character "depth," what makes him "believable," is often precisely this layered performativity. Audiences typically read such performance-within-performance as "realistic," because they themselves adopt multiple roles or personae (literally, "masks") in their everyday dealings with each other. What one might call "getting to know someone" boils down to seeing through these various "characters" to the "actor" beneath, as well as learning to predict which particular role the actor will adopt under what circumstances. Audiences in the theatre (or in front of a movie screen or television set, for that matter) typically enjoy reading and decoding the various layers of a character, because it is a game in which one practices for real life. *Short Eyes* is full of such role-playing; and in fact, this is what makes the play so compellingly scary. The characters are *always* performing for each other, adopting various poses and postures, bluffing, threatening, manipulating, etc., and the reason becomes clear: they are terrified. One might say, turning this observation around, that Piñero manages to convey the scariness of prison so compellingly because his method is indirect: he shows us a world in which *no one is ever safe to be himself.* One's very survival in this world depends upon one's *ability to act*, and in particular, to act tough, confident, invulnerable, brave or, in prison lingo, "cool"— in other words, to act precisely contrary to one's true feelings and the true state of affairs in prison, where even the strongest prisoner is subject to the absolute power of the prison guards. Very rarely, and only under very particular circumstances, do we see anyone let down his guard and drop his role.[12]

The difference between this kind of role-playing and megaphoning is something an audience feels immediately, but which can be explained analytically by considering the question of the character's action: What is the character *trying to do* by speaking or behaving in this way? Can we discover, in this particular speech or behavior, a clear intention; and does this intention make sense, i.e. does it line up with this character's intentions in other scenes, to form a coherent overall character *action* for the play? By way of illustration, one might consider a speech Longshoe gives to Clark soon after the latter's appearance on the floor:

> LONGSHOE: Look here, this is our section ... white ... dig? That's the Rican table, you can sit there if they give you permission.... Same goes with the black section.... Black go on the front of the line, we stay in the back.... It's okay to rap with the blacks, but don't get too close with any of them. Ricans too. We're the minority here, so be cool. If you hate yams, keep it to yourself. Don't show it. But also don't let them run over you. Ricans are funny people. Took me a long time to figure them out, and you know something, I found out that I still have a lot to learn about them. I rap spic talk. They get a big-brother attitude about the whites in jail. But they also back the niggers to the T ... [p. 28–29].

Here Longshoe is playing a very specific "role" vis-à-vis Clark: he is the benevolent mentor, whose job, as he says earlier, is to "hip you to what's happening fast" (p. 27). His action is clear: as the only white on the floor besides Clark, he wants to bring Clark under his wing. This will benefit him in a variety of ways, both by increasing his power relative to the other racial groups, and by giving him absolute power over Clark, from whom he will then claim certain material (and quite possibly sexual) favors. The speech makes sense in context, because Clark is in fact ignorant of the things Longshoe is telling him, things he needs and probably wants to know. Moreover, at the macrological level of the play's action, Longshoe's speech performs the essential function of *exposition*: setting forth or creating the "world" of the play. We, the audience, are at this point in essentially the same position as Clark himself: we've been thrown into a world we don't understand, the governing rules and structural principles of which seem obscure and almost baroque in their complexity. We need to be educated in order to understand and appreciate the story that is about to unfold before our eyes, but we can't simply be *told* this information outright. (That would be a particularly odious instance of megaphoning.) We have to be *shown* it, or at least overhear it being given, in a situation and in a manner that is both necessary and real *within the world of the play*. This is exactly what Longshoe's speech does. It is no surprise, then, that the scene in which it occurs is preserved almost verbatim in the film version, where the audience finds itself in an epistemological situation similar to that of their theatre-going predecessors.

What makes *Short Eyes* both interesting and challenging in this regard, however, is that the role-playing these characters engage in is itself rather hyperbolic. The characters speak in a way that everywhere betrays their relentless consciousness of being in front of an audience, namely, each other. Even a dialogue between only two characters, such as the altercation between Longshoe and El Raheem early in Act I, is really a sort of play-within-the play being performed with the other characters as audience. But it is a play with very real consequences. Although often commonplace in dramatic dialogue, a struggle for power is a life-and-death truth for the characters in *Short Eyes*. For them, to lose face is to lose power, and to lose power is to become vulnerable to attack, and vulnerability is tantamount to invitation. The role-playing we see among the characters is thus largely about parading one's strength, and such parades can at times begin to resemble megaphoning. Even in such cases, however, the distinction can be made. By way of example, Mr. Nett, one of the prison guards, delivers a longish speech to Davis in Act I which, on its surface, seems egregiously over-written, almost to the point of self-parody:

NETT: Clark Davis ... Davis.

CLARK: Yes, that's me.

5. From Cell to Celluloid: *Short Eyes* (Crutchfield) 97

> NETT: Come here ... come here ... white trash ... filth.... Let me tell you something and you better listen good cause I'm only going to say it one time ... and one time only. This is a nice floor ... a quiet floor.... There has never been too much trouble on this floor.... With you, I smell trouble ... I don't question the warden's or the captain's motive for putting you on this floor.... But for once I'm gonna ask why they put a sick fucking degenerate like you on my floor.... If you just talk out of the side of your mouth one time ... if you look at me sideways one time ... if you mispronounce my name once, if you pick up more food than you can eat ... if you call me for something I think is unnecessary ... if you oversleep, undersleep ... if ... if ... if ... you give me just one little reason ... I'm gonna break your face up so bad your own mother won't know you....
>
> LONGSHORE: Mr. Nett is being kinda hard...
>
> NETT: Sit down, Murphy ... I'm talking to this ... this scumbag ... yeah, he's a child rapist ... a baby rapist, how old was she? How old? ... Eight? ... seven.... Disgusting bastard ... [p. 30–31].

Thus Mr. Nett, clichés unfurled and snapping ostentatiously in the breeze, announces the arrival of the "short eyes," Clark. Significantly, Young preserves this scene (which goes on for nearly two pages) in the film version, where the demands of the medium are particularly unforgiving of inessential verbiage. As the plot unfolds, however, and we observe Mr. Nett's hand in the final outcome, we realize that here what we were seeing is not in fact megaphoning, but a performance on Mr. Nett's part for the special benefit of the other characters. Mr. Nett, we realize by the final scene, has had it in for Clark all along. Moreover, he has worked in the prison long enough to know how prisoners deal with a fellow they know to be a child rapist, a "short eyes." Nett's speech, in all its over-the-top glory, enacts (with remarkable success) his desire to ensure Clark's eventual murder at the hands of the other prisoners. The speech both alerts the other prisoners as to the nature of Clark's supposed crime, and assures them that he, Nett, will not interfere should they decide to victimize Clark. By the end of the scene, Longshoe, who had moved to take Clark under his wing, now spits in his face. Nett's performance has hit home. Clark is now completely isolated from his only natural ally on the prison floor — the other white man. He has no one to "watch his back." In this way, Mr. Nett's speech does much more than simply express his hatred for Clark. It effects a crucial transition in the plot.

Apart from the occasional megaphoning, Piñero's play presents two other difficulties: the instability of characterization, and the use of the "catwalk" for "silent" conversations between characters. Of the second, little need be said except that they do nothing to advance the plot, and hence are unnecessary, or what's worse, distracting. Of the first, one example should suffice. We are introduced early on to Juan, the main protagonist, and his first words seem to position him squarely in the moral center of the play. With apparent humanity, he comes to the defense of Cupcakes, the young Puerto-Rican upon whom several of the prisoners have lascivious designs. As Cupcakes enters the dayroom, the other prisoners, according to Piñero's stage-directions, "accompany him with simple scat singing to the tune of 'The Stripper,' Ad-libs." Immediately, Juan says, "Why don't you cut that loose? Man, don't you think that kid get tired of hearing that every morning?"(p.11). But a few pages later, we come across the following dialogue, still set in the dayroom:

> CUPCAKES: Told you before that I don't have no complexes.
>
> JUAN: You got no plexes at all?
>
> CUPCAKES: No.
>
> JUAN: Then why not let me fuck you?
>
> CUPCAKES: That's definitely out.
>
> JUAN: People without complexes might as well turn stuff [p. 19–20].

In no other scene in the play does Juan speak with such crude cynicism. This kind of language might well come from Paco, but it is simply out-of-character for Juan. Which is not to say that Juan isn't motivated by the desire we see expressed here (it is implied later that he is), but only that he would never express it this way.

In fact, even if we assume the worst (i.e. that Juan's interest in Cupcakes is essentially amorous), by expressing it so openly, Juan is directly undermining his own action, which in this case would be to seduce Cupcakes under the ruse of being his mentor and protector. Then the problem would not be that there are no good guys here, but that we find this truth out too soon and too baldly. When, late in Act II (indeed, just before the play's conflict becomes a crisis), Paco points out that everyone, including Juan, has designs on Cupcakes, and hence that no one has any right to object to the planned rape of Clark, the effect should be powerful. We should be horrified to see that Juan — even Juan! — has after all been morally compromised by prison life. But the earlier dialogue with Cupcakes has already given this truth away, and the dramatic potential of the final revelation is lost. How much more dramatic to have established Juan as the moral pillar of the play, to have preserved this humane figure of hope as long as possible, until Paco's speech unveiled the bitter truth, with the ensuing dénouement.

Instead, what we have is something more like David Mamet's *Glengarry Glen Ross*, where we know all along that there are no good guys: the question is merely which of the bad guys will do the dirty deed. Accordingly, we are in a universe where morality, if it exists at all, operates abstractly as a structuring principle and not as any particular character's motive. All of Juan's apparent compassion for Clark must be attributed to some nefarious motive, and Clark's memorable expression of gratitude, "Juan, you are the only human being I've met," must be read as inadvertently, and bitterly, ironic.

Perhaps by the time he was working on the screenplay with Young, Piñero realized this was undesirable. In any event, the film omits this earlier exchange with Cupcakes, thus withholding the revelation of Juan's compromised motives until the crucial moment when that revelation can affect the outcome. There, it is implied that if Juan had been able truthfully to deny Paco's accusation, Cupcakes' faith in Juan might have been preserved, he might have sided with Juan against the others who wanted to rape Clark, and thus might have preserved his own humanity, as well as Clark's life. But Juan is too honest to attempt to deny his own share of evil. The effect, then, of these (and many other) cuts in the film version is a much more unified sense of character for Juan, as well as for the others. Though, as we shall see, many incongruities remain.

It is necessary to turn now more explicitly to the film *Short Eyes*, both in order to gain a sense of Robert Young's art as a director, and to see what his version might teach us about the more general relationship between the two media, theatre and film. Comparing in this way a playscript to the visual "script" of a film "based upon" it might best be understood as posing the question of *translation*. As has been observed, theatre is essentially a verbal and vocal medium, though its language is continually and to varying degrees supported by image, non-verbal sound, and movement.[13] In film, this relationship is reversed. Film's power to make meaning derives from images, or rather, from sequences of images, as Lev Kuleshov pointed out long ago. These images may be supported by language and non-verbal sound (especially music), but sound is not essential to the meaning-making of film. Film and theatre are thus distinct semiotic systems which operate according to their own rules. In this way, what Walter Benjamin observed in the relationship between different languages, i.e. that each has its own "way of meaning" (*Art des Meinens*), is also true at the level of semiotic systems in general.[14] What happens, then, when a certain "content" (Benjamin's *Gemeinte*) is "carried over" (*trans-latio*) from one "form" or semiotic system to another? To what degree does the content (in this case, the *story* of the play *Short Eyes*) undergo transformation as it crosses from stage to screen?

It is interesting to observe how frequently the film's contemporary reviewers noted its "theatrical" quality. This was almost always done by way of condemnation, or at best, half-hearted apology. Among the more cogent reviews was a piece by Pauline Kael, which appeared in *The New Yorker*. Kael remarks, "Right from the beginning ... you hear the play coming through the documentary surface." The dialogue has "the rhythm of well-practiced stage readings. And some of the actors love their lines too much." At the same time, Kael admires the directorial "restraint" with which the violent moments are handled, a restraint that "intensifies our terror." Nevertheless, "*Short Eyes* doesn't stay in the mind," she says. "Its potency is in its words. They're live, raw, profane. But a movie that is primarily words tends to evaporate." As a consequence, the whole is "hung up somewhere between photographed play and prison documentary."[15]

Kael's comments are useful in that they draw attention precisely to this question of form, i.e. of the formal differences between theatrical and cinematic "ways of meaning." In effect, she is saying that too much of the story content remains, as it were, untranslated from its original theatrical form. Within the new semiotic system of film, the predominance of spoken language seems out of place. To make matters worse, Kael implies, Young has allowed his actors (several of whom also appeared in the stage version) to indulge themselves in a "theatrical" style of delivery, a style inappropriate to the more nuanced vision of the camera.[16] What this means in practical terms is that the film actor must *do less*. In fact, as Alfred Hitchcock demonstrated so memorably in *Rear Window*, it is possible to tell an emotional story without the actor doing much of anything at all.[17] Robert Young, Kael implies, has not sufficiently coached his cast in how to act for the camera.

A more recent reviewer takes Kael's lead, and goes even further in his dismissal of the film:

> [I]ts theatrical roots show: characters stand in stationary poses and sermonize at each other in melodramatic flights of overcooked prose. Nobody actually has a conversation here. As a screenwriter, Piñero had a tin ear for dialogue and at no time does anything in *Short Eyes* sound close to how people genuinely speak to one another.[18]

One might begin by observing that, as an ex-con himself, Piñero might be fairly well qualified to judge how people "genuinely" speak to one another in prison, but the essential matter lies elsewhere. It's true that, at first, the dialogue in *Short Eyes* sounds oddly self-conscious, even "melodramatic," and that the actors are often seen assuming rather deliberate "poses." But the fact that these "theatrical" elements are off-putting is itself significant, for it tells us that the world we are entering in the film is different from the conventionally "real" world, and different in a specific way: it is *intensified*.

The theatrical element is thus not simply a style that the director might just as well have dropped. *It is not a formal characteristic of the play, but an essential characteristic of the world represented by the play.* Therefore, to fault the film for its "theatricality" is to fall into a category error, i.e. to mistake a content-element for a form-element. What Piñero and Young are trying to show us is not a world seen theatrically, but a world that is itself theatrical in a very particular way.[19]

We see this same category error repeated in reference to another choice Young and his collaborators made, this one having to do with the soundtrack. Curtis Mayfield's score is used only sparingly; for the most part, the score of the film consists of myriad synchronous sounds produced by the actors on set, and includes a surprising (and at times rather disturbing) variety of shouts, cat-calls, murmurs, animal howls and screeches, laughter, flushing toilets, and the ubiquitous grinding and rattling of the metal gates. This texture of background noise is broken by patches of silence, across which the dialogue drifts almost eerily. One obvious reason for this choice is to enhance the sense of "reality" of the world of the film, in a way analogous to the lighting and set design, both of which are minimal. Very rarely in the film is music used in the way it so often is in feature films, i.e. to enhance or qualify the audience's emotional response to the images they see.[20]

But early in the film, Young takes an interesting artistic risk with the sound, and in the view of a number of commentators, it fails miserably. The moment in question occurs during the initial dayroom scene, as we're getting to know the various characters and their world. The inmates are all gathered together in their respective "sections" of the dayroom, when Cupcakes grabs someone's hat, wields it like a microphone, and begins improvising a Latin music radio show. The other *puertorriqueño* inmates join in, beating out a dance rhythm on whatever objects are handy, and before we know it, Freddy Fender is singing a heartfelt ballad, "Break It Down." Not to be shown up, the black inmates soon put up their own crooner, played by Curtis Mayfield. Unlike Fender's song, which is delivered a capella, Mayfield's is layered over a full band arrangement (also by Mayfield), which is obviously not being produced by the actors on stage. This seems to have utterly baffled the film's initial reviewers. According to Martin Mitchell, for example, Mayfield's song "sounds far too sophisticated in view of the participants and their meagre facilities."[21] The song, in other words, isn't presented "realistically." It is, again, theatrical or "staged" in a way that seems to be out of keeping with the conventions of the documentary genre. Such lyrical group sing-a-longs may have their place in Hollywood prison films or nostalgic melodramas of the Old South, but in a serious drama, how can they come across as anything short of ridiculous?

The basis for this objection is the assumption that Young intended for us either not to notice the overdub, or to believe that, hidden away somewhere among the crowd of the dayroom, are an electric guitar, bass, drums, and horn section. However, one can give Young the benefit of the doubt in this case. The objection falls into the same trap as Kael's above: it confuses content and form. The songs are not simply injected out of some misguided desire to present the world of the prison more theatrically. Within the reality of that world itself, these songs *are* theatrical performances in the same way that most of the prisoners' behavior is. Moreover, they arise organically from the scene. The residual tension from the conflict with Go-Go (played with unctuous finesse by Piñero himself) is redirected through humor by Cupcakes, when he begins his Latin disc jockey bit. This evolves into the Latin a capella, which in turn, according to the competitive logic of the prison, gives rise to the Mayfield song. This time, however, the competition is artistic rather than physical. The *puertorriqueños* have shown something of their culture, and now the blacks are invited to show something of theirs, the transition being the moment when Mayfield, who has been shown delighting in Fender's song, rises from the bench to congratulate him, and the two men embrace. The effect is a deft — and dramatically motivated — passing of the musical baton.

Furthermore, a clear dramatic progression leads from Fender's song to Mayfield's: Over the course of the scene (and it is a long one), we see the prisoner's faces gradually relax from pose into authenticity, from grimaces into expressions of genuine emotion — joy, longing, regret, brotherly love. The men smile at each other, hug and pat each other on the back, or simply close their eyes and sway to the music. It is as if, for them, music were the only medium in which the expression of the actual fear, frustration and loneliness they feel, the madness and woundedness, the sense of waste and futility, were permissible. The music marks out a kind of sacred space in which the truth can be told with impunity and felt without reserve. The ritual begins with Fender's song, and by the time Mayfield begins his, the music has carried us far into the heads of the prisoners, into their inner lives, so that what we hear on the soundtrack is what *they* hear in their imaginations. The way Young structures the scene, intercutting shots of the performer with close-ups of the prisoner/audience members, reinforces this. The Mayfield song is a moment of expressionism, a glimpse into the hidden, residual, scarcely articulate humanity of the prisoners. As hardened and brutal and self-protective as they are, they still manage to feel moved by music, to forget their poses for a moment and remember their souls. What we are witnessing here is not, as Mitchell implies, some generic faux-pas, some tasteless decoration foisted upon the material. It *is* the material; and it is presented at the dramatically appropriate time. Without it, we would witness the escalating violence that follows—first against Go-Go, then against Clark—as the work of animals rather than human beings. And that the prisoners be recognizable as human beings, however morally compromised, is essential to the story.

Clearly, then, it was not Young's intention here to conform to some conventional notion of documentary realism, the genre in which his work up to this point in his career had been primarily conceived. (One begins to suspect, in fact, that the critical confusion stemmed from the assumption that Young was and always would be a documentarian, plain and simple.) Instead, what we see him doing is taking the tools of that genre, and putting them into the service of serious drama. And the film is drama, not documentary. That this particular drama is itself the product of a "testimonial" process; that it was filmed on location in an abandoned wing of the Manhattan House of Detention for Men (commonly known as "The Tombs"); that the design elements (lighting, sound and set) are for the most part bleakly naturalistic; and that many of the characters are played by professional and non-professional actors with first-hand knowledge of their roles and of the world represented in the drama, does not change this fact. The film is a drama that exploits many of the conventions of documentary, not a documentary dramatized.[22]

But Young's intention in using these documentary tools seems to go beyond merely heightening the "reality effect" of the film, and to push deeper toward an interrogation of how "reality" and notions of the "realistic" are constructed to begin with. While the harsh natural lighting reveals the unglamorous grubbiness of the characters' faces and bodies; while the set is restricted to the bare day room and the hall of cells, surrounded everywhere by unadorned concrete and iron bars flaking garish paint; while the whole echoes with the squalid, profane sounds of incarceration; in fine, while all of this grounds the film in an ineluctably gritty physical reality, the story is drawing us into a deeper, psychological reality which we would not otherwise want to believe. Like the reality of warfare, which so many works of art have sought to convey, the reality of prison is deeply disturbing; so disturbing, in fact, that it is difficult to accept as "real." To do so would necessitate a radical reimagining of reality itself, or rather, an expansion of it to include its extreme and hidden darkness. Prison and warfare are like "normal life," only, as it were, *more so*. But it is by virtue of this *more*, this excess, this monstrosity, that the darkness within social reality is made perceptible, that the patterns of everyday contemporary life are shown to be pathologies. No wonder, then, that a film like Young's *Short Eyes* encounters such critical resistance. By asking us to see ourselves in these prisoners, and to see our choices in theirs, the film is asking something very repugnant indeed. If our sense of ourselves and of the reality we live in were not so thoroughly predicated upon the denial of this more complex reality, then why would we go to such trouble and expense to criminalize certain people, and conceal them in labyrinths of concrete and iron?

It thus makes perfect sense that, in order to open up the question of social reality, Young has had to modify the conventions of his art form, creating a package uniquely suited to the content of the *Short Eyes* story. This is because such conventions serve, in a complexly symbiotic way, both to construct and to represent that reality. If a new sense of social reality is to be engendered through cinema, a new form must be discovered, a new "way of meaning" within the larger semiotic system of film.

Looking back on Piñero's original *Short Eyes*, it is easy to see that the film fixes many of the dramaturgical problems in the playscript: the story is streamlined and rearranged into a more compelling dramatic shape; the characterization is more consistent; the over-writing is trimmed back considerably. And certainly the overall sense of claustrophobia is greatly intensified by telling the story through the camera's eye, which is for the most part right down among the terrified, murderous faces of the characters, or else beholding them at close range through a lattice of bars. Moreover, what new material has been added — the scenario with Go-Go, the "roach derby," the brief display, at the top of the film, of the homemade knife that will become the murder weapon, the shots panning across the prisoners in their crowded cells — all of this contributes to the plot either directly or indirectly through symbolism or foreshadowing. And the editing of the murder scene itself is certainly a minor tour de force unimaginable on stage.

But *Short Eyes* is by no means a perfect film, and not all of its flaws are attributable to the low budget or volatile circumstances of the production. One of the more unfortunate choices for the film has to do with the way the crucial "confession" scene between Clark and Juan was shot. In the play, as Clark narrates the chilling history of his pedophilia, Juan moves about the empty dayroom doing janitorial chores, as is apparently his job. Piñero is quite specific in his stage directions as to where Juan is and what he is doing at each moment of Clark's speech. Apart from the symbolic value of Juan's task, it has a very practical, dramatic value, or rather, two values. First, it gives the actor playing Juan something specific to do during Clark's speech (which goes on for several pages). This prevents the scene from sinking into stasis. Secondly, and more importantly, however, it allows Piñero to withhold, from both Clark and the audience, Juan's reaction to what he is hearing. This is crucial. The dramatic power of the confession is its seeming innocence and naiveté. We feel encouraged, at one and the same time, to sympathize with the obviously disturbed and distraught Clark (or at least to pity him), and to keep him at arm's length. His story is horrifying, but the way he tells it makes it impossible to dismiss him as a degenerate. This is a delicate and emotionally fraught situation for the audience, and one that points to the central ethical problem posed by the film: understanding that which it would be easier simply to abhor. It is important that the audience be allowed to feel this problem truthfully. We can't have our own private response tampered with by cues from the playwright via Juan. As he has imagined the scene, Piñero has enabled us to experience and observe our own response first, however uncomfortably complex or conflicted it may be, before Juan shows us his. When he finally does react, there is an explosive release of tension — his own, and that of the audience.

For reasons it is difficult to fathom, Young shoots this scene in the conventional manner, as a series of cuts between close-ups of the two actors' faces. Bruce Davison's performance as Clark is beyond reproach, but José Perez's mighty struggle to make his face silently express Juan's contorted feelings is painful to watch. It is obvious that he simply doesn't know what to do with himself. Even preserving the basic shot-structure of the scene, how much better it would have been if Perez had been directed simply to keep his face absolutely neutral — moving, perhaps only his eyes — so that the audience would be left in suspense about what he is really feeling, until the moment of explosive revelation. But even then, the scene would make no sense: Juan has been instructed by the guards to clean the dayroom. His negligence of that task is simply out of character for him. The effect on the audience, in turn, is inadvertently to pull them out of the drama. They are made to feel more concern and sympathy for the hapless Perez himself than for the character he's playing. Given the importance of this scene in the overall plot, this is regrettable indeed.

Piñero's play loses something structurally in translation as well. The most significant is a "framing" device which is totally absent from the film. Early in the play, in a seemingly insignificant ripple in the dialogue, Cupcakes discovers that the communal TV set is broken. Mr. Nett responds by saying he'll put in a repair order (p. 16). The action passes on, and not until the very end, in the play's "Epilogue," does this detail return. After Clark's murder, which Mr. Nett and the inmates have played off as a suicide, Captain Allard is conducting an investigation. He interviews Cupcakes and Longshoe, both of whom lie, saying that while Clark was in the shower cutting his own throat, they were out in the dayroom watching *The Dating Game*. Allard tells Nett he knows they're lying. "What makes you think they're lying?" Nett asks innocently.

> ALLARD: Nett, did you send this TV repair order to the shop or not? This is your signature, isn't it? Then I can assume that the men were not watching TV, because the television was not working.... And can I also assume that Clark Davis's death was not a suicide.... Do you realize what you've gotton yourself into? [p. 115–116].

For a brief moment, it looks as though Allard, who from the beginning seemed to be concerned about the danger he knew Clark would face on the cellblock, will set things right, punish the perfidious Nett and his inmate accomplices. But then:

> ALLARD: ...His parents are downstairs in the warden's office complaining about why he wasn't placed in a special unit ... or given more protection. What are we supposed to say to this family? ... I don't know if I'm doing the right thing, Nett ... but I am going to tear up this repair order. It's the only thing that'll shake up their story, and yours as well....
>
> NETT: Thank you, sir.
>
> ALLARD: There's nothing to thank me for. I didn't do this for you, Nett, but for the Department. Do we understand each other? [p. 116].

All of this is cut from the screenplay, and with it goes a fairly sophisticated and pointed critique of institutional corruption in the prison system, even among well-intentioned administrators. Perhaps this layer was peeled away from the film because Young felt it took the story in a new direction, broadening the context in a way that lessened the power of the drama among the prisoners. And yet, clearly, Clark's fate is not merely an "internal affair." At every stage of the game, from Clark's first moment on the cellblock to his last, Mr. Nett is planning his destruction. Nett introduces Clark to the others in no uncertain terms as a victim, and he basically directs Clark's murder, saying, when Paco wants merely to stab Clark, "No, cut his throat" (p. 95). Here and elsewhere, it is apparent that the prisoners take their cues from Mr. Nett. Interestingly, Young does much in other respects to emphasize this state of affairs. During the early fight between El Raheem and Longshoe, he returns at rapid intervals to close-ups of Nett, who looks on sadistically as the two men go at each other like animals. And in the murder scene, not only do we see Nett in the background keeping lookout and giving instructions, but immediately after the shot of Clark holding his lacerated throat, we have a long take of Mr. Nett as he backs away, followed by a cut to Longshoe and El Raheem staring immobilized down at Clark, then back to Mr. Nett as he turns and walks out. The effect of the sequence is chilling. Like a modern day Iago or low-brow Mephistopheles, Nett has others do his dirty work, then slinks away while those he has manipulated stand aghast with the knife still in their hands.

The last glimpse we get of Nett is during Allard's speech to the prisoners in the dayroom, in which, though Allard says he is "satisfied that it was a suicide," he nevertheless holds the others "morally guilty.... If you had taken some time out of your own problems to help this poor man that was placed in here because of mistaken identity..." (p. 117). Clark, it seems, was not guilty of the crime for which he stood accused. This is presumably disturbing news to Clark's murderers. As if to emphasize the dangerous potential of the situation, Young cuts to Nett, lurking outside the gate and glaring in at the prisoners with his teeth gritted, as if daring any one of them to "rat him out." Nothing happens. Or rather, two nothings: nobody blows the murderers' cover, and nobody relieves their guilt. This second nobody is of course, Juan, who alone knows that, though Clark may not have committed the particular crime of which he stood accused, he is in fact a child molester, and is certainly guilty of many other instances of statutory rape.[23] But Juan holds his peace (Young shows him doing so), leaving the others to suffer the belief that they've killed a man wrongfully, even by their own harsh code of ethics. "Good night, men," says Allard, himself none the wiser. The prisoners return sullenly to their cells. In a few moments, Cupcakes is "on the bail," Juan delivers his last fatherly advice, and the film is over.

In Piñero's original version, we are made to see that people like Nett exist within and *because of* the system. In Young's, they exist within and *in spite of* it. Allard, in Young's version, is the dupe of the cover up; in Piñero's, he is a reluctant accomplice, with the implication that, at every level of society, choices are made which compromise one's morals, and that no one, no matter how removed from the scene of the crime, is free of responsibility for what happens there. The point is emphasized in a final dialogue among the prisoners.

> LONGSHOE: Man, he was guilty, I know, I could tell, I could see it in his eyes.
>
> EL RAHEEM: Man, he was clean.
>
> CUPCAKES: What have we done?
>
> ICE: Ain't no use crying over it now, Cupcakes, be cool, don't blow your cool, kid [p. 118].

Cupcakes then asks Juan for some last words of wisdom, something that will help him understand "what we have done." Longshoe interrupts:

> LONGSHOE: ... [W]hat are you holding up to Juan so much for, will that bring him back?
>
> CUPCAKES: You talk cause you did the killing.
>
> EL RAHEEM: He talks cuz we did the killing.
>
> CUPCAKES: I didn't take his head, I didn't swing the knife, he did.
>
> ICE: Cupcakes, listen to me, you killed him just as much as I did.
>
> CUPCAKES: You? You wasn't even there.
>
> ICE: I was there ... I was there ... No, I didn't swing the knife ... and neither did you, but we're guilty by not stopping it ... we sanctioned it ... Only Juan is free... [p. 119–120].

Here the message is fairly clear, and Juan's final words (the final words of the play) drive home the truth of what Cupcakes' self-preservation at Clark's expense has in fact cost him morally and spiritually. The mentoring relationship with Juan is at an end, and Juan can only pronounce upon its failure: Cupcakes is on his way out, and hopefully for good, but Juan can offer him no advice, no "life-style pearls,"

> ...becuz you, like the rest of us ... became a part of the walls ... an extra bar in the gate ... to remain a number for the rest of your life in the street world ... [...] Cupcake, you went past the money and blew it ... yah, that's right, this is cop and blow ... and you blew it becuz you placed yourself above understanding [p. 121].

The play thus ends squarely in Cupcakes' court. In a sense, it has been his story all along, and it is a tragic story.

All of this is absent from the film version. Instead, the focus is on the inmates' anxiety that, unless Juan tells him something to allay his misgivings, Cupcakes will, as Ice says, "go out there and run this thing on someone who shouldn't hear it." This is an altogether more ambiguous ending than what Piñero had originally imagined. The question of who is to blame and who is "free" never explicitly arises. We never hear Cupcakes express his qualms while attempting to evade blame; we never hear Ice's emphatic denial of that evasion. Without the context of this discussion, and of Juan's speech (quoted above), the film's final words, "[Y]our fear of this place stole your spirit ... and this ain't no pawnshop," are more enigmatic. It's as if Juan has left Cupcakes (and us) with a riddle rather than a clarifyingly moral interpretation of what has happened. Moreover, the scene is filmed with Juan and the other inmates locked once again in their cells, speaking through the bars to Cupcakes as he passes by on his way out, arms full of his hastily gathered possessions. The gate is then unlocked, and Cupcakes slips out, followed by the sound of Paco's sadistic laughter. The final image of the film is identical to the first: we see "The Tombs" from the outside, looking up from a low angle at the huge, dark, ominous face of the building, a face which betrays nothing of what goes on inside. It is a sinister image, suggesting a passage through an infernal darkness that, despite having been lived through, remains an enigma.

And this is perhaps where Young's art is most palpable in its effects on Piñero's story. Where Piñero had imagined an essentially humane and morally unambiguous story that, though tragic, offered some hope of redemption, Young gives us something resistant to easy moralizing. In other words, we might say that Young is less inclined to pass judgment on his characters and less willing to offer any clear answers to the moral problems the story brings its audience up against. It is in this ultimate stance toward the material, perhaps even more than the specific directorial choices along the way, that Young's experience as a documentarian is most clear. His *Short Eyes* is not saying, "Let me tell you a story, and here's the moral," but "Take a good look at this...."

Notes

1. Peary, Gerald. Review of *Short Eyes*, in *American Film*, July–August, 1982.
2. K.B. "Junkie Bond," in *New York Magazine*, March 10, 2003.
3. Ibid.
4. Piñero, Miguel. *Short Eyes*. New York: Hill and Wang, 1975. p.ix. (Introduction).
5. Indeed, this paradox points to one of the central themes of the play: the intersection between two differences: first, the difference between the morality "on the outside" and the morality "on the inside" of prison; and second, the difference between the legal conceptions of Innocence and Guilt, which are both codified within and serve to delimit any society, and the ethical concepts of Good and Evil, which are (arguably) not a function of any particular social setting.
6. Gussow, Mel. "*Short Eyes*: Talent and Authenticity in Play of Prison Life," in *The New York Times Theatre Reviews*, 1973–1974: 168.
7. Piñero, Miguel. *Short Eyes*. New York: Hill and Wang, 1975. p. ix. (Introduction).
8. Roger Platizky and Arnaldo Cruz-Malave are notable among those who have considered the play from this perspective. (See Platizky's "Humane Vision in Miguel Piñero's *Short Eyes*," *The Americas Review*, vol. 19, no.1, Spring 1991, p. 83–91, where he argues that "Piñero exposes and finally censures hegemonic violence, while understanding, first-hand, its social and psychological underpinnings" (p. 83). See also Cruz-Malave's "'What a Tangled Web!' Masculinity, Abjection, and the Foundations of Puerto Rican Literature in the United States" in *Differences: A Journal of Feminist Cultural Studies*, vol. 8, no.1, Spring 1996, p. 132–151, a psychoanalytic reading, which bases part of its argument on a regrettable (and, alas, somewhat symptomatic) misreading of the script: Cruz-Malave quotes the white character Longshoe as saying "If a spic pulls a razor blade on you ... and they ain't no white people around ... get a spic to watch your back, you may have a

chance...." We are then told that "the founding texts of Nuyorican writing ... persistently comment on that porous, treacherous condition that constitutes 'Puerto Ricanness...'" (p. 138). In fact, what Piñero has Longshoe say is, "If a spic pulls a razor blade on you *and you don't have a mop wringer in your hands ... run.... If you have static with a nigger and they ain't no white people around ...* get a spic to watch your back, you may have a chance..." (Piñero, p. 29, italics mine). Piñero is not implying that Puerto Ricans are especially treacherous, only that their presence disrupts the reductive racial dialectic of black/white.

    9. One could of course argue that no work of art is completely whole, and that, in fact, the essence of art is the fragmentary. But (at the risk of sounding more dialectical-than-thou) this kind of fragmentation bears a different relation to wholeness than does the playscript; for though the work of art, in its semantic "openness," can perhaps be considered "fragmentary," still it is *all there is.* Thus, it continually points toward wholeness *in itself.* That is to say, in the work of art, fragmentation at the level of logic is recuperated (experienced) as wholeness at the level of *aesthesis.* But this is of a different order than the more fundamental fragmentation that constitutes the essence of the playscript. Here, the fragment is not an end in itself, but points toward a wholeness *elsewhere.* Such fragments do not yield themselves to recuperation, and thus are not dialectical. They represent rather an irreducible fragmentation that can only become whole with the supplement of the body (or recorded image) of the actor in performance. Only then can one speak of a work of art, and hence, of fragmentation in its higher, aesthetic, generative sense. (Of course, both kinds of fragmentation are subject to the additional defacement that comes about through accident, e.g., the *Venus de Milo.*)

    10. The use of this term here owes somewhat to J.L. Austin's analysis of performative language in *How to Do Things with Words.* Language is *dramatic* (from the Greek δραν, "to do") when its performative aspect is emphasized over its informative aspect. In concrete terms, this means that a character's speech functions primarily as a form of *action*— for example, to seduce, confuse, console, manipulate, or intimidate another character. Even in cases where a character seems to be merely expressing himself or informing another character, his language is dramatic if this expression can be related to an underlying character action.

    11. One might define "dramatic necessity" as a function of the constraints placed upon a character by the crossing of immediate dramatic circumstances with his own *action* (i.e. Aristotle's *praxis*).

    12. The only character who doesn't seem able to find a viable a role is, of course, Clark. From the moment he walks in, his terror is palpable. He doesn't know the rules of the role-playing game, and is continually picking up the wrong role, misreading the other prisoners' cues, and falling out of character and back into himself. Without a *pose,* he is utterly *ex-posed,* "placed-out" into the open; and this is what — perhaps even more than his alleged crime — "marks" him as a victim for the other prisoners.

    13. Dance, and other movement-based performance arts, including "physical theatre" (and one might also mention the infinite variety of other "live entertainment" spectacles, such as sporting events, tractor-pulls, and erotic dancing) while certainly *performative* or "theatrical," are thus not *theatre* in the sense the term is used here.

    14. See Benjamin's "The Task of the Translator," which appears in *Illuminations*— ironically enough (as Paul de Man pointed out) in a singularly inept translation.

    15. Kael, Pauline, Review of *Short Eyes,* in *The New Yorker,* September 26, 1977, pp. 127–133.

    16. A close-up, or even a medium-range shot, will always transcend the theatre-goer's natural ability to perceive the shifting expression on an actor's face as well as the inflection in his voice. Somewhat counter-intuitively, this mechanical power — to shift instantaneously between ranges, angles, perspectives, scenes, etc. in a manner that is utterly

unnatural — is precisely what has given film its "reality effect." One might venture to say that the camera's gaze seems so "real" not because it represents reality as we "really" see it, but because it presents something new: reality as we *would like* to see it, reality as seen through an ideal, omnipotent eye, freed from all constraints of individual human subjectivity. Thus, the real and the natural become divergent — even antagonistic — concepts in film.

17. The scene shows the protagonist, L.B. Jeffries (Jimmy Stewart), looking through binoculars and a telephoto camera lens at his neighbors in the adjacent apartment building. Hitchcock cuts back and forth between what Jeff sees (a musician practicing, newlyweds moving into an apartment, a woman drinking by herself, a ballet dancer doing exercises, and a couple bickering) and Jeff's face, which seems to respond with a range of emotions. In fact, Hitchcock repeated *exactly the same footage* of Jeff's face each time.

18. Hall, Phil. Review of *Short Eyes* for FilmThreat.com, posted March 7, 2003.

19. The beginnings of this understanding can be found in a review which appeared in the *New York Times* on September 28, 1977. Vincent Canby echoes Kael's observations, but interprets them more apologetically. "The theatrical origins are quite apparent in this furious but controlled screen version directed by Robert Young," he writes. "In this case, though, the theatrical origins contribute to the claustrophobic atmosphere that is essential to the point of *Short Eyes*, which is about a kind of overcrowding that is the physical equivalent to emotional desperation. There's no way out. As lines of dialogue overlap in that supercharged way of a theatrical production, so do Mr. Piñero's characters fight for space in the single cellblock where the action takes place." Likewise, Kevin Thomas writes in *The Los Angeles Times* (October 2, 1977) that "because *Short Eyes* asserts its own reality (of a very heightened sort), its theatrical elements never seem inappropriate." What neither reviewer seems to have noticed, however, are the deeper connections between the artistic choices they read as "theatrical," the performative, "role-playing" ethos those choices are intended to elucidate, and the sense of dread that ethos both betrays and, on the side of the audience, induces.

20. In fact, this happens only twice in *Short Eyes*: during the fight between Longshoe and El Raheem, and during the brief promenade of the drag queens.

21. Mitchell, Martin. Review of *Short Eyes* in *After Dark*.

22. An analogous work in the realm of literature is Tim O'Brien's *The Things They Carried*, which deploys many of the conventions of memoir (the dedication to individuals named in the narrative, the centrality of a narrator whose name is the same as the author's, the confessional mode of much of the writing, etc.), but which is nevertheless a work of fiction.

23. Unless, that is, one believes Clark is simply insane, that the "little picture incidents running across [his] mind" (p. 35) are the delusions of a psychopath — a possibility the film, like the play, does not rule out. After all, the only "evidence" concerning Clark is his own disjointed testimony to Juan. In that case, though, Juan's moral dilemma — defending a man he knows will continue, should he get out of prison alive, to molest children — loses its teeth and hence, its interest.

6. *Ballad of Gregorio Cortez*: A Traditional Tale for Postmodern Times

Cecelia Conway

Near dark on a hot spring evening in 1964, a classmate and I walk to the Rialto Theater in racially troubled and disintegrating downtown Durham, North Carolina. My religion professors have already joined the "sit-ins" at Woolworth's in Greensboro on behalf of civil rights. The YWCA meetings at Duke University reaffirm our sense of common humanity and enlighten our understanding of diverse struggles for dignity from *Death Camp to Existentialism* to Mississippi and east Durham. At the same time, my dear but increasingly conservative Texas grandmother, a lawyer, threatens and pleads for me not to take a bus through the Deep South on the way home to Dallas. Long before, she has told me more than once, "Papa said, 'Never sign a petition.' I haven't, and I certainly hope you won't." The ticket I buy that night lets me see *Nothing but a Man*. The film, with an all black cast, brings vividly alive the everyday life of a proud young African American railroad worker and his relationship with a preacher's daughter. We witness the couple's struggles surrounded by racism. Robert M. Young is the director of photography. That night the film's sensitivity and justice to the couple's life deepens my aesthetic and ethical perspectives in ways that continue to resonate.

In 1992, I still remember the film. When we show *Nothing but a Man* (directed by Michael Roemer), in the Appalachian State University "Introduction to Film" class, the work stands up as well as it did so long ago. After I met Robert M. Young in 2003, I learn that he is the co-producer and the co-writer, as well as the director of photography, for this film that has influenced my work in folklore and documentary film and video. At last I get to see *Caught,* a romance set in a fish market (in Hoboken) providing a daily catch from the New York City Fulton Street market; *¡Alambrista!,* about the psychological struggles of an illegal immigrant; and *The Ballad of Gregorio Cortez.* All these diverse, fine films share the same inspiring commitment as *Nothing but a Man* in presenting the dignity of ordinary ethnic individuals.

In his award-winning fiction films, Robert M. Young creates a fascinating paradoxical legacy of the American documentary tradition, inaugurated by Robert Flaherty in 1921—the year Flaherty and the feature length *Nanook of the North* achieved international acclaim. When making a documentary film about the last Netsilik Eskimos, Young risked his life by living above the Arctic Circle in an igloo for five weeks with some temperatures at 50 degrees below zero. *The Eskimo* won an Emmy in 1971. His fiction films are grounded in the extensive experience of his documentary background, and they provide informed historical context. They are not like the popular contemporary historical fiction films that so often fail to do the research required to make a documentary. Young uses realistic wardrobe, contextual details, and background scenery; the original railroad cars were replicated for use in the *Ballad of Gregorio Cortes.* He sets the climactic courtroom scenes in the actual courthouse in Gonzales where Cortez was prosecuted in 1901. The judge also adds to the authenticity, for he had researched the case for 30 years.

When he was a 20-year-old aerial photographer for the Navy, Young remembers being "illumined" by the realization that he was going to be a filmmaker. He would learn to shoot, edit, write, and direct. He began to realize that he couldn't simply "catch" reality, but with the abstract process of filmmaking that preserves "surfaces," he was after "what you understand or remember about what you see. And that meant taking responsibility for the material." He says that what is difficult about documentaries is "trying to find the story."[1]

Like Flaherty, Young is romantic and idealistic, but also genuinely realistic, in his appreciation of the human quest for survival and dignity. His blurring and merging of fictional, dramatic, and documentary techniques enhances his straightforward realism. Young is also sensitive and savvy to the multicultural voices that are crucial for realism. In *Grapes of Wrath* (1940), his first film vignette of a turtle crossing the road foreshadows his sensitive perspective and tone, for the scene is shot from the turtle's point of view. In a 1983 retrospective in Santa Fe, Young said, "I want to give voice to the ordinary person who isn't recognized. All my stories are the same. They're about people to whom life gave a raw deal. But ... [t]hey have dignity."

Robert Young handling the camera as Edward James Olmos prepares to mount and ride in *The Ballad of Gregorio Cortez*.

Young's films carefully use fiction to address issues of social responsibility in cases where written history failed to record ordinary people's lives but where the patterns of their lives remain relevant today. Some of these films, like ¡*Alambrista!*, which won the Camera d'Or award at the Cannes Film Festival in 1978, would be dangerous for the main character, an illegal immigrant, if presented as a documentary. Young respects and honors the subjects of his films.

The accomplished and award-winning *Ballad of Gregorio Cortez* is the first major movie to result from Robert Redford's Sundance Institute — the creation of five resource people coincidentally invited for the 1981 independent filmmakers' workshop. Young's film is about a Mexican who unwillingly becomes an outlaw after he kills a sheriff. In the Rio Grande Valley, this tenant farmer becomes a legend in his own time, for he manages to elude the Texas Rangers and other posses, who use a train as their mobile headquarters in "the biggest manhunt in the history of Texas."[2] A ballad with many variants springs up around the hero who evades his trackers. Like the old Scottish border ballads, *El Corrido de Gregorio Cortez* arises along a culturally contested border — the north side of the Rio Grande — during the century after 1836 when Texas claimed the borderlands from Mexico.[3] *El Corrido de Gregorio Cortez* contains the three factors of the *corridos* created during this century: "*corrido* form, border conflict theme, and a hero that defends his right."[4] The ballad does not "always correspond to fact, but it carries the real man along with it and transforms him into the hero."[5] The film's gritty texture "sets a standard" that reminded one critic of the eagerness of European neorealism "to tell the Audience that they are the true protagonists of life."[6] Young dramatizes this conflict bilingually as he explores the chase and trial of Cortez from both the Anglo-Texan and the Mexican-Texan point of view.

A narrative card — on black — simply and immediately explains: "At the turn of the century, more than fifty years after Texas had then won its independence from Mexico, two cultures — one Anglo and one Mexican — lived side by side in a state of tension and fear. From a time still of that era come different accounts of the same event."

The next narrative card sets the scene that provides the haunting landscape: "Gonzales, Texas."

Then listeners hear two verses of the ballad in Spanish, which are translated into English in white print on the screen. Emblazoning these cues in the mind offers insight into the rest of the film. The differences between the sung *corrido*— an epic narrative folk song of an ordinary person turned into a folk hero — and the English printed translation are crucial. The sound is living language performed, and *corrido* literally means "running." Although well phrased, the print is white and static and a translation:

> *In the country of El Carmen*
> *A great misfortune befell;*
> *The Major Sheriff is dead;*
> *Who killed him no one can tell.*
>
> *At two in the afternoon,*
> *In half an hour or less,*
> *They knew that the man who killed him*
> *Had been Gregorio Cortez.*

The film is about translation and mistranslation — about cultural misunderstanding and its artistic and violent consequences. The two cultural perspectives of the story unfold naturally and complexly in two different, and usually untranslated, languages. The bilingualism serves as a literal and metaphorical signal that border dwellers need to learn each other's ways. Like Cortez, viewers become embroiled in the difficulties of translation, for about one-third of the film is in untranslated Spanish. We understand most of what is happening but misunderstandings occur. Like Cortez, in a land now strangely run by Anglos under their alien law, we English-speaking viewers might unwittingly end up on the run through a simple misunderstanding of a foreign language. With this double cultural view, reinforced by the bilingualism, Young offers participatory realism and receives well-deserved acclaim.

Young also exemplifies the symphony tradition of cinema inaugurated with the 1927 release *Berlin: The Symphony of a Great City*. The British social critic John Grierson considers the symphony tradition of cinema dangerous and *Berlin* "the most dangerous of all film models to follow." He believes that *Berlin* is highly attractive visually because of its swinging "wheels and pistons" and comfortable because it "has little to say about the man who tends it" or issues of "underpaid labour and meaningless production."[7] But critic Richard Meran Barsam has identified the unobtrusive theme of the film to which Grierson's good intentions blinded him. In the pace and tone of the rhythmic visual images, the critic observes, "Movement becomes madness, hurrying becomes hysteria, men become machines."[8] Young does not employ the symphony tradition gone astray, as Grierson feared, but handles it with great social, as well as artistic, responsibility. Young stunningly renders the Antonionesque beauty of contemporary industry on film, but he also shows the absurdist dehumanization of postmodernism exacerbated, willy nilly, by the geometrically increasing pace of technological change.

The filmmaker finds ways to visually project these challenges and confusions into the 1901 arrival of the train into the old nineteenth century traditional cattle culture. Cultural conflict is signaled not only by the written narrative card, the ballad stanzas, their translation, and the bilingual progression of the film, but also by the powerful images that immediately introduce the machine into the breathtaking border landscape of the film and the culture of the cattlemen. Young says that the train provides the story of the film and "tells the form it should take, and the truth of *Gregorio Cortez*."

In *Gregorio Cortez*, the narrative action is launched when the train looms close and shiny and still amidst the fog. The train sequence perhaps suggests the excitement of a journey. But then the engine slowly moves closer, still surrounded by fog and bearing down upon the audience. Close-ups of the train, the wail of the engine, abstract patterns on the ground begin to rush by. Young said that the train "is a beast with its pant, pant, panting. It's always following the guy, there waiting to take him away from the community of family and friends."[9] The belching smoke and "piercing cry of steam and sound" convert the 1901 Iron Horse into a fearsome and living "clanging, chugging iron dragon."[10] With close ups and sound, Young creates a poetic intimacy with the train that symbolizes the new ways and powers that are bearing down upon ordinary men like Gregorio Cortez. The train motif echoes the images also unfurled exquisitely, harrowingly, and relentlessly during a journey in *¡Alambrista!* In the same region at a later time, two illegal immigrants ride the rails under the cars. When the train stops, only one man has survived the battering ride below the boxcar to reach his destination.

As Grierson developed his theories about the documentary as "the creative treatment of actuality," he observed that to make a film about a system, the power is in the specifics. A film about the postal system may best be dramatized by following one letter through the entire system. Grierson based many of his still-relevant theories upon the fine work of Flaherty like *Nanook of the North*, *Man of Aran*, and the *Louisiana Story*. Flaherty unifies his films by focusing upon the difficulties of one man like Nanook and his family. Likewise, Young focuses upon Gregorio Cortez, an ordinary man transformed into the legendary ballad hero. Young understands the power of the specific character, and he immediately moves in this film to his main character. During the sound montage, the camera dissolves "to include and center on a lonely rider" with close-ups above the saddle of a rider. The close-up shots shift to the horse and then to the face of the man.[11] Like Flaherty, a photographer sensitive to the beauty of human life and abstract patterns, Young is a master of close-up visuals and drama with little narration. Both skills were honed in Young's early films about subjects without language — his documentaries for Marineland like *Secrets of the Reef* (1956) and *National Geographic*'s, *The Great Apes* (1975) — the first film about orangutans in the wild. The camera moves slowly across the rugged country following the man. With "his culture's use of nature ... on his side," the rider moves naturally through the landscape.[12]

The next shot shows a train car filled with heavily armed men with stars pinned to their vests. The Texas Rangers are smirking, talking, or sleeping. Men in the caboose car read the June 20, 1901 *Daily Express* from San Antonio: "Hot Chase after Cortez.... Every foot of country is being scoured." Anglos read aloud snatches from the sensationalized newspaper accounts about the hunt for a gang of Mexicans who shot two sheriffs and are horse thieves.

Again the narrative perspective shifts as the camera moves across the unforgiving landscape, closer and closer, for viewers to see the exhaustion of the handsome rider and horse. The camera often anticipates gestures of exhaustion or delight. Later, the man sleeps against the neck of the horse and eventually slides off onto the ground. The camera allows viewers to witness the reality of the lone Cortez's escape, despite the beauty of the forbidding canyons, and in contrast to the exaggerated media representations. This is the second of many times that the camera will undercut the exaggeration of the Anglo news reports with the real situation.

These earliest film images suggests how industry will change the old rhythms of the cattle culture that developed after the arrival of the Spanish and the horse that are now practiced even by both Anglo and Mexican cowboys.¹³ On horseback, the Texas Rangers are tracking a man they think is a horse thief. A posse of dark figures chases the rider night and day; shadows and starless nights cover the riders. The camera often highlights Cortez against the sky and sometimes his pursuers. Both Anglo and Mexican wranglers tend and soothe the excited horses as the train speeds on. Despite the ethnic differences on the border, cattle culture is shared. Broken by railroad car slats, light falls on the quivering bodies of the horses. All these images foreshadow the industrial revolution arriving in the borderlands of Texas. At the same time, the Anglos are the ones introducing the machine into the landscape. This sequence dramatizes another basic conflict, for the Anglo culture of technology with the train as its hallmark is once again invading border culture and surrounding Cortez, the horse, and Mexican traditions. In the film, Young provides not stereotypes but complex reality. This conflict between shared and changing cattle culture is played out in the film through the situation of the ballad hero Gregorio Cortez who is pursued by both rangers and the train.

The film cuts to the reporter from the *San Antonio Daily Express* in another symbol of industrialization as he meets the train in an improbable automobile. Before the rangers ride away, the captain takes a few moments to explain that the Mexican gang will head south to cross the Border and thus must cross the train track. The Rangers are using the train to provide fresh horses and supplies. The telegram and telephone allow them to stay in touch with all the posses and trackers.

The train is not only a dangerous beast but also a dehumanizing tool for the overzealous Texas Rangers. Posses and Texas Rangers chase Cortez and "his gang," arrest Mexicans so they can't warn the hero, shoot Mexicans by mistake, and hang others. The second Major Sheriff reprimands these vigilantes (deputized with tin stars and protected by the law) for pulling a young boy up with a rope to try to make him talk. The cultural conflict of these times in the borderland region displays increasingly "the cruel capriciousness of frontier justice."¹⁴

Young beautifully writes the half of the script that covers the desperate chase and capture.¹⁵ There are always changes between script and film — sometimes because the written plan does not translate visually, sometimes to sharpen drama and viewer understanding, and oftentimes due to pressing constraints of time and money during production. The opening shifts in the film that differ from the script heighten clarity. Humanizing references to cowboys cooking bacon and eggs and a meeting with a lovely woman are postponed until the essential clash between Anglo culture and Cortez is set. Emphasizing the complexities of translation, the train, the harassing of an unsuspecting Mexican, and the inaccuracy and exaggeration from the press are all techniques that foreground the two conflicting cultural perspectives.

Another shift in the script is the fact that although Sheriff Fly is seen, the translator (Tom Bower) is introduced in more detail before him. This change foregrounds the theme of miscommunication quickly. We see the translator drive a wagon into town with two dead men wrapped in sheets. He too familiarly takes advantage of comforting the grieving wife of the sheriff, who was likely killed by friendly fire — probably the translator's. Soon the translator says, ironically and cynically, that he's "sick of senseless killing." Also, the law is holding the immediate family of Cortez in jail as hostages.

With the Texas Rangers, the translator chases three Mexicans with horses; the posse shoots two of them. They do not kill these Mexicans, but they do violently harass them and soon kill others. When the translator, who was with the sheriff who was shot, explains that none of these men are Cortez, the reporter again serves as a device to give the audience information. Another strategic alteration is the omission, at least in English, of an explicit passage in the script for a voice-over from the newspaper that reveals the widespread path of racism and the belittling of women: "Viewers also hear news of the lynching of an evangelical Negro preacher in Shreveport, LA, for stirring up trouble against whites, of Mrs. McKinley's illness, and of laxatives to solve the over dramatized illnesses of women."[16] Instead, another visual intimidation makes the point and keeps the story well focused. Mid- and close-up silent shots show an unsuspecting local Mexican threatened with a noose attached to the saddle horn intended to drag him, likely to death, across the range. (The reference to women is far more realistically and intensely dealt with late in the film when Rosana DeSota translates for the lawyer with a "quiet dignity" that transmits the tragedy and "her own role in an unequal power relationship.")[17]

The translator's narration of the past encounter shifts into a flashback dramatization that both elaborates and complicates the translator's story. Critic David Ehrenstein found the flashback structure "confusing," and Michael Saenz found the flashbacks fracturing.[18] They actually signal Young's progressive, bilingual narrative skill. In a key sequence, when the sheriff and translator arrive suspecting Cortez may be a horse thief, a man quiets a barking dog, and a woman takes the children inside. The translator says that the brother told Cortez that he "was wanted" rather than they wanted to talk to him. Viewers witness a miscommunication — perhaps initiated by the translator. In reply to "has he traded a horse lately?" Cortez says "*Un caballo*? No." For non–Spanish speakers, his crucial remark will be explained later. The non–Spanish speaking sheriff, on the trail of a horse thief, decides Cortez is lying and tells the translator to say, "he's under arrest." In Spanish, Gregorio says that no man can arrest him. His brother rushes the sheriff and Gregorio pulls a pistol. Everything is confusing, but the sheriff shoots the unarmed brother, and Cortez, "with a pistol in his hand" shoots the sheriff. The unarmed translator runs away, back to the sheriff's nephew left near the gate. The flashback provides complex and realistic characterization and offers a reminder of the difficulty of presenting actuality. The film is about who holds physical power and who controls the telling of the story.

> *They let loose the bloodhound dogs,*
> *They followed him from afar.*
> *But trying to catch Cortez*
> *Was like following a star.*

For wanting to preserve the dignity of human life and work honed by long standing cattle country traditions, Gregorio Cortez, like the steel driving man John Henry, is forced into a race that takes on industrialization. Like "a star," Cortez is endowed with natural and cosmic qualities. His knowledge of horse culture and the land help him elude, time and again, the *rinches*—who include not only the Texas Rangers, but also the Major Sheriff, other posses, trackers, and much later the border patrols and immigration officers.[19] Like some African American banjo songs, including *John Henry*, the antagonist in the *corrido* is sometimes seen as the industrial system. But even more often the legal system is symbolized in man-against-the law songs by the "High Sheriff," or here by the "Major Sheriff." In the ballad, sometimes called "Sheriff Killer," Cortez's home ground has a new law in the land. The system is endless and the men responsible are usually absentee and hard to identify or hold responsible. One Major Sheriff is killed in the first stanza, but a few stanzas later another Major Sheriff wants to capture Cortez alive. As in history so in the film, after two Major Sheriffs are killed (perhaps the second by friendly fire), another arrives. The savvy Cortez, "like a star," first eludes the *rinches* by traveling north before he starts south for the border—often in spiraling patterns.

With *Nanook*, Flaherty explored man's struggle against nature. In the *Ballad*, Young shows Cortez's closeness to nature and the land. The film also explores his struggle against cultural misunderstanding and the miscarriage of justice by Anglo society. The sensationalized exaggeration and scandalized tone of the media coverage reveals Anglo stereotyping. Young also shows the dehumanization of Anglos through the extravagance of this manhunt with its industrial tools, and by favoring expediency and capitalism more so than individuals or justice. As their institutionalism continues to expand, there is talk that the Texas Rangers are becoming obsolete. As the *rinches* rush to arrest innocent bystanders at an industrial speed, stereotyping is unmasked as racism exacerbated by fear. In contrast, Cortez becomes a guiding star of a man to inspire Mexican followers.

Critic Donald Hoffman acclaims the film's genuine presentation of diversity. He observes that "the Hollywood that ignores African Americans and glamorizes and demonizes Native Americans, seems to treat Mexicans ... to an unusually vindictive program of degradation and defamation."[20] In this western, Young moves well beyond *Dances with Wolves*, which emphasized the benefit of Indian culture to two disaffected Anglos. The *Ballad of Gregorio Cortez* is one of the first exceptional films to convincingly and realistically include diverse ethnic characters — other than Young's earlier works.

Like Flaherty, Young knows the people he reveals. By the time of this film, Young had already made *¡Alambrista!* and was finding other ways to understand Mexican culture. In this film, he tells a real history about a man already respected by his peers. One major contribution to the Latino point of view is that Young based the film upon Americo Paredes' landmark 1958 book *"With a Pistol in His Hand": A Border Ballad and Its Hero*. Paredes, a scholar raised within the culture, details the history of the land, the legend, the man, the ballad, its almost one dozen collected variations, and he provides extensive cultural interpretation. He dedicates the book to his father and the "old men ... talking in low, gentle voices about violent things" while he listened. Paredes was a good listener, for his voice actually sings the *corrido* in the film.

Reviewer and University of California Chancellor Tomas Rivera — often a spokesperson for the Chicano community — observes that legends "are an accumulation of communal and individual passion, historical precedence and cultural perspectives, and ... the basis of spiritual and actual history."[21] Aptly named Americo, Paredes offered a unique insider study of ballads in the making that brought "Mexican-American historical perspective ... within the context of the American ... experience."[22] Cortez is the last Mexican, for he was born into and represents cattle culture, but he is also the first Chicano. He must tangle with Anglo law, but he does so with great agility and dignity. For fifty years, cattle culture had been declining after Texas took over the border from Mexico. The ballad represents the first sign of Mexicans living on the Texas side of the border taking on the identity of border Americans. With the extensive and sensitive resource of Paredes' cultural study, Young translates and reinterprets the insider significance of the history of Gregorio Cortez in border culture context for outsiders. The film also shows what will be lost to Anglo and Mexican cowboy culture as the train replaces and becomes the iron horse of the Texans. Industrial losses will increase as the cattlemen of the depressed area of Gonzalez are put to work in a cash economy as hand laborers in the new cotton gin that opens for the first time during the trial of Gregorio Cortez.[23]

The high production values of the film are set by Young and the dedication he inspires. In addition to relying upon and translating Paredes' study and sharpening the script as he moves to film, Young achieves an insider's sensibility in the film with the casting of Mexicans. Especially fortunate was the casting of Edward James Olmos, starring as the hero, Gregorio Cortez. Raised in the barrios of L.A., Olmos had recently been nominated for a Tony for his star role in *Zoot Suit* (1981) as the street savvy and mystical El Pachuco. After his success, Olmos became an actor-turned-activist.[24] He realized that the symbol of Latin machismo and that film had incredible power when he could quiet the entire school of the Central Juvenile Hall in downtown Los Angeles. But Olmos also understood the limits of the "tough guy" image. He told the students that "it's good to be proud and self-respectful, but don't wear it as a shield.... You're safe but you are alone."[25] The American Theater Wing acknowledged his contribution to Latino culture by declaring him one of the three definitive American characters along with Marlon Brando's Stanley Kowalsky and Lee Cobb's Willy Loman. Olmos brought all of these talents and cultural wisdom to the role of Gregorio Cortez. Olmos explained that the atmosphere of the group's work each night before the shoot was "incredible." "Everyone committed themselves to the picture — from the gaffer ... to the producer."[26]

At the telegraph office, the reporter overhears a judge fussing because Cortez has not been caught in a week in spite of the threats and intimidation. The injured pride of the Texas Rangers leads to their brandishing capitalistic monetary incentives. As another weapon in their armory, along with the train and Anglo law, the judge announces a $1000 reward to smoke out the killer.

> *All the rangers of the country*
> *Were flying, they rode so hard;*
> *What they wanted was to get*
> *The thousand-dollar reward.*

The reporter introduces himself to Sheriff Fly, who has taken up the chase because the second Major Sheriff Glover was a friend. The naïve reporter seeks accurate information but is surprised to learn of false arrest because there is no gang. Fly, played by James Ganon, explains that tracks don't lie and they are tracking a lone rider — Cortez. The honesty and personal involvement of Fly allow him to become a worthy antagonist to the legendary Cortez.

Finally, Fly almost catches the lone rider but not, as the media hype claims, with Cortez cutting all the barbed wire fences. Instead, Cortez lays his serape across the wire to soften the barbs, and then the little mare responds to Gregorio's talking and closeness and jumps the fence. Just as Fly and the other trackers arrive, Cortez slowly swings his arm down to reclaim his serape and ride away. In fact, the Anglos are the ones who do not jump but cut the barbed wire fence. The Anglos fence the land aggressively and proprietarily. Like the train, they cut up, divide, and parcel the land. Cutting their own boundary line wires suggests the confusion of their approach.

As a means of deepening character, Young often creates masterful erotic love scenes beautifully and passionately portrayed whether they take place in a luxurious bed, in a handy closet (*Caught*), or on a pallet on the floor (*¡Alambrista!*). This film is somewhat subdued in romantic relationships. Gregorio Cortez is married but away from his wife on the run from the law or in a prison cell during all but a few moments of the film. Like most westerns, this ballad hero stands alone against great odds. But Young does find a way to suggest the passionate and playful relationship between Gregorio and his wife in one of Cortez's fantasies, which is well placed during the water section of the film that provides relief from the drought of the desert chase.

Since the Texas Rangers have staked out all the waterholes and men and horses cannot cross the country without water, they are sure it is just a matter of time until they catch the bandits. The film then cuts to the gurgling of a rushing brook. Young's use of natural sound is as powerful as his close up photography and bilingual narration. A man's hat enters the frame, drops in the water, and rushes around the bend and on to a woman washing clothes. Viewers recognize the wife as she calls out, "Gregorio." Abruptly he emerges, she whirls about, and they fall laughing into the water and kiss.[27] The camera cuts to the horse nuzzling the sleeping Gregorio. He awakens from the dream and smiles — perhaps with humor and irony. Just as the camera revealed the shift between media exaggeration and reality, here it reveals the shift between human fantasy and reality. This may not be an example of Olmos's appreciation of the film's "subtle humor," but Young makes a witty self-reflective comment on the western film genre and a cowboy's love of his horse. Cortez feeds and strokes the mare. Still a tool of realism and without words, the camera characterizes the man, his romantic imagination, his humor, and his competence with horses. Eventually Cortez rounds up some cattle and drives them to a waterhole. The horse and sole rider are able to drink among the cattle while armed men stand guard. Gregorio looks as harmless to the *rinches* as the ordinary man he once was.

Later, the Sheriff asks why the translator and the nephew, who was armed, didn't go back for the wounded Major Sheriff. (Before the major sheriff died abandoned, he had crawled away into the brush.) The translator claims he thought the Sheriff was dead. But another crucial flashback contradicts his story. This scene shows the nephew who wants to return, but the translator, riding double, is afraid and probably intentionally lying about the size of the gang and the certainty of the sheriff's death. Increasingly the (mis)translator becomes a literal and metaphoric symbol of the basis for these murders and the chase to capture and execute Cortez unjustly. The film cuts to Cortez, who is thanking his exhausted little brown mare and letting her go; then he covers his tracks and begins walking. Soon Gregorio grabs Fly's partner, the nephew, and takes his gun and horse but does not shoot the boy. Cortez's restraint and humanity, in contrast to the translator's and many others' is evident. When Fly finds the nephew, he says, "God Almighty, what a horse! What a man!"[28]

Even Latino detractors of the film, like Michael Saenz, praise the scenes of the fugitive riding across the Texan landscape for catching "the spirit behind Cortez's heroism."[29] Likewise the critic finds that "Olmos' quiet portrayal of Cortez masterfully conciliates a killer's resolve with a paradoxically streak of tenderness and sensibility." He and David Ehrenstein both find Olmos is "becomingly restrained as the unwitting outlaw." He "deftly hones in on the character's decency and salt-of-the-earth nobility."[30] Olmos explains about the quiet desperate man Cortez, "We were all committed ... to capturing reality in a way we had never been allowed to do before.... These people [in the film] are whole people, true and active people — factual, real people. There are too many stereotypes."[31] Again Young is a master of few words. Cortez speaks hardly at all, and, despite Anglos and Mexicans naturally speaking their native language, "the viewer understands the soliloquy."[32]

Later, the little brown mare finds Cortez, who shakes his head, remounts her, and rides on. At another water hole, Cortez eventually exchanges her for another brown mare that bucks and whirls but comes eventually to obey him. Fly and the others are still tracking Cortez and drawing closer. Young heightens the suspense of the classic chase. Suddenly, a line of thirty Texas Rangers come from the right as the train is coming from the left. Cortez rides across the range flying toward the train. He seems trapped on three sides. The mare flies over the range — giving herself as did the last one. As Gregorio seems about to collide with the train, it rushes across a trestle bridge and he rushes below. Now Fly and the Rangers chase him to the deep river. Gregorio blindfolds the mare, she leaps into the current, and then swims across; he waves to Fly as he disappears on the other side.

A national spokesman for bilingual education, Olmos hails the film's fluid languages, its celebration of the "most sung hero on the border ever," and especially its portrayal of perhaps the first "lead character [in] an American [film] who doesn't speak English."[33]

Edward James Olmos eluding the pursuing posse in *The Ballad of Gregorio Cortez.*

> And in the county of Kiansis
> They cornered him after all;
> Though there were more than three hundred
> He leaped out of the corral.

Whereas the verse about the $1000 specifically comments on the capitalism of the trackers, this stanza draws the simple and apt metaphor of "the corral" from cattleman culture to identify the three-sided pincher movement against Gregorio.

In their largest manhunt, the Rangers next plan to cordon Cortez with a circle of 300 men. Increasingly fueled by racism and fear that the Rangers will be disbanded, the *rinches'* attacks grow more and more extreme. The exhausted Fly eats with ranchers. Their young son asks, "How come you can't catch the Mexican?" Fly asks the definition of a Texas Ranger. The boy replies, "A man who tracks like an Indian, shoots like a Tennessean, and ... rides like a Mexican."[34] Cortez's skills as a cattleman appear again and again. Many uncut scenes emphasize the skills of the horseman, who masterfully outwits the trackers time and again. These uncut scenes strengthen viewers' recognition of their inexperience with these survival skills necessary in the desert land and their respect for Cortez's cattle culture competence.

Cortez walks exhausted but unrecognized into a crowded cafe in a small town. Saenz considers the racial conflict "the aspect of Cortez's ordeal best treated by the film" and this poignant scene illustrative: "a voice reads from an English newspaper the accounts of Cortez the mad fugitive. Then two other voices read a more restrained account in Spanish."[35] A young boy runs in to announce that the Rangers had Cortez surrounded, but he escaped on foot in the dark. Cortez overhears that his family is held in the prison and his brother has died.

A woman then says to Cortez, "They are looking for a man who looks very much like you.... You can come to my house."[36] As they leave, the reporter walks in. All is happening with only a moment to spare. But, the methodical, massive Roman legion approach used by the Anglos, the extensive numbers of the Texas Rangers, their determination, their access to industrial power, the exaggeration of the media, the expedient use of the law, and the wielding of money eventually overwhelms the lone Cortez—with only a pistol in his hand.

At dawn, Cortez leaves the edge of town and walks up a hill. He stares across the Rio Grande to the other side at Mexico. The stunning open landscape that symbolizes the resources of traditional cattle culture offers freedom. Is he dreaming again? Or, thinking of his family, does he decide to turn his guns over?

The Texas Rangers believe Cortez has crossed the border. But after eleven days, 150 miles running on foot, and 450 miles on three horses, a Judas comes to the Rangers at the border. For the reward, a shepherd leads them to his camp and points out a small hut.

> *Then the Major Sheriff said,*
> *As if he was going to cry,*
> *"Cortez, hand over your weapons;*
> *We want to take you alive."*

They push open the door and ask the unarmed man if he is Cortez. He replies, "Yes."[37] As with Jesse James (betrayed by "that dirty little coward"), Gregorio is betrayed by an insider as so often is the case. Most Mexicans protected him, covered for him, gave him food and shelter, but one—like the aggressors—wanted to profit personally. In the film, as in history, Cortez is taken alive. Gregorio Cortez's plight extended the life of the Texas Rangers.

Before Paredes even had a chance to see the film, the *San Antonio Light*—much like the *San Antonio Express* in the film—wanted to interview him about his reactions to the film, and the *Dial* tried to talk him into saying the film was too "fictional." There was some Mexican criticism of the film — particularly for a few moments of sentimentality surrounding Cortez. During the fast-paced eleven week shooting and production of the film, Paredes began having heart treatment for angina and was unable to accept invitations to visit the sets in Santa Fe or Gonzalez.[38] No doubt this misfortune contributed to these problems. He did do some publicity shots for the film in Austin, and when the multitalented Olmos was co-creating the musical score, Paredes provided a recording of the *corrido*. Olmos found the initial draft of the script by the young Chicano novelist Victor Villasenor at Sundance, but Paredes thought it "very unsatisfactory." Olmos explains that the original script dealt with the legend, and it was like "El Pachuco rides again — on a horse." Rather than the legend and ballad, Young chose to emphasize the man and the historical facts. Olmos explains, "A lot of Hispanics are very angry at this story because they only know the legend version." The definition of a legend is a story that is believed true by the people who tell it. Thus, it is no surprise that one lady said, "You know the way I've heard it Cortez got away."[39] Folk legends and ballads express not history but the values and fears of those who sing them thus they offer a significant window upon historical perspective. Certainly the poignancy of Cortez's actual life deserved realistic and historical presentation. The historical reality was, no doubt, harder for Hispanics than for Anglo interpreters of the events.

The film includes early verses of the ballad, but does not use the last few verses of the ballad. Using the last well-wrought and understated stanzas of the ballad, as well as the actual history, might have sidestepped even this criticism. The ballad ends:

> *Then said Gregorio Cortez,*
> *And his voice was like a bell,*
> *"You will never get my weapons*
> *Till you put me in a cell."*
>
> *Then said Gregorio Cortez,*
> *With his pistol in his hand,*
> *"Ah so many mounted Rangers*
> *Just to take one Mexican!"*

The ballad hero is distinctive in that he neither becomes a Robin Hood, who robs from the rich to give to the poor, nor repents to provide a moral. He is a "peaceful man, finally goaded into violence by the *rinches* and rising in wrath to kill great numbers of his enemy."[40] But Cortez does not kill wantonly — only to defend family and self. The version of the ballad that Paredes sings is traditional. The ballad hero has the last word twice — once in each stanza. One stanza concludes with the hero's voice "like a bell" unafraid and unrepentant. Whether he lives or dies or is arrested by an alien, untranslatable law, Cortez is a man who has "defended his rights." The ballad ends, suspended in history, with a celebration of the wiliness of the legendary hero and his ironic remark that he has managed to sidestep the vast forces of the Texas Rangers (and their train) for so long.

Before Cortez was released, the *corrido* was sung in the border *cantinas*. The legendary ballad hero is dead, but still today—more than 100 years later—the song of Gregorio Cortez, and his story, lives on. This version of the ballad does not contradict history but with artistic ambiguity emphasizes the Chicano values and expands our bilingual perspective on actual events. Gregorio Cortez is celebrated as a real man, "with a pistol in his hand," who "stood for his rights" in border battle times.

After the capture, Fly comes over the hill too late to participate in the arrest. In Gonzales, Cortez arrives on "a flatcar, in a cage" and "in chains." At the station house, Fly takes charge of Cortez. More close-ups of the train reemphasize the Anglo world. During the chase on horseback, there were many dark and mysterious shots—often in complete silhouette—but the shots were all in warm earth tones. Once Cortez is imprisoned, many shots are within a cell with white light coming through black crisscrossed bars. The warm tones vanish; black and white harshness and oversimplification cover the screen.

Like Flaherty, the ballad, and Paredes, Young organizes and alters reality to create a more accurate presentation of his subject—border cattle culture and the hero. Rather than recording the events and story consecutively, Young structures the film around bilingualism, translation, and the miscommunication between Anglo and Mexican culture along the Texan border. He emphasizes the chase by the Rangers and the train which documents the traditional skills of Cortez as a cattleman. The detailed structure of the film creates the two cultural perspectives in historical context: 1) Song and translation of the ballad; 2) the train—how the Rangers use industrialization and cattle culture is changed by it; 3) the media exaggeration created by the reporter who also arrives by car; 4) the lone rider; 5) the Major Sheriffs—1, 2, 3—representatives of Anglo law; 6) the incompetent or worse translator and other harassers; 7) the barbed wire hindrance to cattlemen; 8) the nephew misled but unharmed; 9) waterholes amidst drought—a fantasy; 10) 300 men become the corral; and 11) the lone hero.

The *corrido* is both an artistic symbol of bilingual translation and the song of the legendary hero. In the *corrido*, the hero is left standing, not yet arrested, with a voice of his own. In history and the film, once the capture finally occurs, it not only interrupts Cortez's escape and life but signals the interruption of traditional cattleman life by industrialization.

Young quickly delineates the extent of the mistranslation at the core of all the injustice. A good woman translator explains that Cortez made a distinction maintained by Spanish ranchers; he had bought a mare—*un caballo*—not a horse. He was speaking precisely—not lying. Cortez stood firm against injustice by standards from his peer border cattlemen and singers to post-modern Derrida, who believes no man should be tried in a language he does not understand. Neither the sheriff nor the translator placing him under arrest accurately understood Cortez or his language. He proclaimed and enacted his right to defend himself and his family, to use his own language precisely, and to carry on his ways of life amidst the long-standing border conflict with the Anglos. The court-appointed lawyer now understands why Cortez's brother died and that Cortez was not a horse thief but simply resisting an illegal arrest—with a pistol in his hand.

Young also foreshortens the trial to the closing remarks. Some critics found the post-chase section of the film slow and thought the court scene would have provided drama. However, despite the lawyer's eloquent efforts to defend Cortez, the results of inadequate justice in an Anglo border court were inevitable. The film is about Hispanic life in realistic but unjust times—not an exploration dramatizing Anglo systems and their power. The film ends quickly with a verdict of murder without malice against Cortez and imprisonment for 50 years. He shouts out against the injustice and struggles against his captors, but still outnumbered, he is carried away. Then the film portrays the dramatization and singing about Cortez that took place and would lead to many complete but different ballad variants within the decade. Late that night, like the one juror who refused to let them hang Cortez, Fly protects Cortez against a bloodthirsty crowd equally dissatisfied with this outcome and trying to lynch Cortez—as they did his godson. The next day Sheriff Fly escorts Cortez and his family back to the train. The walk shows the border people, brown and white, with all their similarities—beautiful individuals and many children—sad and curious—many standing in respect. The camera focuses on the close-up of the train face and then tilts to all going up in smoke. The train carries Cortez and Fly away to a law that does eventually overturn the verdict. But due to six retrials on other charges, Cortez remained in jail for manslaughter of one sheriff and for stealing the horse he escaped on. After 12 years he was found innocent and freed, but he died a few years later.

Young likes the security of imagining how he will shoot a feature film photographically, but is committed to "dialogue between [the actors'] instincts" and his own.[41] Young and Olmos carefully drew the viewers' sympathy to the complex history and character of Cortez and demonstrated that the ballad hero does defend his rights. Young points out that Cortez was not an immigrant even though he needed a translator at court. He "always lived in this country, ... was here before we were, and he has become an alien in his own country."[42] Apparently, Paredes was impressed with Young. Young adapted this script into a 30-page manuscript covering the chase and capture shown in the final film. Paredes considered Young's "plans for the movie" "quite good."[43] Young explains that his revision was guided by replacing the tone of "too much anger" with an Anglo-Texan as well as Mexican perspective.[44] Rivera says that "legends are continued invention" and concludes that the study "by Paredes creates the myth and adds to the legend. The film with Olmos in his very best interpretation recreates a spiritual history and allows Gregorio Cortez to converse silently throughout history. The film is ... a different metaphor as human as the one wrought by the book. It is clear and true poetry, the stuff of humans."[45]

Great power resides in the reality of a documentary. When we learn that a few years after Flaherty's film, Nanook died of starvation, viewers understand more about the intensity and reality of the challenges he faced, and mourn his death. When we think about Cortez's wily escape, surrender, twelve years struggle for justice, and death within a few years of his release, viewers mourn his actual loss of freedom, family, and life. With luck, the *corrido* and the story help us understand the injustice of today, as well as yesterday, and understand the power of each storyteller. Robert Young's film about a legendary hero with a pistol in his hand reclaims a real Latino man's place in American history and art.

Olmos usually views his films like *Zoot Suit* only once, but he has seen *The Ballad of Gregorio Cortez* more than 200 times! After the film showed on PBS, the filmmakers paid $5500 to rent a theater for one week in San Antonio, the home of many of the descendants of Cortez. But the majors didn't know how to market the film. In Los Angeles, Olmos rented the Los Feliz Theater for Labor Day weekend for $250, and 300 people attended. The screenings continued, and eventually Olmos and costar Tom Bower took the film on a free tour to more than 30 cities across the country. Olmos turned down a half-million dollars worth of film roles in the following two years to continue speaking at schools, prisons, and community groups. This grass roots effort showed the film to 70,000 people, and as a result, for the first time a film largely financed (for $1,300,000) by and aired on PBS was released for theatrical distribution.[46] Embassy Picture's vice president and general manager said, "It's the first movie I know of with a Hispanic hero that has the potential to reach an Anglo audience.... It works on an emotional level."[47]

Young has explained that his "style is to play the facts" and his "documentary tenet" is not to "want to tell people what to think," but he is an activist too. Olmos, like Gregorio Cortez, like Americo Paredes, and like Robert M. Young, is an ordinary man turned activist. Young, like the *corrido,* presents in ballad and film form the legendary hero of the Mexican cattlemen. With Paredes and Olmos, he brings *The Ballad of Gregorio Cortez* to the Anglo world on behalf of the Mexican border cattlemen and all who can appreciate a man who is willing to stand and defend his rights in confusing and oppressive times.

Young came of age as an independent filmmaker late in the era of the first great film giants — Flaherty, the creative documentarist; Grierson, the filmmaker of social responsibility; and Eisenstein, the genius of montage. Young has carried forward the legacy of all three into the themes of postmodern life with great skill. In the film of Gregorio Cortez, Young offers us a visual and bilingual border ballad for our times with great accomplishment, dignity, and responsibility. He well deserves his reputation as America's acclaimed and foremost independent filmmaker.

Notes

1. Varney, "Robert Young: Film as Real Life." Interview, *LA Weekly,* October 14–20, 1983, p. 31.
2. Olmos and Young, 1983 p. 50.
3. Paredes, *With His Pistol in His Hand,* 132.
4. Paredes, p. 150.
5. Paredes, p. 149.
6. Aufderheide, "True Grit: From a Committed Band of Independent Filmmakers Comes One of the Best Westerns in Years," *The Movies,* Oct. 1983, pp. 72–73.
7. Hardy, *Grierson on Documentary,* p. 13.
8. Barsam, *Nonfiction Film,* p. 23.
9. Varney, p. 31.
10. Unless otherwise noted, quotes are from Young's screenplay manuscript, p. 1.
11. Ibid., p. 3.
12. Saenz, "'Cortez' Film Falls Short," *Daily Texan,* April 24, 1983.
13. Paredes.
14. *People Weekly,* Oct 24, 1983, p. 10.
15. Paredes papers.
16. Young ms., pp. 4–5.
17. *True Grit.*
18. Ehrenstein, "Good Intentions Go Awry in *Ballad of Gregorio Cortez,*" "Movies," *Los Angeles Herald-Examiner,* October 7, 1983, D.6. Saenz, "'Cortez' Film Falls short," p. 17, 28.
19. Paredes, p. 150.
20. Hoffman, "Whose Home on the Range? *Melus* 22 no. 2 (Summer 1997), p. 45.
21. Rivera, p. 32.
22. Ibid.
23. *Hispanic Conventioneer,* p. 50 or 52.
24. Aufderheide, "Strategies: An Actor Turn Activist," *Mother Jones,* Nov. 1983, p. 60.
25. Ibid.

26. Olmos.
27. Young ms, p. 7.
28. Ibid., p. 21.
29. Saenz, p. 28
30. Ehrenstein.
31. Aufderheide, p. 60.
32. Rivera, p 33.
33. Hispanic Conventioneer, p. 50.
34. Young ms, p. 26.
35. Saenz, p. 28
36. Young ms, p. 28.
37. Ibid., p. 29.
38. Paredes papers.
39. Paredes, p. 8.
40. Paredes, p. 149.
41. Varney, p. 32.
42. Varney, p. 31.
43. Paredes papers.
44. Loynd, "How a Sundance Step Spawned a 'Ballad.'" *Variety*, June 13, 1983, p. 72.
45. Rivera, p. 33.
46. Loynd, p.72.
47. Aufderhiede, p. 60.

Bibliography

Aufderhiede, Pat. "Strategies: An Actor Turns Activist." *Mother Jones,* Nov. 1983, p. 60.
_____. "True Grit: From a Committed Band of Independent Filmmakers Comes One of the Best Westerns in Years." *The Movies*, Oct. 1983, pp. 72–73.
Barsam, Richard Meran. *Nonfiction Film: A Critical History*. New York: Dutton, 1973.
Ehrenstein, David. "Good Intentions Go Awry in 'Ballad of Gregorio Cortez.'" *Los Angeles Herald-Examiner*, October 7, 1983.
Hardy, Forsyth, ed. *Grierson on Documentary*. New York: Faber & Faber, 1966.
Hoffman, Donald. "Whose Home on the Range? Finding Room for Native Americans, African Americans, and Latino Americans in the Revisionist Western." *Melus 22, no. 2* (Summer 1997) p. 45.
Loynd, Ray. "How a Sundance Step Spawned a 'Ballad.'" *Variety*, June 13, 1983, p. 72.
Olmos, Edward James, and Robert Young. "With 21 Reasons Why You Should See: *The Ballad of Gregorio Cortez*." *Hispanic Conventioneer*, 1983, pp. 50, 52.
Paredes, Americo. *Papers in the Americo Paredes Collection*. Benson Latin American Collection. The University of Texas, Austin.
_____. *With His Pistol in His Hand: A Border Ballad and Its Hero*. Austin: University of Texas Press, 1958.
People Weekly, Oct 24, 1983, p. 10.
Rivera, Tomas. "A Clash of Cultures: The Ballad of Gregorio Cortez." *Caribbean Review*.
Saenz, Michael. "Cortez" Film Falls Short of Giving Legend its Due." *Daily Texan*, April 24, 1983, pp. 17, 28.
"Star of 'Zoot Suit' Blowing into Town." *Pasatiempo* (Santa Fe, New Mexico), April 30, 1983.
Varney, Ginger. "Robert Young: Film as Real Life." Interview, *LA Weekly*, October 14–20, 1983, pp. 31–32.
Young, Robert M. Papers. *The Ballad of Gregorio Cortez: Production Information*.

7. Love, Death, and Healing: Some Psychoanalytic Themes in *Extremities*

Roger James Stilling

> *The modern critical tradition, for all its variety, has one continuous element, the search for occulted sense in texts of whatever period.*
>
> — Frank Kermode

Director Robert M. Young's film *Extremities* (1986) tells a deceptively simple story: Marjorie Easton (Farrah Fawcett) is kidnapped at knife point by a unmasked attacker (James Russo) hiding in her car. He attempts to rape her, but she escapes. Upon reporting the incident to the police, she is told by a well-meaning female officer that without witnesses or physical evidence, the charge will come down to her word against his and the attacker will go free. Marjorie then points out that the attacker has her wallet, I.D., and address. She is told that the police can come only after the attacker has intruded on her home. This leaves Marjorie and her two housemates, Terry (Diana Scarwid) and Patricia (Alfre Woodard), without protection. Disappointed, angry, and frightened, Marjorie storms out of the police station without signing the official complaint and goes home to wait for what she believes is the inevitable second attack. A fade to black follows, and a week passes.

During the week, there has been no evident sign of the man, but when the narrative resumes we can see the aftereffects of the incident on Marjorie's everyday life: open hostility to a male visitor with whom Terry is flirting; new locks and keys for everybody; staying home from work for more than a week; and long, anxious, sleepless nights. Then, on a morning after the others have gone to work, the attacker (later called Joe) shows up and walks through an unlocked door. Since he is not masked, it takes her a few moments to realize whom she is facing; but then the war begins, with Joe calling the shots. Joe's idea of foreplay is to parade her through the house, sadistically intimidating her into humiliating acts (such as changing into black lingerie while standing on her bed like a Victoria's Secret model on a runway) before pushing her to the floor to complete the rape. Marjorie, as she did in the car, plays a tricky game — controlling her fear, giving in just enough to keep his displays of anger manageable, and waiting for him to make a mistake. And, again, he does, giving Marjorie a chance to grab a can of wasp spray, blind him with it, and grapple him to the floor. She then succeeds in binding his hands, neck and feet in a spider web of lamp cords and kitchen twine. She stuffs him in the fireplace, which she bars up with an iron bed headboard. Marjorie's first impulse is to go back to the police, but Terry has borrowed her car. And, in the meantime, Joe has begun to brag that the police will let him out because he has committed no crime and that then he will return to kill all three women. Marjorie has been controlling her anger pretty well until she hears this, but then she snaps and begins crazily digging a grave for Joe in the garden.

Marjorie is now beyond reason. When her housemates come home, their loyalties are divided when the bound, blinded, bleeding but cunning killer tries to present himself as an innocent victim. A long, passionate debate over what to do with him ensues, and Joe seems about to turn Terry and Patricia against Marjorie when Marjorie discovers his hunting knife concealed under his work vest. Joe loses all credibility, and Terry and Patricia leave him to Marjorie's far from tender mercies. After a brutal, face-slapping, knife-wielding confrontation, Joe breaks and spills all his secrets. Utterly beaten, he is nudged back into the fireplace while Terry and Patricia go for the police and Marjorie slowly relaxes into the faintest hint of a smile. Her last act is to quietly turn on a handy floor lamp to light the growing dusk. The movie ends.

By his own account, Robert M. Young[1] got involved in this project reluctantly at first — not because of doubts about the project but because of the powerful emotional conflicts the story aroused in him for personal reasons. When his daughter was sixteen, she was sexually assaulted, and Young admits to having conflicted feelings about the task of dealing with such harsh subject matter and the associated personal memories. In the end, his daughter encouraged him to do the project, and he later told Ed Kelleher, "In this film, I wanted to honor not only my daughter but all women and other people who are victims" (40).

Once in, Young brought to the film his demonstrated commitment to social issues and independent filmmaking; his mastery of an unsparing documentary cinematic style; and what one might call his literacy — his ability to make dramatic, strongly visualized films out of highly literary texts. Young's work with the playwright, William Mastrosimone, strengthened the cinematic structure of the work and enhanced the story's power to embody and express a content that is as old as Greek tragedy and as contemporary as today's headlines and culture wars.[2]

Extremities was released in the summer of 1986, and from the start the film generated considerable commentary. Much of this commentary was of the ephemeral sort generally referred to as "buzz" and concerned Farrah Fawcett's career and personal life, but this pre-release material also indicated a thematic faultline around which commentary would continue to develop after the film's release. The core issues were generated by the film's brutal and direct presentation of a confrontation between a man and a woman for the control and use of the woman's body. The intensity of the popular commentary was further escalated by the reversal of power that occurs in the middle of the film, putting the woman in power over the male body and beginning a dramatic and discursive debate over how she should use this unexpected and somewhat shocking new configuration of male-female power relations.

There were, then, two dramatic situations presented in the film that were both highly emotional and highly topical in the mid-eighties: (1) rape as a psychological and social problem and (2) women's rage over male abuse and whether or not the established institutions of education, social support, and justice administration were up to the Herculean task of managing — to say nothing of eliminating — this wrenching individual and societal problem. But in regard to the film itself, commentators were most often drawn to the rough, physically confrontational style of the movie (powerfully visualized by director Young, with fierce yet subtle performances by Fawcett and Russo). Very few reviewers were unmoved by *Extremities*. Walter Goodman of the *New York Times* maligned it (Rev. Aug, 1986) and was quickly and rightly taken to the woodshed by the reviewer from *NOW–NYC* (Tedesco 1986). Richard Corliss's acute and enthusiastic review for *Time* also produced the most dramatic statement of the film's theme: "The most obscene phrase a woman can utter is 'I love you' when it is forced from her at rape point" (Rev. Aug. 1986). And two reviewers' comments provided almost exactly the same lifestyle messages for their female readership: (a) "Lock your car doors, ladies, it's not safe out there" (Russell 1986), and (b) "The message of *Extremities* is clear: Women, don't go out at night because you'll get raped. And if you do, the law won't help you" (M.H. 1986). One might hope they were being ironic. Most of the commentary has focused on either criminal justice or gender issues.

This essay takes a different track, though it eventually leads back by indirection to these matters. Myth, mystery and therapeutic themes have always enriched the work of the dramatic/performance genres. The therapy of art may come through the purgation of fear and pity in tragedy, the leavening of the spirit in comedy, or — more common in our time — a combination of these. Regardless of its mechanism, the working assumption of art is that we all exist in a precarious spiritual state, assaulted by the shocks and anxieties of life at every turn. Thoughtful, formally accomplished film artists like Robert M. Young are popular healers whose work keeps our spiritual and mental immune systems up and running effectively.

Young's film *Extremities* is no exception. The making of it tested the health of its makers, and the harshness of its extremes of feeling has shocked and baffled its interpreters. At its heart, though, is a deep therapeutic intention and design, and the primary aim of this essay will be to uncover this greater motive in the midst of the film's highly emotional dramatic action. To aid in this effort I will draw on language and concepts from archetypal psychology, historical and applied mythology, and psychoanalysis.

The solid foundation of Freud's total theory (no matter what one may think of specific aspects of it) resides in its insistence on the evolutionary connection of all life forms through genetics and the concept of primal instincts. These instincts evolved with the first stirrings of life into proliferating and complex forms with the higher animals. They still move through our psyches in ways we can hardly perceive except when they are expressed in overt and manifestly symbolic forms, as in film, for instance. One particular example is a slyly designed shot near the beginning of *Extremities*. We see into the hallway of a museum of natural history. It is closing time, and, as we watch, Marjorie moves into the frame, exchanging civilities with a friendly museum guard. As she moves out of the frame, the guard catches our eye as the only human in the frame. Behind him, however, looms the skeleton of an ancient mastodon, its huge, menacing, phallic tusks stretching across the screen. This shot is intercut with shots of Marjorie's attacker-to-be. The shot has an appropriate foreshadowing effect, but even by itself the image of the mastodon subliminally reminds us of the world from which we evolved and can all too quickly return.

In this context, several other animal images in the film have interesting and mysterious functions. For example, the pets of the three women (patterns of three have meaning in and of themselves in this movie), are a fish, a bird, and a cat. Now, it is possible to read them as symbols of the personalities of the three roommates — the fish as Terry, the gulper; the bird as Patricia, the high flyer; the cat as Marjorie, the fighter with the leonine hair. One could imagine Carl Jung seeing them as their natural elements: water, air, and earth. He would also note the absence of a fire animal and expect to see that gap filled at some point. And he would be right, for in his anger and lust, the attacker Joe is the fire animal, and about halfway through the film Marjorie (who begins to call him "the animal") shuts him up in the fireplace.

The Mythic Resonances of the Mise-en-Scène

Small, meaningful images such as these are like semi-precious stones; they are all over the place in good filmmaking but hard to notice in the clamor of the drama and the allure of abstractions. Before moving on to other aspects of the art of *Extremities*, I would like to mention a particular conception of Freud's which has helped me understand the design of the film: his great pairing of opposites — Love and Death, or, in their Greek names, Eros and Thanatos. In *The Ego and the Id* (30–37), Freud named Eros and Thanatos as the source instincts behind all others, not only functioning separately but also intertwined in an immense variety of psychological and cultural manifestations.

To Eros, we owe the sexual instincts. In addition, ideas of romantic love, marriage/family institutions, all sorts of social relations (including those for work and play), and even culture itself are built out of the associative dimensions of Eros. And, of course, there are the arts that express different aspects of this great, evolving, instinctual force. To state that civilization or culture is generated by instinct is not to say that the form each takes is inevitable or unchangeable. It is to say that they have evolved as barriers to extinction and are therefore very deeply rooted indeed.

The primary form of the death instinct is to be found in aggression, and, indeed, so many of our cultural energies are given over to it worldwide that its perversions have to be counted as perhaps humanity's most destructive mental illness. But violence, aggression, and the death instinct are also part of our personal psychic make-up, and they manifest themselves in multitudinous ways in our artistic and popular culture. Of course, when these two great powers, Eros and Thanatos, are intertwined as they are in rape and sexually motivated homicide — and in the film *Extremities*— the result can be particularly thought-provoking and emotionally disturbing. It is, of course, not necessary to see Eros and Thanatos as clearly defined psychological entities to recognize their power as rhetorical presences in literature and film. The value that they have is to bring concrete images and abstract ideations together, enabling them to be identified and pondered. They work this way for artist and audience alike, forming a ground of communication.

In *Extremities* we first see Death riding a growling motorcycle, his features encased in black plastic. At that point we cannot absolutely identify him with death, because we don't have enough context: bikers are as American as apple pie these days. But this biker does carry an aura of danger with him. Our sense of a deeper level of morbidity in his nature comes when we are forced by the POV shots in the opening parking lot sequence to eye in a furtive, but predatory, manner three successive women. The camera shows us Joe rejecting the first two, but as filmgoers we can intuit that the man in black will take the blonde in the shorts. And, since we have seen the attractive blonde woman at work, in athletic activity, and always surrounded by light, we understand her both consciously and at the level of the unconscious to be a symbolic representation of life, even as we know she has a personal identity that we have not yet learned about. Then, in her car, the swift hand that clamps down on her mouth and the gleaming hunting knife confirm the composite portrait of Eros and Thanatos which the sequence is building. Director Robert Young's tight two-shot of the dark, masked man with the knife at the bright blonde woman's throat forces us to feel in our viscera the struggle of death against life in that car.

Symbols this fundamental tend to exist not only in the moment but also through their iconographic resemblances to other like instances. For instance, this biker (before he pulls a knife) is reminiscent of Marlon Brando in *The Wild One* (Kramer 1954), although Brando doesn't make one think of Death. However, Joe does conjure images of Death in Christian iconography; the knife and the hidden face link him to the Grim Reaper (though Joe has cooler clothes), and his "darkness visible" reminds one of the Great Adversary, Satan. The darkness and the threat to an innocent prompts one to recall Death in *The Seventh Seal* (Bergman 1957), though that association brings home how alone Marjorie is in her struggles with Death. No knight in battered armor comes to play chess with Death until the innocent living can escape. Marjorie will have to be her own knight.

The theme of escape brings me to the mythic resonance of locations. Joe has Marjorie drive to a dark spot under a highway bridge. The genius of this location is that it could be driven to on ground level, yet had the claustrophobic atmosphere of a cave, of the Underworld, because of the roadway overhead. After a struggle of wills and wiles, Marjorie breaks free from her attacker and escapes — not by running down a dark street — but by running upwards to air, space, and sky. This expresses the woman's desire to be free from the rapist as something so elemental that it couldn't be lived without. It also helps identify the attacker with the Underworld, as an analogue of Hades, dragging Persephone into the Earth, only to see her strive to escape despite the offer of a throne (Reid v. 2 858; Jung 97). Marjorie became of that company in that moment. It is therefore of some mythic interest to see Marjorie herself become an agent of Hades later in the film when, with fitting emotional symmetry but questionable ethics, she begins to dig a deep grave in her garden in which to bury Joe alive.

If Thanatos is behind the symbolism of the prior scene, the house chosen to be the residence of Marjorie, Terry, and Patricia is full of Life resonances. Those who have seen the film will recall the airy, high-ceilinged rooms as the perfect contrast, even perfect antidote, to the claustrophobic darkness of the car attack scene. This sense of freedom is further emphasized by the large windows and long vistas that unfold from those windows. These are freedom exemplified, and freedom is as much a sign of life as confinement is of death. Part of the pathos of the week Marjorie lives after the attack is that it is a week of fear, particularly when night closes in, space loses its visibility and visual reach, and even the wind chimes unsettle the nerves.

Additionally, the house (and the way certain scenes were shot in it) invites the audience to see it as a warm, social space. The breakfast scene moves fluidly within the kitchen-dining area to remind the audience how much of love and life is invested in simple social interactions and conducted in humble spaces with everyday things. Such absolutely mundane items as the refrigerator, a coffee cup, or a key hook take on an aura of living warmth because of the way they look in the house, which is itself easy and unforced; the way they look in all that natural daylight (which is not easy to shoot); and, most of all, because of the affectionate way they are used in the house. One scene that exemplifies this effect is the simple exchange of key rings between responsible, reliable Marjorie and the flaky, semi-employed Terry. Terry unexpectedly asks to borrow Marjorie's car (a plot point with significance) since Marjorie is skipping work again. Marjorie resists a bit but gives in when Terry agrees to pick up her laundry. As Diana Scarwid (Terry) leaves — indeed has left, because she's out of camera view — she suddenly ducks back in to give Marjorie a quick, girlish kiss. It happens so quickly that even Farrah Fawcett seems surprised. This spontaneity, no matter how often rehearsed (if it was rehearsed), expresses the natural spontaneity of life itself, the proliferating, primal vitality of body and spirit.

One cannot leave the topic of place and resonances of life without mentioning the gardens that literally surround the house. The Edenic symbolism is too obvious to mention, but it does not hurt to recall that Adam and Eve cultivated their garden and that cultivation is also Civilization in one of Freud's many senses of the term. So the garden signifies, through a carefully cultivated complex of signs, that human life, fully lived, is an interactive process with nature. Finally, one should note the great tree that seems to stand like one of the angels guarding the Garden of Eden. The noble mass and wing-span of that tree link it mythically to the Tree of the World of the Kabbalah, but its guardian role exists only in the world of wishful imagination. The tree is not seen once Joe enters the house.

Counter-Will, or the Psychopathology of Everyday Life

Joe brings Death into this house of Life. He wrecks the kitchen, crashes over the fishbowl and the birdcage, and abuses Marjorie in every meaningful part of the home that she and her housemates have put so much effort into making a place of love and freedom. Joe also abuses her, putting her through a bruising series of ritual, sexual humiliations before pushing her to the floor where he plans to complete the rape. Marjorie, while telling Joe over and over what he has ordered her to say — that she loves him — slyly and desperately reaches for the insect spray and uses it to blind and immobilize him. Throughout the whole ordeal she stays in control of herself, barely seeming to have the strength and will to survive, yet finding both as soon as the time to counterattack is right.

On first view, Joe's control of the situation seems overwhelming, but subsequent viewings reveal Marjorie's subtle defensive tactics. And from a mythic, archetypal, and psychoanalytical perspective, the whole sequence during which Death in the form of the serial rapist-murderer Joe is defeated seems to have been Fated, for reasons I will now explore.

The question one might raise, then, is — Why (since we know that Marjorie has lived in fear for a week) is it so easy for Joe to simply walk into the house unobstructed? Was it through carelessness on Marjorie's part, or did she, at some unconscious or subconscious level, "invite"[3] him into her lair specifically to engage him in mortal combat and defeat him again, this time for good, in every sense of the word?

To resolve that question, one needs an open mind, open eyes and a few more psychoanalytic insights into human complexity.

The first step is to be able to accept that despite the bruising encounter in the car and the more extended tortures she endures in her home, Marjorie may not be simply a poster-girl for victimhood. What follows is an account of *Extremities* in an article using a cultural studies approach to the evolving iconography of Farrah Fawcett herself:

> Looking at *Extremities*, it seems that ten years after Charlie's Angels, the dream of feminine independence had turned into a full-blown nightmare.... Fawcett as Marjorie becomes a prisoner in her own home. Afraid to sleep,

7. Love, Death and Healing: Themes in *Extremities* (Stilling)

she is confined to the domestic sphere by her fears of monstrous masculine desire.... Her attacker ends her active life, takes her independence, and then invades her home to torture her there [Roberts 9].

The description goes on with more and more lurid details about her abuse but never pauses to discuss how or where this victim found the strength to reverse the situation completely and take so much control of the situation that by the halfway point in the film, she is acting as jailer, prosecutor, witness, judge, jury, and would-be executioner to this exemplar of "monstrous masculine desire."

James Russo (Joe) in a taunting posture in *Extremities*.

Psychologically, the answer is that the film's Marjorie has more complexity than the image-analyst's exaggerated stereotypes. First, one might argue that despite her fear — and all the apparent dislocations of her life that Joe's first attack wrought — Marjorie is still a fighter inside. And anyone carefully studying Fawcett's performance as an actress (rather than a mere icon) would see in the complexity of her facial expression and body language that Marjorie is paradoxically both a bruised victim and a woman warrior in one complex dramatic character.

Furthermore, these two aspects of the self may be acting as they do for the contradictory and paradoxical reasons that Freud wrote about as "counter-will," his term for that unconscious motivation that leads people to say and do things that they consciously cannot avow.

In other words, simultaneously, Marjorie wishes both to avoid confrontation with her attacker (who is also Death) and (unconsciously or subconsciously) to invite the confrontation and make sure it is in her own territory. What better way to achieve the latter than by seeming to be the traumatized victim, changing all the locks, and staying home from work?

This reading of Marjorie's doubleness (which in psychoanalytic terms is really only her *humanness* as a being who functions unconsciously and consciously at every moment of her waking life) can be supported by analyzing some of the details of her behavior on the morning of the attack.

First, while having breakfast with Terry and Patricia, Marjorie reveals that she is looking at an advertisement that promotes handguns to provide both "security" and a sense of "adventure." Now the appeal to "security" suggests the fearful reading of Marjorie, with, however, the added observation that buying a gun is a pretty aggressive form of defensive intention. However, the appeal to "adventure" adds a counter-perspective, suggesting someone who is on the verge of growing into a new incarnation of herself. This new person will not be confined to the "domestic sphere" and avoid life; instead, she is inwardly preparing to take a hero's archetypal journey, with great risks but also great rewards if the ordeal is survived (Vogler 13–31; Voytilla 5–12).

We can see this doubleness in her activities during the rest of the morning before Joe arrives, but we must first address the question of how and why — after all the fuss over new locks and keys — a door which had been conspicuously locked when her housemates left was just as conspicuously unlocked when Joe stepped through it as if he owned the place.

Again we need to trace the sequence of events. Marjorie, after locking herself in the house, changes out of her bathrobe into shorts and shirt to go outside and do weeding and transplanting in her garden. This may suggest someone feeling confined to the "domestic sphere," but it also suggests someone not afraid to be outside, someone used to lifting heavy weights and using potentially dangerous implements (all of which she is shown doing), and someone very much at home in — and in charge of — her own space.

Then she runs afoul of a random wasp that stings her high on the inside of her thigh (carefully shown in close-up). She responds to this insect version of aggression by rushing inside, getting out the can of bug spray she will later use to blind and disable Joe, and unlocking the front door (the one she had carefully locked earlier and through which Joe will enter later) in order to spray a wasp's nest above the door. Marjorie then leaves the door unlocked, rushes upstairs to take a languid shower, and comes back downstairs to drink coffee and read, again passing right by the same front door without remembering to secure it.

There are several ways of reading this sequence. One is that all of this is pure chance, but since movies are written, one must assume an effort to communicate meaning.

The second would be that the sting on her inner thigh so violently reminded her of Joe's first knife-wielding sexual attack that she became temporarily unhinged, abandoning her garden and then showering to symbolically wash away the memories of her prior experience. This reading would support viewing Marjorie as fearfully fleeing back to a defensive, avoidance mode. There is a definite logic in this reading, except that it does not explain her unlocking the door, leaving it unlocked while going upstairs to take a (Hitchcockian?) shower, and then walking right past the same door and again ignoring a second opportunity to relock it.

The third interpretive option would be that at some point after Marjorie locked the door, her fear began to be displaced by a growing and positive inner state of courage, resolution, and a subconscious desire to face her enemy and defeat him. In this reading, the open display of herself in the garden was a sign that she was home and thus a target. The conspicuously unlocked door would seem to signify that she was an accessible target. And her reappearance in the living room in her bathrobe would suggest that she was an unready target. All of these signs would make her the perfect bait for a predatory animal. This concept—or one like it—has been used in hundreds of movies, including one of Mr. Young's all-time favorites, *King Kong* (Cooper 1933). In the customary bait-and-trap movie (the Jurassic Park films are useful recent exemplars, particularly when we recollect the mastodon scene in *Extremities*), there is a hunter nearby. In *Extremities*, though, Marjorie is both hunter and hunted. This is certainly a paradoxical formulation, but one that suggests the complexity of the movie's psychological and mythological vision. One might suggest, therefore, that even before her physical battle with Joe, the inner "hero" in Marjorie is beginning to become manifest.

In the middle section of *Extremities*, there is a protagonist and an antagonist, and the struggle is about life and death. Civilization and its imperatives seem far away.

When Terry and Patricia re-enter the scene, they bring the socialized world and its concerns with them. At first, only Joe changes his game plan. He now tries—with some success—to play the innocent victim for the newcomers, but there is no truth in him. Marjorie stays with her intention to kill Joe, and her homicidal intensity shocks, frightens, and to some degree alienates her friends. Terry tries to intervene on the side of a lawful solution out of fear of the legal system, and Patricia pleads the case of civilization from her perspective as a dedicated public servant. But among the four of them, there is no one believable truth, no single, clear and convincing insight within this mundane world that will help them find a way clear to the path of Life.

However, it is part of the elegant psychology behind the passionate surface of the film's action that the four of them together (including sick, lying, murdering Joe) will force healing truths out of the alchemical furnace of their confrontation.

Alfre Woodard (Patricia) facing an enraged Farrah Fawcett (Marjorie) in *Extremities.*

But to appreciate fully the force of this process, we must return to Freud, this time to one of his most elusive, imaginative, and interesting essays, "The Theme of the Three Caskets" (1913). Here, Freud explores the motif of three women or three sisters in literature and myth as a path to wisdom and healing.

Terry, Patricia, and Marjorie and the Goddess Within

No summary will do justice to the complexity of Freud's "Three Caskets" essay, and there is no reason, on this occasion, to follow every step of its intricate argument. Suffice it to say that Freud found it fascinating that in the stories of Shakespeare's *The Merchant of Venice* and *King Lear* (and in other works as well) there were two different but related patterns involving female threesomes. In *The Merchant of Venice*, a crucial moment turned on the paradox that Bassanio's choice of the palest and least outwardly appealing of three boxes or caskets turned out to be the one that brought him the rich prize of the beautiful, wise, and wealthy Portia. In *King Lear*, however, Lear unexpectedly refuses to choose as his favored heir the beautiful and good Cordelia (the best among three sisters) because she gave the least eloquent and ego-flattering answer to his question about which sister loves him most. The result of Lear's short-sighted unwisdom was to be punished with suffering and death. The moral for Freud was that in literature, fairy tale, or myth, this situation meant that men were actually choosing among the Three Fates — the sister goddesses Lachesis, Clotho, and Atropos. Different sources give different nuances to the first two, but are unanimous about the third. In Freud's essay, Lachesis was the element of choice at birth or in life, and Clotho was the distributor of the thread from which the Fates spun every human being's life. Atropos, however, was the "ineluctable" or inevitable ("Caskets," 519), the holder of the shears that cut off the thread of life and brought death.

The moral of Freud's story, actually, is that by choosing one of the three sisters (and particularly Atropos), one is psychologically accommodating oneself to the Reality principle, the inevitability that life will end. To Freud, this understanding enriched life, giving it an authentic value that formal religions (he called himself a godless Jew) could not offer. He called this understanding "Eternal Wisdom," a most un–Freudian-seeming — but sincerely meant — formulation.

However, this fable of Freud's is significant for this essay because its elements — three women and a man who chooses among three women — are the core characters of *Extremities*. It is not until Joe is faced with the gaze of all three women together that he gives up his evil truth and breaks the impasse of the three sisters in their choice of life/love or death. It is also at this moment of truth that the all too human women achieve a spiritual transformation within themselves that re-creates them as the Fates and animates the goddesses within — changing each into something beyond what she had been. This happens most of all to Marjorie, but the beneficence is realized by the other two as well.

Now, this sounds neat in theory, but may seem questionable in practical application to the film. So let us trace the motif through the movie.

We recall, then, that Joe at the very start chose among three women, rejecting the domestic-looking lady and the slightly plump teenager (too much like his wife and daughter?) before seizing and losing the beautiful Marjorie, but keeping her wallet. Joe is nothing if not consistent, and when he fingers through her wallet, he fixes/fixates on a picture of all three women. He still chooses Marjorie first, but he ups the ante on himself by deciding to rape and kill all three. Of course, following the pattern which the Shakespearean precursor myths exemplify, Joe again chooses the most overtly appealing woman, and by doing so ends up choosing his own personal Atropos or Death.

Now, how do we know which woman is which goddess? Freud's association of Lachesis with chance fits with Terry's flaky, inconsistent personality. Clotho, who keeps the threads of life flowing, seems consistent with the generous, social worker side of Patricia's personality. Also, by some accounts, both Lachesis and Clotho wore clothes that were either variegated or decorated with stars. By chance, intuition, or cinematic design, both Terry and Patricia wear outfits which — though different from each other's — are consistent with the descriptions above.

Atropos generally wears black and carries shears. Marjorie, however, tends to wear white and/or light colors that express her life/eros symbolism (like her racquetball, gardening, or bathrobe outfits). However, there is an important exception to this rule.

The exception comes when Joe forces her to change to a stereotypically sexy black negligee. Of course, unwittingly he is also dressing her in the color of Death and of Atropos. And, indeed, after a short time he becomes disturbed with the black garment and tries to get her to take it off. To his cost, she refuses.

The other key to the Marjorie/Atropos identity comes from Patricia, who absolutely insists on getting Atropine as the antidote for the bug poison that Marjorie used to blind Joe. As it turns out, Atropos (the goddess of death) and Atropine (the antidote) both derive from the same Greek root word for "bitter." The identification of Marjorie with Atropos is supported by Patricia's insistence, specifically and repeatedly, on Atropine to reverse the damage caused by Atropos, that is, Marjorie.

There are two other interesting details. The Fates are also known as the Spinners, because they weave life skein by skein. When Marjorie turns the tables on Joe, she immobilizes him by "spinning" him up in a web of household cords. She is spinning him to his death — at least to the Death of what he has been — the serial rapist-killer he confesses to being at his breakdown.

But Marjorie is also the person who — at the end — carries the implement with which to cut the threads. It is Marjorie who discovers the knife hidden in Joe's clothes, and it is the presence of this knife that erases all doubt from Terry and Patricia's minds that Joe might not be guilty of the crimes that Marjorie accuses him of committing.

And, of course, it is Marjorie who uses the knife to actually cut some of the cords and then — in the astonishing parodic repetition of the scene she endured with Joe in the first attack — wields the knife in such a way that he can indeed see not only a mirror image of his own mocking, hateful, horrific self, but can actually see his fate — his Death, his personal Atropos — with her knife, first in his face and then jammed under his crotch. Seeing and feeling all this, he spews out all his secrets, and the three women friends achieve a stronger bond of trust than ever before. Their faces radiate this resolution.

The final moments of the film belong to Marjorie first, with a little to

Joe. For Joe, there are few hints that by confessing and by achieving self-knowledge and humility, he can be purged of his sickness and achieve redemption. One could argue that by persistently pursuing his Atropos, Marjorie, he was unconsciously following a path towards the death of the killer within him. However, the signs for this interpretation are weak. Joe's spiritual fate is as ambiguous as his bodily state seems inevitable — a death sentence, either present or deferred.

The last moments of the film are deservedly Marjorie's. Joe retreats to his fireplace. Terry and Patricia go to the police. Marjorie's black lingerie — the sign of her oppression and of her will to fight back in the Atropos mode — is now mostly covered by a more characteristic, light-colored garment. She is no longer Atropos, but she seems to have incorporated some the dark wisdom of Atropos into her own humanity.

In the film's final compelling moments, Marjorie pulls a floor lamp into the foreground and lights it, bringing a protective circle of light, life, reason and calm around herself and — to a lesser degree — Joe. She settles down beside the fireplace and Joe's limp, fetally posed body. As the camera moves in for one of Robert M. Young's signature close-ups, the play of emotions across Marjorie's face settles into a tentative, hard-won calm and peace. Her mouth shows the barest hint of a Mona Lisa smile. The movie ends.

Notes

1. I wish to thank Robert M. Young for giving me the benefit of his personal reflections on the making of *Extremities* and of his wisdom and expertise about life, human nature, and making movies during an exchange of e-mails and a long, wide-ranging phone call on December 28, 2003.

2. For insights into feminist attitudes from the period on rape, theater, and media, see the works listed below by Bart and Moran, Keyssar, and Projansky.

3. It should be completely clear that no invitation for sexual pleasure is intended here; consciously and unconsciously, Marjorie is Joe's implacable enemy.

Works Cited

Bart, Pauline B., and Eileen Geil Moran, eds. *Violence Against Women: The Bloody Footprints.* Newbury Park, CA: Sage, 1993.
Corliss, Richard. Rev. of *Extremities*, dir. Robert M. Young. *Time* 25 Aug. 1986: 62.
"*Extremities*: Sneak Preview." Photographs by Kelvin Jones. *Picture Week* 28 July 1986: 32–4.
Freud, Sigmund. Trans. Joan Riviere. *The Ego and the Id.* Rev. and ed. James Strachey. New York: Norton, 1962.
_____. Trans. Alan Tyson. *The Psychopathology of Everyday Life.* Ed. James Strachey. New York: Norton, 1960.

———. "The Theme of the Three Caskets." *The Freud Reader*. Ed. Peter Gay. Norton, 1989. 514–22.
Goodman, Walter. "Screen: *Extremities*, with Farrah Fawcett." Rev. of *Extremities*, dir. Robert M. Young. *New York Times* 22 Aug. 1986: n. pag.
Hill, Geoffrey. *Illuminating Shadows: The Mythic Power of Film*. Boston: Shambala, 1992.
Jung, Carl. Trans. R. F. C. Hall. *The Spirit in Man, Art, and Literature*. Bollingen Series, XX. Princeton, NJ: Princeton UP, 1966.
Kelleher, Ed. "Young, Fawcett Court Danger in Atlantic's Tense *Extremities*." *Film Journal* 89.8 (August 1986): 6, 40.
Kermode, Frank. *The Art of Telling: Essays on Fiction*. Cambridge: Harvard UP, 1983. P. 24. Quoted in *Making Meaning: Inference and Rhetoric in the Interpretation of Cinema*. By David Bordwell. Cambridge: Harvard UP, 1989. P. 2.
Keyssar, Helene, ed. *Feminist Theatre and Theory*. New Casebooks. New York: St. Martin's, 1996.
Lurker, Manfred. *Dictionary of Gods and Goddesses, Devils and Demons*. London: Routledge and Kegan Paul, 1987.
M.H. "Rape of the Schlock." Rev. of *Extremities*, dir. Robert M. Young. *Vogue* Aug. 1986: n. pag.
Mastrosimone, William. *Extremities: A Play in Two Acts*. Garden City, NY: Nelson Doubleday, 1978.
Projansky, Sarah. *Watching Rape: Film and Television in Postfeminist Culture*. New York: New York UP, 2001.
Reid, Jane Davidson. *The Oxford Guide to Classical Mythology in the Arts, 1300–1990s*. 2 vols. New York: Oxford UP, 1993.
Roberts, Chadwick. "The Politics of Farrah's Body: The Female Icon as Cultural Embodiment." *Journal of Popular Culture* 37.1 (August 2003): 83–104. *InfoTrac OneFile*. 14 Dec. 2003 <http://infotrac.galegroup.com>
Russell, Candice. "*Extremities* Feeds on Sadistic Violence." *Showtime* 22 Aug. 1986: 6.
Tedesco, Joan. "*Extremities*: Do See It!" *NOW—NYC* [newsletter], [1986?]: n. pag.
Vogler, Christopher. *The Writer's Journey: Mythic Structure for Storytellers and Screenwriters*. Studio City, CA: Wiese Productions, 1992.
Voytilla, Stuart. *Myth and the Movies: Discovering the Mythic Structure of 50 Unforgettable Films*. Studio City, CA: Michael Wiese Productions, 1999.

8. "Don't Let Anybody Hurt Anybody": Working-Class Masculinity in *Dominick and Eugene*
Alexander H. Pitofsky

When *Dominick and Eugene* (directed by Robert M. Young; screenplay by Alvin Sargent and Corey Blechman) was released in 1988, dozens of reviewers extolled its emotional power. Roger Ebert wrote that "[in] the way it shows ... two brothers caring for each other, it captures a tenderness and intimacy that few love stories ever reach."[1] Leonard Maltin called the film a "completely affecting story of love, compassion and responsibility."[2] Bruce Kirkland described it as "pure of heart ... so caring, so tender."[3] In their eagerness to praise *Dominick and Eugene*'s warm heart, these and many other commentators overlooked the film's formidable intellect. More specifically, *Dominick and Eugene* delivers a relentless critique of working-class masculinity in the 1980s. The American popular culture of the period frequently emphasized the integrity of blue-collar characters, but *Dominick and Eugene* takes a hard, extended look at the brutality of men in an urban working-class community.

Twenty-six-year-old Eugene Luciano (Ray Liotta) is a medical student at the University of Pittsburgh. He lives in an apartment above a meat and poultry market with his fraternal twin Dominick, or "Nicky" (Tom Hulce), a brain-damaged sanitation worker. Their mother died in childbirth; their father, a steelworker, "had to go away" several years later. Early in the film, Eugene learns that he has been admitted to an internship program at Stanford. He wants to accept the offer, but feels uneasy about moving to California because he has cared for and protected Nicky for years and because Nicky has, with immense pride and generosity, paid for his education. Moreover,

149

Eugene is burdened with guilt because he has helped to cover up the true cause of his brother's disability. Contrary to the family's well-established myth, Nicky did not "fall and strike his head" during his childhood: he was assaulted and nearly beaten to death by his father. The elder Luciano battered Eugene, Nicky tried to defend his brother, and the result of his intervention was a brain injury that has permanently rendered him childlike and "slow." During a garbage run, Nicky sees his closest friend, a sixth-grader named Mike Chernak, thrown down a flight of basement stairs by his father. The incident stuns Nicky, who simultaneously grieves for his friend and remembers that he was a victim of domestic violence during his own childhood. After Mike is pronounced dead, his father threatens to kill Nicky if he reveals what he has witnessed. Nicky responds by stealing a gun from his employer's truck and, in a bizarre re-enactment of his childhood defense of Eugene, abducts Mike's infant brother to protect him from his father. At the end of an emotionally charged scene filmed in an abandoned ironworks, Eugene persuades Nicky to surrender the baby to the police. Mike's father is arrested, Nicky's well-intentioned kidnapping is pardoned, and Eugene drives to California (alone, and with Nicky's blessing) to continue his medical training.

This synopsis might suggest that *Dominick and Eugene* is something akin to a network movie-of-the-week melodrama, but Young's direction and the cast's performances are strikingly unsentimental. The film is "better than the standard-issue heartwarmer it may sound like," Janet Maslin observes, primarily because of its "refreshing plainness and ... welcome unwillingness to milk the story for more pathos than is warranted."[4] Young foregrounds the tenderness of the brothers' relationship, but never allows the audience to forget that the relationship is an anomaly. The other male characters in the film, with very few exceptions, are extraordinarily destructive and coarse. First of all, the film suggests that domestic violence is commonplace in the South Side, the neighborhood in which Nicky and Eugene have come of age. Both brothers were abused as children but survived. The beatings suffered by Nicky's friend Mike, by contrast, prove to be fatal. The end comes suddenly, but the audience knows that Mike's victimization has been escalating for some time. The boy is injured repeatedly by his father — a bruised chin is followed by a black eye, which is in turn followed by the deadly attack. (Mike's mother must have been aware of the boy's ordeal, but she is apparently too intimidated to intervene. Perhaps she, too, is a survivor of domestic violence and Mike, like Nicky many years earlier, has become a victim after a brave but futile attempt to make it stop.) Nicky notices Mike's injuries, but appears to take his friend's evasions about "falling down" and "walking into doors" at face value. In a particularly moving scene, Nicky articulates a possible explanation for his friend's latest injury and Mike wearily endorses it:

8. Masculinity in *Dominick and Eugene* (Pitofsky)

Ray Liotta (Eugene) and Tom Hulce (Dominick) in *Dominick and Eugene*.

NICKY: What happened to your chin? Fall down again?

MIKE: Yeah....

NICKY: Yeah? I fall down sometimes, too.

Although Nicky does not know for certain that his father injured him until his suppressed memories are forced into the open by Mike's death, he is extremely fearful of sudden outbursts of violence. Early in the film, he stops at church after work and concludes his prayers by asking God not to "let anybody hurt anybody." (Religion and violence often intersect in Nicky's imagination. At home, he mutters, "They were so bad to Jesus"; at church, he reproaches God, insisting that he would have prevented the crucifixion had Christ been his son.) During a conversation with Eugene, Nicky — a devoted fan of the television series *The Incredible Hulk* — asks why the action hero seems so angry and speculates that "maybe somebody did something bad to him once; maybe somebody hurt him." These scenes intimate that no one in this community, not even a man as innocent and kindhearted as Nicky, can remain unaware of the violence that surrounds him.

Dominick and Eugene's most disturbing moments involve child abuse, but several other forms of violence darken the brothers' lives. In the opening scene, Eugene helps a team of nurses and orderlies rush a dying man (apparently the victim of a gunshot wound in the chest) into an emergency room, rinses off the blood that covers his hands, and watches a surgeon struggle to revive the patient. Eugene's neighbors view his education as a golden opportunity to lift himself and his brother out of the dangerous environment in which they have been raised, but the audience learns immediately that the physician-in-training, like a police detective or a gang member, sees the results of street violence on a routine basis. At a garbage dump, Nicky's co-worker Larry Higgins (Todd Graff) shoots rats with a handgun and dares Nicky to prove he isn't "chickenshit" by contributing to the massacre. Nicky refuses to kill, of course; like Laurence Sterne's Uncle Toby, he literally wouldn't hurt a fly. Nevertheless, it is telling that even he is pressured to contribute to the South Side's culture of violence.

Nicky mentions more than once that Larry knocked out one of his teeth by dropping a garbage can on him from the top of a truck. Nicky accepts his co-worker's claim that "the can slipped out of my hands," just as he appears to accept the notion that his friend Mike is clumsy and accident-prone, but the viewer cannot help wondering if Larry's appetite for destruction caused him to hurt Nicky intentionally. *Dominick and Eugene* portrays violence as an ineluctable threat: it looms at home, in the workplace, in church, on television, and in the streets. (Even the brothers' surname elicits thoughts of Charles "Lucky" Luciano, the Sicilian immigrant who become one of the most powerful figures in the history of the Mafia and helped to form Murder, Inc.)

In spite of his indisputable devotion to his brother, Eugene proves to be one of the most violent characters in *Dominick and Eugene*. When he learns that a scrap yard worker named Guido has been using Nicky as a drug runner (he conceals packets of heroin in newspapers and pays Nicky to deliver

8. Masculinity in *Dominick and Eugene* (Pitofsky)   153

Jamie Lee Curtis (Jennifer) and Ray Liotta (Eugene) in *Dominick and Eugene*.

them to "my main man Sal"), Eugene tracks Guido down and punches him in the face through a window. Later on, Nicky startles Eugene's med school classmate and girlfriend Jennifer Reston (Jamie Lee Curtis) by explaining that Eugene once nearly killed a man: "One time when Frankie the Squirrel was bothering me, Geno came after him. You should have seen Frankie's face. His nose was bleedin,' his lips was bleedin,' his eyes was bleedin.' I thought Eugene was gonna kill him." After Eugene attacks Guido, moreover, he slams Nicky into a fence and berates him for failing to keep his distance from the "Guidos" in the neighborhood:

> NICKY: Eugene? What'd I do. Huh? What'd I do? Don't be mad at me, I....
>
> EUGENE: What'd you do? What'd you do? You have a life! You have a life! I can only take so much care of you, Nicky! You know he's shit! You can see he's shit! He's a *drug* dealer! You have a responsibility — do you understand me? Huh? *Do you understand me*? I can't watch you every minute! I'm not God!

In short, Eugene is unmistakably a product of the South Side. He knows he is in danger of becoming "just like" his father, yet he seems unable to contain his violent impulses. Is his rage a matter of heredity? Does it arise from his complicity in the fiction that Nicky was injured in an accident, or, perhaps, from his fears that he can never ensure his brother's safety? Is it generated from the frustration of spending day after day with privileged medical students oblivious to the difficulty of living on a garbage man's salary, or from the years he has spent despising his father? The film does not offer a simple explanation, but it emphasizes that within Eugene's psyche a seething Hyde coexists with a respectable Jekyll who dreads his alter ego's next convulsion. Or, to put it another way, Eugene is a real-life analogue of Nicky's idol the Incredible Hulk: a talented man of science who becomes a violent brute when he loses his temper.

Eugene's struggle to control his rage helps to explain why he looks so worn and unhappy throughout the film. *Dominick and Eugene* is, among other things, a late twentieth-century Horatio Alger narrative — a story about a young man on the verge of escaping from urban poverty through hard work, determination, and luck. Eugene's white-collar aspirations are within reach, yet he never pauses for a moment of celebration. He occasionally speaks vaguely about a pleasant future in which he will become a "rich doctor" and live with Nicky "by a lake in the country," but that is the closest he comes to acknowledging his success. There is little doubt that Eugene will earn his MD, and the offer from Stanford suggests that he might be on the path to a distinguished career. Nonetheless, he always seems anxious and overburdened — even when he smiles. In scene after scene, he looks like a beaten man, exhausted by 22-hour shifts in the emergency room and beset by domestic pressures he can't explain to Jennifer and professional pressures he can't explain to Nicky.

Throughout *Dominick and Eugene*, Young also underscores the boorish manners of working men. Larry proves to be a surprisingly empathetic friend during the chain of crises initiated by Mike's death, but until then he is the film's most glaring example of the vulgarity of the South Side. He calls Nicky "Birdbrain" and "Nick-nut" and warns him to beware of "Black Plague." He uses a racial slur to describe their employer, Mr. Johnson. He takes Nicky to the home of Mrs. Vinson, a lonely woman who exchanges sex for companionship, and has an encounter (loud enough for the neighbors to hear) with her while Nicky watches television downstairs. Moreover, Larry seems determined to drive a wedge between Nicky and Eugene. When Nicky mentions his brother's relationship with Jennifer, for example, Larry insists that the romance will inevitably give rise to Nicky's abandonment:

> LARRY: All right, so she's got this great bod ... long legs. Cool car. I'm tellin' ya, Nick — the writin's on the wall.
>
> NICKY: What wall?
>
> LARRY: Two's company, three's a crowd. You put him through medical school — he's dumping you like a rock.
>
> NICKY: Huh?
>
> LARRY: Don't be dumb, Nick.... It won't be long before you get a postcard from Atlantic City: "Having a wonderful time. Glad you're not here."

In spite of Larry's abysmal judgment and endless supply of crude remarks, he usually seems more pathetic than harmful. He is manifestly a feeble-minded bigot, humiliated to find that he works for a black man, shoulder to shoulder with a disabled co-worker. In fact, because of Larry's I'll-do-the-minimum work ethic and ceaseless complaints about working conditions and benefits, Mr. Johnson appears to regard him as a less valuable employee than Nicky, who, as Maslin writes, works "cheerfully and at the height of his abilities."[5] The audience winces when Larry tells Nicky his brain is "in reverse," but Larry's disparaging remarks are less startling than his numerous boasts that he is more street-smart than a man who has suffered a catastrophic brain injury:

> LARRY: That's your biggest problem, Nick — you like everybody.
>
> NICKY: No, I don't.
>
> LARRY: And you believe anything anybody tells you.
>
> NICKY: I do not!
>
> LARRY: No? How about the time I told you there was nitroglycerin in the middle of golf balls?

NICKY: I didn't believe you that time.

LARRY: No? Then how come you ducked when I tossed one at ya? Look — you can't trust nobody.

In some ways, Larry is a brilliantly twisted parody of the working-class protagonists of the pop culture of the late seventies and eighties. He likes to use the word "Yo" — with the intonation of the title character of *Rocky* (1976), not that of an eighties rapper — but he lacks the talent and determination of Sylvester Stallone's club fighter. Stallone persuades the audience that Rocky Balboa is a diamond in the rough, a local athlete with world-class physical and mental toughness. Larry, by contrast, is unimpressive to the core. In his sleeveless denim jacket (adorned with a Jack Daniel's patch), black T-shirts, cheap sunglasses, and bandanna headband, Larry looks like a character in an anthem by Bob Seger or Steve Earle, yet he is devoid of the dignity and longing for better times audiences expect to find in "blue-collar rock." The narrator of Earle's "Guitar Town" is a journeyman musician who transcends his limits through live performances: "When my boots hit the boards, I'm a brand-new man/With my back to the risers I'll make my stand."[6] For Larry, there will be no moment of transcendence — he is a "full-time sleazoid,"[7] and, despite his uncharacteristic moments of compassion late in the film, he seems unlikely to change.

Larry's behavior is distasteful, but by no means unusual. In an early scene, three teenagers surround Nicky, steal his treasured Pirates cap (a gift from Mr. Johnson), taunt him mercilessly, and knock his bag of groceries on the street when Eugene happens to drive by and chase them away. When Eugene confronts Guido and announces that he is Nicky's brother, the drug dealer smirks and asks, "Are you retarded, too?" When Mike's father comes home unexpectedly in the afternoon and sees his son reading a comic book with Nicky, he sends the terrified boy into the house — to prepare for yet another beating, the audience fears — and assails Nicky with a vicious string of insults: "What're you lookin' at, goofy? Huh? What's your problem? What're you doin'? Playin' with your dick out here?" Even the local priest uses a watered-down version of the neighborhood's in-your-face vernacular. During a conversation with Nicky, "Father T" facetiously threatens to attack Eugene:

FATHER T: Hello, Nicky. How's my boy?

NICKY: Good, Father T.

FATHER T: How's Geno? I never see him around here anymore....

NICKY: He's really busy.

8. Masculinity in *Dominick and Eugene* (Pitofsky) 157

FATHER T (smiling approvingly): You stand up for him. Listen. Tell him if he don't start comin' to church, I'm gonna kick his butt from here to heaven.

Most of *Dominick and Eugene*'s male characters fill their leisure time with entertainment that reflects the belligerent ethos of the South Side. Nicky is a professional wrestling fan (he does not seem to understand the difference between the Incredible Hulk and Hulk Hogan, the wrestling celebrity) and he and Mike are avid readers of violent comic books. Larry's black Anthrax and Megadeth T-shirts signal that he enjoys the blood-soaked fantasies of eighties speed metal, and when he takes Nicky to a pool hall, he repeats his prediction that Eugene will abandon Nicky while a raunchy country and western song blares on the jukebox.[8]

One of the most striking features of Young's representation of working men is the way it diverges from most of the popular culture of the 1980s. During the ten years before *Dominick and Eugene* was released, Hollywood studios released a spate of films that highlighted the dignity of working Americans.[9] They valorized blue-collar women (*Norma Rae* [1979], *Coal Miner's Daughter* [1980], *Silkwood* [1983]) and men (*Breaking Away* [1979], *Matewan* [1987], *Wall Street* [1987]). They found working-class heroes in post-industrial cities, in rural America, and in small towns.[10] Hollywood's turn toward sympathetic portrayals of working people was echoed on network television (*Hill Street Blues* [NBC, 1981–87], *Cheers* [NBC, 1982–93], *Cagney & Lacey* [CBS, 1982–88]) and in rock music (albums by Bruce Springsteen, Steve Earle, Los Lobos, the Del Lords, the Blasters, the Bus Boys, and many others). Nicky's innocence and Eugene's determination are often poignant, but never seem representative of working-class culture. The warmth of the brothers' relationship — Young shows them sharing silly jokes, cuddling at bedtime, and showering together like happy six-year-olds — marks them as outsiders in a film teeming with abusive fathers, sadists, bullies, and drug dealers. *Dominick and Eugene* also differs from other working-class narratives of the period in that it never places the title characters' struggles in a bleak or menacing setting. To the contrary, the film's establishing and location shots of the skyline, rivers, bridges, train yards, and hills of Pittsburgh must rank among the most tranquil, attractive images of "Steel Town" ever captured on film. In Young's Pittsburgh, every prospect pleases and only man is vile.[11]

Another unusual aspect of *Dominick and Eugene*'s investigation of working-class life is the fact that Young shows virtually no interest in the women of the South Side. Jennifer Reston, the most carefully developed female character in the film, is a Saab-driving Harvard graduate; every moment she spends in the brothers' neighborhood is a moment of slumming.

Mrs. Gianelli, an elderly neighbor who sings Italian folk songs and feeds the brothers tortellini and cake, appears in only a handful of scenes. Mike's mother, Theresa Chernak, appears so infrequently that she barely qualifies to be labeled a character. Larry's "girlfriend" Mrs. Vinson is by far the most intriguing South Side woman in the film. When Larry and Nicky visit her home, Young emphasizes that her personality is a blend of contradictions. She is fun-loving and unhappy, carnal and ashamed, energetic and indifferent:

> LARRY (calling from upstairs): Nicky! Bring my baby back up here! It's time for you to prove yourself to be a man.
>
> NICKY: I *am* a man!
>
> MRS. VINSON: Of course you're a man! You can join in the fun if you want to. I don't really care.... I just enjoy the company, that's all.

The women in *Dominick and Eugene* seldom call attention to themselves. To the contrary, they are used primarily to sharpen the audience's understanding of the film's male characters. Jennifer, for instance, embodies Eugene's fears that his responsibilities at home and at work have become a trap. The two medical students are drawn to each other, but "dating" is simply not an option for Eugene. He works around the clock. He intends to move to California. Nicky is terrified by the thought of his brother in a second loving relationship. Accordingly, Jennifer usually resembles a member of the audience more than a full-fledged participant in the narrative. She observes the brothers' relationship, wishes them well, and appears to understand that she will remain on the sidelines until Eugene finds a way to become settled in a medical career without hurting Nicky. Mrs. Gianelli's attempts to nurture "the boys" remind the audience that Nicky and Eugene have no family beyond each other. They never knew their mother. Their father is long gone. (Is he dead? In a penitentiary? Did he abandon his sons immediately after he injured Nicky, or did he try to make amends for his crime? The film leaves these questions unanswered. The elder Luciano is just a painful memory, Young implies, and that is all the audience needs to know about him.) The brief appearances of Teresa Chernak and Mrs. Vinson, moreover, highlight the brutality of Mike's father and the coarseness of Larry Higgins. In several other films (*Nothing but a Man* [1964] and *Caught* [1996] are among the first that come to mind) Young pays a great deal of attention to the effects hard work and financial insecurity can have on women's lives. In *Dominick and Eugene*, by contrast, Young is almost exclusively concerned with the behavior and attitudes of working-class men.

Young's critique of working-class masculinity in *Dominick and Eugene* is uncompromising, but never one-dimensional. For every male perpetrator of violence in the film, Young includes a corresponding male victim. The nameless emergency-room patient in the opening scene expires before our eyes. The audience knows that three male characters — Mike, Nicky, and Eugene — have been victims of domestic abuse; it seems likely that others have endured similar attacks. Larry's sadism, Guido's amorality, and the cruelty of the three boys on the street and Frankie the Squirrel do not plague Nicky by chance, the film implies. All of the men in the South Side have, to greater or lesser degrees, been influenced by brutal behavior and coarse attitudes. When I think about the violent men in the film, an image that recurs again and again is the face of Mike's father (David Strathairn). The audience is given many reasons to despise the elder Chernak, yet he often looks more desperate than sinister. The military jacket he wears hints that he may be a Vietnam combat veteran, and he appears to be unemployed. Everything about him, from his haunted eyes to his dilapidated pick-up truck, signals that he is miserable, overwhelmed, and possibly deranged. The fact that he, too, has suffered does not mitigate his guilt, but it adds another layer of complexity to *Dominick and Eugene*'s portrait of working-class masculinity.

Notes

1. *New York Post*, 18 March 1988.
2. *Leonard Maltin's 2000 Movie & Video Guide* (New York: Signet, 1999), 365.
3. *Toronto Sun*, 18 March 1988.
4. *New York Times*, 18 March 1988. Similarly, reviewer Jeff Strickler observes that "heavily laden with opportunities to play to sentimentalism, the film aims much higher and achieves very effective, very human drama." *Minneapolis Star Tribune*, 20 May 1988.
5. *New York Times*, 18 March 1988.
6. "Guitar Town," *Guitar Town* (MCA 1986).
7. Sheila Benson, *Los Angeles Times*, 18 March 1988.
8. The song heard is "The I-95 Song," written by Fred Campbell and performed by August Campbell and the Spur of the Moment Band.
9. In the late seventies and eighties "plebeians are not cast on a lonely and highly singular struggle as gangsters, fallen women, or boxers, but they are now part of groups seeking measures of justice and respect that rightfully belonged to them." John Bodnar, *Blue-Collar Hollywood: Liberalism, Democracy, and Working People in American Film* (Baltimore: John Hopkins University Press, 2003), 200. In another recent study of Hollywood's representations of working people, Steven J. Ross points out that directors of the eighties had no illusions about the box-office appeal of blue-collar characters. When John Sayles wrote *Matewan*, for instance, "[he] understood that most filmgoers would not pay to see a movie unless it was entertaining. Consequently, like worker filmmakers of the 1920s, he presents his political messages in the form of an action-packed movie that

builds to a dramatic climax right out of *High Noon* (1952) in which the sheriff and his union allies walk to the center of town and shoot it out with coal company gunmen." *Working-Class Hollywood: Silent Film and the Shaping of Class in America* (Princeton: Princeton University Press, 1998), 253.

10. *Raging Bull* (1980), *Alamo Bay* (1985), and a few other films of the period featured the kinds of working-class violence and boorishness that recur throughout *Dominick and Eugene*, but these films, it seems to me, are exceptions that prove the rule. Throughout the 1980s, Hollywood studios seemed eager to avoid narratives highlighting what Bodnar defines as "[the] common man's inability to manage his violent drives." *Blue-Collar Hollywood*, 191.

11. Film historian Peter Stead calls Pittsburgh the "most filmically neglected of all American cities" and censures *Flashdance* (1983) for failing to present convincing images of the city's "working-class industrial" character. *Film and the Working Class: The Feature Film in British and American Society* (London: Routledge, 1989), 225. Of all the commentators who reviewed *Dominick and Eugene* when it was intially released, only one, Lynn Darling, appears to have noticed Young's surprisingly serene representation of Pittsburgh: "...the shots of [the city's] hilly working-class neighborhoods somehow fail to capture its grit. Pittsburgh, a city of rough-talking fiercely independent immigrants surrounded by dying steel mills, knows a little bit about the disadvantages people can labor under and still triumph: it's too bad the filmmakers didn't take more advantage of so well-chosen a setting." *New York Newsday*, 18 March 1988.

9. Memory and History in *Triumph of the Spirit*
Zohara Boyd and Rosemary Horowitz

Robert M. Young's *Triumph of the Spirit* has not gained the public fame or critical acclaim accorded to other serious Holocaust films such as *Schindler's List*, *The Pianist*, or even the controversially feel-good *Life is Beautiful*. Its obscurity and poor reception are grossly unfair to an intelligent, powerful work of art that contains three groundbreaking features: It is the only movie filmed entirely on location at Auschwitz, with a supporting cast consisting largely of concentration camp survivors and sons of former Nazi officers. While other films limit the Holocaust to the destruction of East European Jewry, *Triumph* depicts the virtual extermination of the ancient Greek Sephardic community of Salonika. The Porrajmos (the Devouring) of the European Gypsies has largely been ignored in history as well as in art. Young has at least partially redressed the wrong of that silence.

Salamo Arouch, a Greek Jew from Thessaloniki (Salonika), was the middleweight boxing champion of the Balkans when he and his family were deported to Auschwitz. There, the SS, who whiled away the time between murders with a variety of amusements such as orchestral concerts and operatic performances by the inmates, found yet another diversion by arranging boxing matches between Arouch and a series of contenders who were gassed when they were defeated. Nicknamed "The Ballerina" for his swift and graceful footwork, Arouch fought and won approximately two hundred such bouts. In the film, if not in life, Arouch's boxing triumphs were aided by a gypsy camp inmate who became his manager. Arouch, who received extra, life-saving rations as reward for his victories, emigrated to Israel after the liberation of Auschwitz, married, and became the owner of a transport company. He returned to Auschwitz to serve as a consultant on the

Willem Dafoe as Salamo Arouch in *Triumph of the Spirit*.

filming of *Triumph of the Spirit*, a somewhat fictionalized version of his experiences.

Arnold Kopelson, the film's producer, learned Arouch's story in 1983 when it was presented to him by Shimon Arama, who had produced films in France and Israel and who became co-producer of *Triumph*. Together with script writer Zion Haen, Arama researched and wrote the first version of the story, which was then scripted by a writer named Larry Heath. In November of 1987, Kopelson and Heath presented a draft to Robert Young and asked him if he would be interested in directing it. Young was interested in the story but felt that Kopelson and Heath's script treatment of the camp experience was too "frontal" and "explicit," to use Young's own words from his letter to the Writers Guild of America dated May 30, 1988. In the original script, which Young likened to a cross between *Rocky* and *The Guns of Navarone*, Salamo "kills his Nazi oppressor and is reunited with the woman he loves as the Allies (like the Seventh Cavalry) liberate the camp." Young wanted the film "to serve the truth rather than the wish-fulfillment fantasies of the audience."

When the collaboration with Larry Heath failed to produce a satisfactory script, Robert Young enlisted the aid of Arthur Coburn, who had worked closely with Young on a previous project, *Dominick and Eugene*. Yet another writer, Millard Lampell, was brought in to help create the film's early scenes, which were set in Salonika. However, even the new draft — a combination of the writing done by Heath, Young, Coburn, and Lampell — proved inadequate to the truths and emotions presented by the film's shooting location, Auschwitz's Cell Block 11 and the remains of Birkenau with its ten square miles of barracks, ruins of four crematoria, cremation pyres, and train platform where new arrivals were selected for life or death. Permission to use the site was obtained through the assistance of the government-owned Poltel (Polish Television). Eddie Surkin, special effects director, acknowledged that the shooting could have been done in Hollywood and Auschwitz recreated through special effects, but he felt that filming on-site evoked a psychological phenomenon that could not be created in any other way. No other film depicting the Holocaust, before or after *Triumph of the Spirit*, has been filmed on-site.

Realizing that the script "needed to be even more rooted in the moment to moment life of the camp," Young set about revising it each night after the day's shooting had been completed. According to his own account of the weeks on location, he took no days off and rewrote until two or three in the morning to create an emotionally valid account of how one man could survive under impossible circumstances. His criteria for creating such an account were to "be true to the reality of Auschwitz, be experiential, do not moralize, and do not tell the audience what to think or feel."

The actors, too, were overwhelmed by the setting. Pat H. Broeske documented their reactions in a detailed article for the *Calendar* section of the *Los Angeles Times*, April 23, 1989. Edward James Olmos, who played Salamo Arouch's gypsy boxing manager, said he went to the crematoria pits almost daily to pray: "You come here to pay homage. It's like going to church." Willem Dafoe, who portrayed the lead character Salamo Arouch, noted, "Being here is special.... It gets you closer to the ghosts. They do creep up on you, I think.... Occasionally, I'd wake up in a cold sweat."

Many of the extras playing SS officers were in reality Jews and Poles who were either themselves survivors of Auschwitz, or children and grandchildren of survivors and therefore had to harden themselves to resist the emotions the setting aroused. Dorota Bialy-Wieczorek, who portrayed an SS guard and was also a translator for the film, was married to a man whose mother and grandmother had been prisoners: "I should be playing a prisoner ... but I am also an actress. So I must try to imagine what it would have been like to be on the other side."

Hartmut Becker, who portrayed SS Major Rauscher, and Burkhard Heyl, Rauscher's aide SS Lieutenant Heinrich in the film, were two actors who did not have to "imagine what it would have been like to be on the other side." The only two Germans in the cast, they were both sons of German

World War II officers, albeit in the regular army and not SS members. They were prepared for jokes from the rest of the cast but not for the anger and tears of tourist groups comprised of survivors and their offspring. Becker told interviewer Boeske that he probably would not have agreed to appear in the film had he known the effect Auschwitz would have on him: "I was not prepared for what I would feel when I got here," he said. "You know, when I was young, I saw the documentaries about the camps.... But this place ... and Birkenau ... when I saw it for the first time, well, it is so huge."

Affected so strongly by the setting, actors found that in order to give a truthful portrayal, they had to abandon many aspects of their training and technique. Robert Loggia, Papa Arouch, whose life Salamo vainly tried to save through his boxing victories, described to Broeske his reactions: "It was snowing, there were hundreds and hundreds of extras. We had on frayed clothes and our Jewish stars and had to jump from the boxcars. And we were freezing. We re-created that scene — we didn't act it.... With this movie, if you start to do any acting out there, other than just dealing with the cold and the craziness of the situation, you're going to look phony.... The way [Bob] Young is making this movie, it's as if you're inside the vortex — in the maelstrom." One scene that Loggia and Young agreed had to be cut depicted Papa Arouch as doing a Greek dance on his way to the gas chamber. Loggia told Broeske, "That scene would never work — not the way we're doing this picture now. I told them that's 'Zorba the Greek' time.... But it's not for me — not here."

Young stated that he was careful not to turn Salamo Arouch into a heroic or self-sacrificing figure: "He chooses to live, to survive.... He does not say no to becoming a Sonderkommando, as does his brother Avram, who pays with his life for his refusal. Nor does Salamo join his friend Jacko Levy in the resistance movement in the steelmill.... Nor is he a hero in the revolt at the crematorium. I resisted all attempts to have Salamo do some heroic or redeeming act near the end of the film before his liberation. He is simply a witness.... Salamo is a survivor, and as such provides the possibility of a future." He further explained Arouch's predicament by comparing him to "a cork bobbing on the surface of the sea in a storm."

Kopelson's first choice of director for *Triumph of the Spirit* was Oliver Stone, who had previously worked with Willem Dafoe on Kopelson's Oscar-winning *Platoon*. Kopelson acknowledged it would have been a very different film under Stone's direction: "He might have been out there bulldozing the bodies, going into those aspects." Kopelson, in fact, had "become obsessed" with the descriptions of gassings given by surviving Sonderkommandos who spoke of naked victims jammed into the chambers "so tight that they had to raise their hands" and of children and babies tossed in above the dying crowd. He wanted to film such a scene, but "Saint Bob," as Kopelson referred to Young, refused to do it. "I think it's like pornography," he said. "I'm not going to turn this movie into a horror picture — which is what it would become if I showed atrocities." His refusal to film a sequence that followed the victims into the gas chamber had personal reasons as well: "I don't want to psychologically experience that moment myself. That scene also involves a child. Well, I'm not going to terrorize a child by subjecting him to something like that. I happen to have children."

Young understood the perils of his refusal to turn *Triumph of the Spirit* into a horror show or an Auschwitz-based *Rocky* or *Guns of Navarone*. As he acknowledged in his letter to the Writers Guild, "It may turn out that I made all the wrong choices, but I can honestly say that I shaped and led and forged this script out of my guts and deepest thinking.... In the end, I took the responsibility for making this story the way it is. I was extremely fortunate in having producers who believed in me and who gave me the freedom to do as I saw fit."

Robert Young, his cast, and his producers paid dearly for their integrity. *Triumph of the Spirit* was independently financed and had a hard time finding a distributor. When it was released by Nova International Films on December 8, 1989, critics were almost uniformly unimpressed and harsh in their judgment of the film. Willem Dafoe had predicted this reception in his April 1989 interview with Broeske. He understood that the "ambiguous morality" and "documentary style" of the film might not find wide audience appeal: "When people start judging films on what they should be rather than what they are, then we're in trouble." Citing audience reactions to two of his previous films, *Mississippi Burning* and *The Last Temptation of Christ*, he joked, "Movies that nobody will touch are becoming my specialty."

New York Times film critic Janet Maslin began her review by acknowledging that *Triumph of the Spirit*, while "not especially graphic or brutal, ... depicts aspects of the concentration camp experience that are not ordinarily seen on film." She also stated that "it serves as a reminder of why the tattoos being inflicted, the prisoners being marched to the showers, the release of the poison gas and the bodies on their way to the crematorium are not usually shown.... Horror like this cannot be reduced to the level of routine fiction...." She then excoriated the film for not doing precisely what she said should not be done. She described Young's principled refusal to show atrocities as "a thoroughly mundane approach to its material, an approach better suited to television films about dread afflictions than to a subject of this magnitude." Arouch's "remarkable experience" has been reduced "to the level of easy irony and lifeless cliché." Young's direction "seldom sounds an unusual note when a familiar one will do." Even Cliff Eidelman's musical score failed to escape Maslin's scorn. She described it as "outstandingly intrusive, wringing emotion at every possible moment with weepy laments and ominous choral flourishes: ...[the music] pre-empts the viewer's emotional response. Television routinely treats its audiences this way. Feature films of real gravity don't have to." According to Maslin, then, the horrors of Auschwitz should not be depicted too graphically, but *Triumph of the Spirit* is inferior television fare because it has not done so. Reading this review, one can only wonder at its inner contradictions.

Roger Ebert's review for the *Chicago Sun-Times*, dated February 2, 1990, was not much kinder. While acknowledging the uniqueness of the location, the authenticity of the script, and the director's attention to accurate details, Ebert stated, "Every serious story, especially one about a subject such as the Holocaust, must find its own inner truth, and on the inside, 'Triumph of the Spirit' is hollow. It is never able to decide exactly what its story is saying, or should say. Blinded by the fact that the story is based on a man's life, that it 'actually happened,' the film seems to assume that the message is in the very accuracy itself. But at the end we feel confused and unsatisfied.... Salamo, we learn, won enough fights that he was still alive at the end of the war; he survived to tell his story, and this is the film of his story. But what does it mean? ... Did the filmmakers ever consider placing the fights offscreen, or dwelling on them less, and considering the implications of the situation Salamo finds himself in?" By asking several such pointless questions, Ebert tried to rewrite the script rather than to review the film, judging it on what he thought it should be rather than what it was, exactly the reaction Willem Dafoe predicted and deplored. Ebert repeatedly stated that he did not know what meaning he should derive from the events depicted in the film. Apparently, he was left befuddled by Robert Young's decision not to tell the audience what to think or feel.

Rolling Stone's undated review by Peter Travers described the film as "earnest but woefully misguided" and as a melodramatic "Holocaust Gothic — a fiction that trivializes unspeakable horror by adding entertainment elements." Cliff Eidelman's score again is derided as "intrusive" and designed to "pump" the viewer's emotions "to a fever pitch." This last bit of criticism from a publication largely dedicated to music reviews is baffling. Isn't emotional arousal the function of a film's musical score? *Variety*'s staff review of January 1, 1990, called the story "murkily underplayed" and "very slow." Ryan Cracknell, reviewer for the online *Apollo Guide*, found *Triumph of the Spirit* too emotionally detached and Willem Dafoe's performance too "stoic": "As a viewer, you will want to empathize with everyone, but you don't really get to know any of them, so how could you? *Triumph of the Spirit* lacks a soul, so fails to rise beyond the realm of a mediocre Holocaust-themed movie." Brett Willis, a volunteer guest reviewer for the *Christian Spotlight on the Movies*, deplored the film's lack of Christian or Jewish "moral content" and described it as "not particularly uplifting even at the end; any 'triumph' consists of a few prisoners surviving and going on with life after the war.... This movie tries to do something historically worthwhile, but in my opinion it never quite succeeds." While these reviews failed to understand *Triumph*'s uniqueness and power, the reviewers did, at least, use the film as some sort of Rorschach test of their own emotional needs in relation to the Holocaust. Peter Travers wanted less melodrama and more detachment while the *Variety* staffers and Ryan Cracknell wanted the exact opposite, and Brett Willis craved a heroic and uplifting ending, precisely the "wish-fulfillment fantasies" that Robert Young rejected in favor of the truth.

Since its 2002 release on DVD, *Triumph of the Spirit* has slowly started to garner the critical acclaim it always deserved. Robert Young may be even more gratified to find that the favorable reviews come not from professional critics but from viewers who have taken the time to express their appreciation at various online sites. An anonymous writer to *Channel 4 Film* describes *Triumph* as "an uncompromisingly gruesome film which thankfully doesn't gloss over the protagonist's darker sides.... Dafoe's performance and the harrowing setting make this compelling viewing." *DVD Talk*'s reviewer Gil Jawetz understands the uniqueness of the film in its portrayal of Greek and Gypsy inmates at Auschwitz. In a review dated May 15, 2002, he praises Young's use of subtlety in place of overt emotion: "It's not a film that tugs at the viewer's heart-strings in a cheap, easy way, but bald, honest emotion, while difficult to pull off, is the only way to make an audience really feel for the characters." However, Jawetz also feels the film does not always make an emotional connection with the viewer and "is more likely to make a viewer understand without really getting under the skin." *TV Guide Online* praises Robert Young's "judicious use of his setting—neither shrine, nor stage set, it gives the film a firm grounding in history and a corresponding commitment to truth." This review is one that meets Young's film on the terms he set out to fulfill. Customer reviews for *The Online Shopping Center* are uniformly favorable. While some of these reviews may be a bit generic and lacking in detail, they reflect the enthusiasm of the audience Robert Young truly intended to reach, the "amateur" reviewer who is open to honest emotion, not the critic who makes his own reputation by scoffing at artistry he himself could never achieve. A few samples of such heartfelt, if nonprofessional, reviews follow:

> This is an outstanding film with an excellent cast and the deepest power I have seen for a while. All I can say is see it for yourself and enjoy the best.

> I cautiously recommend this film for any serious student of the Holocaust and urge that the message therein never be forgotten or repeated. Thank you.
>
> *Triumph of the Spirit* is probably the most realistic dramatic recreation of the horrors of Auschwitz I've seen. Director Robert Young is a pro at bringing controversial independent films to fruition, and Dafoe gives one of his best performances here.... Again there is an intensity and realism to this film that makes *Schindler's List* pale in comparison.
>
> A good touch of realism is the languages. The Germans speak German, the Poles speak Polish, and the Russians speak Russian all without subtitles [compare this to *Schindler's List*].
>
> If you want to know about the Holocaust this drama is near the top of the list with the best documentaries.

Even Cliff Eidelman's music, derided by Janet Maslin and Peter Travers, has been rehabilitated by *Filmtracks,* an online reviewer of movie scores, which praises its emotional power and intensity, calling it the strongest of the composer's early works. His research of the "instrumentation and language of the Greek Jewish culture" and his "attention to ethnic detail" are also praised.

Eidelman's research of the Greco-Jewish culture and his attention to ethnic detail are a mirror of Robert Young's own work in creating *Triumph of the Spirit.* Most filmmakers, as well as most historians, have chronicled the destruction of Ashkenazi Jewry in Eastern and Western Europe. The fate of the Sephardic communities of Spain, Portugal, Italy, and Greece has not been so thoroughly examined in literature or onscreen. Even Primo Levi in *Survival in Auschwitz* has more to say about the Ashkenazi prisoners he met despite his own Italian Jewish origins.

Jewish settlement in Greece can be authenticated as far back as 85 B.C. and may go back as far as 586 B.C., the beginning of the Babylonian exile. According to one tradition, Jews first arrived in Salamo Arouch's community of Salonika (Thessaloniki), in 315 B.C. when Cassandros, brother-in-law of Alexander the Great, asked King Ptolemy of Egypt to send him some Jewish artisans. The expulsion of Jews from Spain in 1492 swelled the small community into "the Jerusalem of the Balkans." By the end of the nineteenth century, approximately half of Thessaloniki's population was Jewish and thoroughly identified with its Islamic Ottoman rulers who had shown religious tolerance toward Jew and Christian alike. When Thessaloniki fell under Greek rule in 1913, the Jewish community was promised full equality by King George I of Greece, a promise partly broken in the 1930s when the exclusive use of the Greek language was mandated and Sunday was proclaimed the country's official day of rest. Such decrees disrupted the ancient community's way of life, and Jews began to emigrate from Thessaloniki, with many of them deciding to settle in Palestine.

When the Germans occupied Thessaloniki on April 9, 1941, the Jewish population there numbered approximately 50,000. Of the 46,091 Thessaloniki Jews who were sent to the death camps, only 1,950 survived, Salamo Arouch among them. In 1945, only 10,000 or so Jews remained in all of Greece, and today the community has vanished almost entirely. Their story has not been told because hardly anyone was left to tell it. Again, in *Triumph of the Spirit*, Robert M. Young has created a tale as unique as the film's use of the real Auschwitz as its setting.

Edward James Olmos (Gypsy) in front of the barbed wire and a guard tower in *Triumph of the Spirit*.

The third precedent-setting accomplishment of *Triumph of the Spirit* has been to present a portion of the Holocaust ignored even by the Museum in Washington, D.C., despite its best attempts at inclusiveness. The Museum has done a good job of documenting and memorializing Nazi persecution of Slavs, Jehovah's Witnesses, whereas the Porrajmos (The Devouring), as the Roma call the attempted eradication of the European Gypsies, has been ignored almost completely by historians, writers, and filmmakers alike. Salamo Arouch's boxing manager at Auschwitz, magnificently portrayed by Edward James Olmos, is known only as "the Gypsy." All the other major characters and almost all of the minor ones, too, are given names in the story. The Gypsy's anonymity is symbolic of the almost invisible role accorded to the Sinti (German Gypsies) and Roma who were murdered in the death camps. As the Sinti and Roma were not a highly literate society, the survivors did not create their own record or written memorial either, unwittingly abetting the obliteration of their story from the annals of the Holocaust.

The Roma and Sinti, as they prefer to be known, are thought to be descendants of a group of wandering craftsmen and artisans who moved into Europe from the Indian province of Punjab approximately 1,000 years ago. The light-skinned inhabitants of the European countries through which they traveled thought the dark-skinned Roma might be Egyptians, a name that eventually transmuted into Gypsy. (An alternate theory of the origin of the word "Gypsy" is the belief that after leaving India, the Roma may first have settled near the Greek village of Gyppe.) Like the Jews, the Roma were sporadically persecuted throughout Europe and endured pogroms known as "Gypsy hunts." Killing the men, whipping and branding the women, and presenting the children to gadje (non–Roma) families were common practices. In Romania, Roma slavery was practiced for about 550 years and finally abolished in 1864.

When Hitler became Chancellor of Germany in 1933, he inherited a legalized German tradition of persecuting the Roma. In 1890, a German conference dealing with *Zigeunergeschmeiss* ("Gypsy scum") empowered the military to regulate the movement of Gypsies. In 1909, another government policy conference recommended that all Gypsies be branded for easy identification. While this policy suggestion was never carried out, photographing and fingerprinting all Roma was mandated throughout the German territories. This followed Karl Binding and Alfred Hoche's 1920 suggestion that Gypsies be sterilized to ensure their eventual disappearance. Binding and Hoche were the originators of the concept of "lives unworthy of life," which later led to the elimination of mentally retarded and physically handicapped Germans under the race purification program of the Third Reich. In 1927, Bavaria placed 8,000 Gypsies in special isolation camps. By 1934, Gypsies were being sterilized, castrated, and sent to the concentration camps of Dachau, Dieselstrasse and Sachsenhausen. June 12 through June 18, 1938, was proclaimed *Zigeuneraufraumnugwoche* ("Gypsy clean-up week"), during which hundreds of Gypsies in Germany and Austria were arrested, beaten, and imprisoned. All of these actions may now be seen as rehearsals for the Nuremberg Laws, Kristallnacht, and the death camps that soon followed.

Actually, the Nazis found themselves a bit at a loss as to how they should classify Sinti and Roma within their racial scheme of things. According to the Nazi racial categories, Gypsies were Aryans. When trying to determine their ultimate fate, Heinrich Himmler considered the option of preserving a small group of "pure" Gypsies for the purpose of ethnic studies. While being a Jewish mischling might actually provide some measure of safety, Roma mischlinge were considered racially more dangerous than pureblooded ones and were, therefore, exterminated all the faster. On December 8, 1938, Himmler issued a circular, *Combating the Gypsy Nuisance*. Under this directive the state had an obligation "to defend the homogeneity of the German nation" and therefore was obliged to create "the physical separation of Gypsydom from the German nation.... The necessary legal foundation can only be created through a Gypsy Law which prevents further intermingling of blood, and which regulates all the most pressing questions which go together with the existence of Gypsies in the living space of the German nation." The separation was soon achieved by shipping off the Sinti and Roma to occupied Poland, where many of them were placed in ghettos alongside the Jews. On December 16, 1942, Himmler issued an order to send all Gypsies to the death camps, where approximately one and a half million of them perished.

Robert M. Young, through the character of the Gypsy, has resurrected at least a small part of their story. At Auschwitz-Birkenau, the Roma were first placed in a special family camp and urged to carry on the daily business of their lives so that they might become objects of ethnic study and medical experimentation before they were destroyed. Just as Salamo Arouch mistakenly believes he can keep his family alive by boxing for the entertainment of the SS, so does the Gypsy believe he can protect his family by playing the clown for the Germans. When interviewed by Pat H. Broeske, Edward James Olmos said he worked with a group of gypsy consultants who helped him learn the Romany song he performed in the film. "All the gypsies of the world will understand what I'm singing," said Olmos. The lyrics tell the Nazis "to go to hell, to rot and die — and that sort of thing." The Nazis don't understand the subversiveness and defiance of his performance because he smiles at them as he sings. The Gypsy is an ambiguous character whose motivation for helping Arouch even as he ingratiates himself with the SS killers is unclear to the audience until we see him returning to the Roma family camp with a stolen toy for his child. Again, Robert Young has created another cinematic and historic first. The Jew and the Gypsy are equally victims, equally human. The film honors both cultures and presents the grim realities and ultimate horrors that overtook them.

But not all societies remember the past in the same way. The importance of cultural memory for Jews in particular has its roots in Deuteronomy, where the Jews fleeing Egypt are instructed to write a book in remembrance of their defeat by Amalek. This longstanding Jewish injunction to remember has been studied by many scholars from a variety of perspectives. Books such as *Zakhor: Jewish History and Jewish Memory*, which looks at Jewish concepts of the past, and *Storm From Paradise*, which investigates memory and Jewish identity, are useful for learning about Jewish memory in general. In addition, texts such as *Holocaust Testimonies: The Ruins of Memory*, which analyzes the recollections of Holocaust survivors; *The Texture of Memory: Holocaust Memorials and Meanings*, which examines memory and public art; and *Popular Culture and the Shaping of Holocaust Memory in America*, which focuses on the Americanization of the Holocaust, are invaluable for learning about representations of the Holocaust.

Overall, these works point to a number of distinct approaches to shaping the cultural memory of the Holocaust. One looks for meaning by focusing on uplifting stories; the other rejects the notion that the Holocaust teaches lessons of any kind. Commercial films usually take the first approach, and Robert Young's *Triumph of the Spirit* is no exception. The film portrays the ways in which people decided how much of their dignity they could sacrifice to survive in Auschwitz and the various strategies they used in making those decisions. This perspective assumes that concentration camp inmates did have a measure of control over their lives. Although a number of scenes in the film, notably the arrival by train of new prisoners at Auschwitz, do underscore the lack of prisoner control in light of the randomness of the concentration camp, the film ultimately emphasizes the power of endurance. However, the reality of concentration camp life was very different, as one scholar, Ilan Avisar, writes:

> The Nazis' disregard for human life nearly perfected the mechanism of entrapment and destruction, and their utilization of methods of starvation, slave labor, and random, arbitrary killing made their grip on their victims absolute. The few who were saved from the death camps attribute their survival to mere chance or blind faith.[1]

Furthermore, in his study of Holocaust films, Avisar points out the dangers inherent in producing any film, such as the reliance on aesthetics and the convention of the happy ending. In the case of Holocaust films, especially, heeding Avisar's warning is particularly important given the magnitude of the catastrophe. Even more forcefully, Langer constantly notes that many people survived by luck or even by stupidity and that there is not a linear transition between one's prewar and postwar life. This should serve as a caution against producing films that stray too far from the historical facts, and thus create an unrealistic image of life and death in the camps and afterwards. This section of the essay focuses on the ways in which *Triumph of the Spirit* promotes the illusion of prisoner control and the way in which the film contributes to the cultural memory of the Holocaust.

Avram's refusal to clean the crematorium is one example of an attempt to preserve a degree of dignity. When he was selected from the lineup for an unspecified work assignment, Salamo told him not to create any trouble. This advice was predicated on the notion that Avram could control the outcome of the selection. However, at that point, the brothers did not know that Avram would be assigned to clean the ovens. As Avram enters the crematorium building and gets close to the ovens, the lighting in the film changes from indoor lighting to black and then to red, clearly signifying his nearness to the inferno. When Avram realizes the nature of the task, he simply says: "I won't do it." It is not clear if he knew that his refusal meant death.

Later, we learn that the entire crew was killed, when the film shows one prisoner in the yard telling another what happened. This prisoner then tells Salamo and Poppa what happened to the men. Of course, in actuality, Avram could have been killed earlier in a roll call when he was hit for requesting help for a sick prisoner. Avram's refusal to clean the ovens is completely sane given the horrifying request, yet others complied with it before and after. In fact, there was only one uprising of prisoners assigned to work in the Auschwitz crematoria, which Young also incorporates into his film. Since the film does not supply this background knowledge, viewers do not understand the uniqueness of Avram's decision. This may lead viewers to question why other prisoners did not simply refuse the assignment, masking the fact that the decision to choose was a luxury.

Poppa tries to keep his dignity by protecting and comforting his family. Until he is deemed unfit for work, he valiantly tries to maintain his family life. The scene in which he touches Avram and Salamo, while they are resting from their work, is an extremely moving example. Although he is hungry and tired himself, he reaches out to comfort his sons. The scene in which Poppa and Salamo hold each other after learning about Avram's death also shows that having a loved one nearby helps, even if only temporarily. But, in Auschwitz, roles are reversed. Sometimes sons have to protect fathers. In the film, this role reversal occurs when Salamo tries to persuade the Gypsy to spare Poppa's life. The number of people killed had to match the list of people selected to be killed. However, one person could replace another if someone switched the names on the lists, as the Gypsy suggests in the following exchange:

> SALAMO: My father has been selected. Is there something you can do?
>
> GYPSY: Someone would have to take his place on the list.
>
> SALAMO: Can you do that?
>
> GYPSY: It's too late.

The bargaining that takes place between Salamo and the Gypsy here is horrific. The selection of the men was partially, but not exclusively, based on their physical condition and age. Chance also played a role. For example, maybe the Gypsy could have found a substitute for Poppa. Maybe he did not feel like it at that moment. Maybe he did not feel like taking the risk that day. In this case, even Salamo's special position as the boxer for the Nazis could not spare Poppa because the lists were already issued, and the Gypsy did not act. Even after Poppa knows he is going to die, he continues comforting Salamo. In fact, one of his last acts is to give Salamo a photograph of their family. By some unclear means, Poppa managed to hold onto a family photograph during his entire stay in the camp, and by handing the picture to Salamo, Poppa is passing the custody of the family to Salamo. Given that the prisoners were stripped of all their personal belongings when they entered the camps, Poppa's ability to salvage the photograph seems unlikely. Ultimately, Poppa cannot protect his family and is killed, as were millions of others in Auschwitz.

In another instance of trying to preserve one's dignity, Elena claims pregnancy as a way to survive. She uses the normal reaction towards pregnant women to get sympathy from Allegra and the others. After telling an elaborate story about the pregnancy to Allegra, Elena does gain the expected reaction, at least from her sister, for a while. However, since Elena's pregnancy jeopardizes herself and possibly the others, one of the women in the barracks offers to abort the child as a safeguard. Elena's secret is revealed when a group of women pin her down to confirm her pregnancy and discover her lie. She learns that the pretense of motherhood does not shield her. On the contrary, motherhood in Auschwitz was dangerous because the Nazis conducted experiments on mothers — a diabolical reversal of its role in normal society when pregnant women are often granted a degree of protection by their friends, family members, coworkers, and associates.

Allegra maintains her dignity in an arbitrary world by several means. For example, she tries to distract her sister with stories from the past. At one point, Allegra and Elena are struggling to pull the cart, and Elena is about to fall. They have this conversation:

> ALLEGRA: Remember that summer we spent with Grita? Her boyfriend? What was his name?
>
> ELENA: I know what you're up to. I don't wanna play…. I can't do this.
>
> ALLEGRA: Yes, you can. Elena, get up.

Allegra pulls Elena to her feet, refusing to let her sister fall. Later, Allegra wrestles with the woman who is accused of stealing Elena's shoes. Fighting over shoes was a serious matter because although having a good pair of shoes in Auschwitz might help with one's life, not having shoes meant death. So, when Elena mentions that the woman will die without shoes, Allegra says: "It was her or you." After giving her bread to Elena, who was still presumed to be pregnant, Allegra steals bread from a dying woman and is betrayed by the woman from whom she retrieved Elena's shoes. Even though Allegra fought for her sister and stole for the baby, Elena could only watch while Allegra was whipped for stealing bread. Actions on behalf of one's family were likely to be punished, not rewarded, in the concentration camp.

Although the Gypsy is in a relatively fortunate position relative to the Jews, he has to struggle to maintain a degree of integrity despite his role as a guard. Taking the stuffed animal from the pile of confiscated belongings is an example. One night, while walking with Salamo and another guard on the grounds of the men's barracks, within sight of the women's barracks, he mentions that "some of my people" are in there. Holding the toy, he says, "I want to give this to someone special." He then whistles a tune and a woman and child emerge from the building. He tosses the toy across the barbed wire to the child. This gesture of giving a toy to a child is commonplace, but in Auschwitz, it might mean death. Very likely, the Gypsy bribed his companion, because the other guard moves away from the fence during the encounter with the woman and child. The Gypsy learns that even his role as a guard does not really offer protection when the Russians move toward Auschwitz. He tells Salamo that those not fit for work will go up the chimney, including the Gypsies. This realization may account for the Gypsy's involvement in the uprising in the crematorium. He finally understands and acknowledges his fate. However, juxtaposing the fate of the Gypsies and the Jews is fundamentally inaccurate since the Gypsies, along with political prisoners, homosexuals, and other non–Jewish victims, were not Hitler's prime target. The final solution was solely for the Jews.

Like the others, Salamo, the central character of the film, tries to maintain a degree of personal and professional integrity. When he starts boxing for the Germans, his first question is about rules.

SALAMO: How many rounds?

OFFICER: Rounds? No rounds. You fight till one goes down and can't get up.

Salamo wants to box according to standards, whereas the Nazis want a fight to the death. He is their entertainment as long as he continues to win. Although Salamo wins over 200 fights in the camp and survives, he could have been killed randomly at any point. Or after his father's death, he could have just given up and stopped caring about life. By shooting the fight scenes after the father's death in slow motion, for instance, the film suggests that Salamo keeps fighting, without thinking and without caring. In Auschwitz, sometimes people simply gave up caring. Known as musslemaner, these people were oblivious to their surroundings. Although Salamo never reaches that extreme state, many did.

Salamo tries to retain his prewar personal integrity as well. He still believes in friendship, for example. When Salamo sees Jacko, his best friend from Salonika, he calls out his name to establish their relationship. However, since Jacko has decided to collaborate with the Nazis, he does not acknowledge his old friend. Their former friendship has no currency in Auschwitz. Near the end of the story, Salamo is also selected to work in the crematorium during the uprising. Although he has an unspecified role in the uprising, he is caught and tortured. His role as a prize boxer did not prevent his ill-treatment. After the defeat of the Nazis, Salamo is released from his cell and goes outside. He looks at the dead bodies in the wheelbarrows and remarks, "How can we do this to our brothers?" The use of the first person in this question implies the Nazis and their collaborators are not solely responsible for the atrocity. It implicates everyone, a very disturbing premise. In the last scene in the film, Salamo walks out of the camp by himself. There is a long shot of the road out of Auschwitz, indicating that Salamo is taking his first steps toward a return to a normal future. He says, "All I have left is my love for Allegra. I will find her and begin again." In reality, there was really no place for him to go because the Jewish life in Eastern Europe, as well as in Greece, had been destroyed. There was even a pogrom in Poland in 1946. Displaced persons facilities were created, and after the war, many Jewish organizations, such as the Joint Distribution Committee, helped resettle survivors. This final scene, a testament to individual survival, leaves the impression that Salamo resumes his normal life. Although for some liberation was the beginning of their problems, not the end, the film glosses over the postwar difficulties faced by survivors. By ending with the words that Salamo finds Allegra and lives in Israel with their four children and twelve grandchildren, the film leaves no room for postwar unhappiness. However, Langer's work with the narratives of Holocaust survivors suggests that postwar normalcy is not necessarily a given. Our understanding of the postwar condition of the survivors needs to include the recognition that normalcy did not simply return after Auschwitz. The happy ending is not the entire story.

The film contains several messages about the Holocaust that shape the representation of the Holocaust in the film. These are that personal dignity is possible in extreme circumstances; individual control in an arbitrary system is the norm; survival is a matter of endurance; and there is a seamless transition between prewar and postwar life. Perhaps from the experiences of certain individuals, these conclusions may be drawn, but they are ultimately illusions. Despite that, Young intelligently juggles the grave realities of the Holocaust with the need to make a film that audiences could handle.

Triumph of the Spirit did not receive the critical and popular acclaim it so richly deserves when it was first released to theaters in 1989. One hopes that its DVD release will finally give the film and its director their groundbreaking due and the artistic triumph they truly merit.

Notes

1. Ilan Avistar. *Screening the Holocaust: Cinema's Images of the Unimaginable*. Bloomington and Indianapolis: Indiana University Press, 1988, p. 76.

References

American-Israeli Cooperative Enterprise, Gypsies in the Holocaust [online] [Cited 9/28/2003]. Available from: http://www.us-israel.org/jsource/Holocaust/gypsies.html.
American-Israeli Cooperative Enterprise. Gypsies in the Holocaust [online] Jewish Virtual Library. [Cited 8/31/2003]. Available from: http://www.us-israel.org/jsource/Holocaust/gypsies.html Excerpted from "Accounting for Genocide: Victims — and Survivors — of the Holocaust" (New York: Free Press, 1979) Helen Fein.
Anderson, Jim. "Triumph of the Spirit" [online] *Binary Flix* [Cited 8/16/2003]. Available from: *http://www.binaryflix.com/movie.asp?scope=t&ID=1062*.
Austin, Ben S. Introduction. [online] The Holocaust\Shoah Page [Cited 8/31/2003]. Available from: *http://www.mtsu.edu/~baustin/gypsies.html*.
Avisar, Ilan. *Screening the Holocaust: Cinema's Images of the Unimaginable*. Bloomington and Indianapolis: Indiana University Press. 1988.
Bandy, Alex. The Forgotten Holocaust [online] *Patrin Web Journal* [Cited 8/31/2003]. Available from: *http://www.geocities.com/Paris/5121/forgotten.html*
Boyarin, Jonathan. *Storm from Paradise: The Politics of Jewish Memory*. Minneapolis: University of Minnesota Press. 1992.
Broeske, Pat H. "On Location. Auschwitz." *Los Angeles Times* 23 April 1989, Calendar sec., pp. 6–7; 88–91.
Channel 4 Film. "Triumph of the Spirit" [online] *Channel 4 Films*, [Cited 8/15/2003]. Available from: *http://www.channel4.com/film/reviews/film.jsp?id=109564*.
Cinebooks Database [online] *TV Guide Online*, 2003 [Cited 8/15/2003]. Available from: http://www.tvguide.com/movies/database/ShowMovie.asp?MI=31789.
Clemmensen, Christian. "Triumph of the Spirit" [online] 2001–2003, www.filmtracks.com/titles/triumph_spirit.html.
Cracknell, Ryan. Triumph of the Spirit [online] Apollo Guide [Cited 8/15/2003]. Available from: *http://apolloguide.com/mov_fullrev.asp?CID=4218&RID=4980*.
Cybrary of the Holocaust. Gypsies in Auschwitz [online] Witnesses. [Cited 8/31/2003]. Available from: *http://remember.org/witness/wit.vic.gyp1.html*.
Cybrary of the Holocaust. On Gypsies [online] Witnesses. [Cited 8/31/2003]. Available from: http://remember.org/witness/wit.vic.gyp.html.
Ebert, Roger. Triumph of the Spirit [online] *Chicago Sun-Times*. 2 Feb. 1990 [Cited 8/15/2003]. Available from: *http://www.suntimes.com/ebert/ebert_reviews/1990/02/529563.html*.
Filmtracks. Triumph of the Spirit (Cliff Eidelman) [online] *Filmtracks: Modern Soundtrack Reviews* [Cited 8/15/2003]. Available from: *http://www.filmtracks.com/titles/triumph_spirit.html*.
Hancock, Ian. A Brief Romani Holocaust Chronology [online] [Cited 8/31/2003]. Available from: *http://www.osi.hu/rpp/holocaust.html* condensed from "Gypsy History in Germany and Neighboring Lands: A Chronology to the Holocaust and Beyond," in Nationalities Papers, 19(3): 395–412 (1991), a special issue on Gypsies.
____. Genocide of the Roma in the Holocaust [online] *Patrin Web Journal* [Cited 8/31/2003]. Available from: http://www.geocities.com/Paris/5121/genocide.htm.

Excerpted from Encyclopedia of Genocide (1997) by Israel W. Charny (ed.) Reprinted by the Patrin Web Journal with permission of the author, Ian Hancock. Posted 1 March 1997.

Hecht, Esther. The Jewish Traveler: Thessaloniki, Hadassah Magazine [online], March 2001 Vol. 82, No. 7 [Cited 8/16/2003]. Available from: http://www.hadassah.org/news/content/per_hadassah/archive/2001/march01/traveler.htm.

Himmler's Circular of December 8, 1938: "Combatting the Gypsy Nuisance" [online] [Cited 8/31/2003]. Available from: http://www.holocaust-trc.org/nuisance.htm. Translated in Michael Burleigh and Wolfgang Wipperman, The Racial State: Germany 1933–1945 (New York, 1991), pp. 120–21.

The Holocaust in Greece: The Thessoloniki [online] United States Holocaust Memorial Museum [Cited 9/28/2003]. Available from: http://www.ushmm.org/greece/eng/salonika.htm.

The Holocaust O Porrajmos [online] *Patrin Web Journal* [Cited 9/28/2003] Available from: http://www.geocities.com/Paris/5121/holocaust.htm.

Holocaust Teacher Resource Center. Sinti and Roma ("Gypsies"): Victims of the Nazi Era [online] [Cited 8/31/2003]. Available from: http://www.holocaust-trc.org/sinti.htm originally published by the United States Holocaust Memorial Museum as a pamphlet titled "Sinti & Roma."

Insdorf, Annette. *Indelible Shadows: Film and the Holocaust.* Third Edition. Cambridge University Press. 2003.

Jawetz, Gil. "Triumph of the Spirit" [online] *DVD Talk,* 16 April 2002 [Cited 8/31/2003]. Available from: *http://www.dvdtalk.com/reviews/read.php?id=3878.*

The Jewish Community of Thessalonika. The History of the Thessaloniki Jews [online] [Cited 8/18/2003]. Available from: www.jct.gr/History/page01.htm.

Jewish Heritage Video Club. Triumph of the Spirit [online] Jewish Media Fund, 2002 [Cited 8/31/2003]. Available from: *http://www.jhvc.org/video_library/index.php?film_id=119.*

Kocanda, Petr. Cliff Eidelman: one true voice [online] [Cited 8/15/2003]. Available from: *http://mujweb.atlas.cz/zabava/lokutus/filmmusic/eidelman/eidelman-interview.htm.*

Langer, Lawrence. *Holocaust Testimonies: The Ruins of Memory.* New Haven: Yale University Press. 1991.

Lipman, Steve. The Gypsy "Final Solution" [online] Patrin Web Journal [Cited 8/31/2003]. Available from: http://www.geocities.com/Paris/5121/othervictims.htm. Excerpted from Hitler's Other Victims: There wasn't, some say, just one Final Solution. Steve Lipman, Staff Writer. The Jewish Week, 2 May 1997.

Macedonian Press Agency: News in English, 98–05–31, Foreign Minstry to Publish History of the Greek Jews. Thessaloniki, 31/05/1998 (MPA) [online] [Cited 9/28/2003]. Available from: http://www.hri.org/news/greek/mpa/1998/98–05–31.mpa.html.

Margalit, Gilad. Forty Years for German Recognition of Persecution to Gypsies [online] *Patrin Web Journal* [Cited 8/31/2003]. Available from: http://www.geocities.com/Paris/5121/recognition.htm.

Maslin, Janet. Review/Film; The Camps as Not Often Seen [online] *New York Times* [Cited 8/15/2003]. Available from: http://movies2.nytimes.com/gst/movies/review.html?title1=&title2=TRIUMPH+OF+THE+SPIRIT+%28MOVIE%29&reviewer=Janet+Maslin&v_id=51039.

———. Triumph of the Spirit [online] New York Times [Cited 8/15/2003]. Available from: *http://movies2.nytimes.com/gst/movies/movie.html?v_id=51039.*

Miller, Shirley A. The Road to Porrajmos, the Gypsy Holocaust [online] *Patrin Web Journal,* Posted 29 January 1999, [Cited 8/31/2003]. Available from: http://www.geocities.com/Paris/5121/road-to-porrajmos.htm.

Mintz, Alan. *Popular Culture and the Shaping of Holocaust Memory in America.* Seattle: University of Washington Press. 2001.

Novitch, Myriam. Gypsy Victims of the Nazi Terror [online] *Patrin Web Journal* [Cited 8/31/2003]. Available from: *http://www.geocities.com/Paris/5121/terror.htm.* Excerpted from the UNESCO Courier, Oct. 1984.

Pond, Elizabeth. Romanies: Hitler's Other Victims [online] *Patrin Web Journal* [Cited 8/31/2003]. Available from: http://www.geocities.com/Paris/5121/othervictims.htm.

The Simon Wiesenthal Center. Gypsies [online] [Cited 8/31/2003]. Available from: http://motlc.wiesenthal.com/text/x25/xm2525.html. Courtesy of: "Encyclopedia of the Holocaust," 1990. Macmillan Publishing Company.

Sinti & Roma: Victims of the Nazi Era, 1933–1945 [online] Florida Center for Instructional Technology, College of Education, University of South Florida [Cited 9/1/2003]. Available from: http://fcit.coedu.usf.edu/holocaust/people/USHMMROM.HTM. Source: Sinti & Roma: Victims of the Nazi Era, 1933–1945 published by the United States Holocaust Memorial Museum.

Stavrolakis, Nikos. A Short History of Jews of Greece [online] [Cited 8/18/2003] Available from: www.greecetravel.com/jewishhistory/athens.html.

Tanner, Harold. The Roma Persecution [online] *Patrin Web Journal* [Cited 8/31/2003]. http://www.geocities.com/Paris/5121/porrajmos.htm

Travers, Peter. Triumph of the Spirit. [online] RollingStone [Cited 8/15/2003]. Available from: *http://www.rollingstone.com/reviews/movie/review.asp?mid=1999804.*

Triumph of the Spirit [online] Jewish Heritage Video Collection, 2002, Jewish Media Fund. http://www.jhvc.org/video_library/index.php?film_id=119.

Triumph of the Spirit [online] Category.org [Cited 8/31/2003]. Available from: *http://www.category.org/browse/video/161677/.*

Variety. "Triumph of the Spirit" [online] Variety.com [Cited 8/31/2003]. Available from: *http://www.variety.com/index.asp?layout=print_review&reviewid=VE1117795888&categoryid=31.*

Willis, Brett. "Movie Review: Triumph of the Spirit" [online] Christian Spotlight on Entertainment [Cited 8/15/2003]. Available from: http://www.christiananswers.net/spotlight/movies/pre2000/triumph-of-the-Spirit.

Yerushalmi, Yosef Hayim. *Zakhor: Jewish History and Jewish Memory.* Seattle: University of Washington Press. 1982.

Young, James. *The Texture of Memory: Holocaust Memorials and Meaning.* New Haven: Yale University Press. 1993.

Young, Robert. Letter to the Writers Guild of America. West, 30 May 1989.

10. "California Dreamin'": *Talent for the Game*
Eugene L. Miller

Robert Young's *Talent for the Game* (1991) begins like no other baseball film: in an Idaho mine shaft. Without context, without benefit of introduction or explanation, without voiceover, Young tracks his camera on a group of miners in hard hats as they approach the shaft's entrance; their conversation speaks obscurely of "management" and the refusal of "management" to give the guys "time off" for whatever event is about to take place. One of the guys, played by craggy-faced Edward James Olmos, quips enigmatically, "I hope he's good." With ear-popping velocity, the car descends into the depths of the mine and halts in a watery cavern where a kid named Lester awaits the arrival of Olmos and the others, whose helmet lamps now penetrate the darkness with crisscrossing shafts of light worthy of an eerie science fiction film. Only then, as Olmos unrolls a portable home plate on the muddy tunnel floor, steps off sixty feet and six inches with a tape measure, and dons a catcher's mask and mitt, does Young reveal the dramatic secret: Lester, a baseball pitching prospect, is being put to the test by Olmos, a professional scout. After the kid hurls three or four pitches, punctuated by applause from fellow miners, the suspense is quickly over: the kid's fastball falls "a little short," he just doesn't have what it takes. But Olmos, adjusting his California Angels cap, leaves him with encouraging words and sound advice, advice which becomes thematically central to the film's meaning: "You did good, kid; you got a dream, you hold on to it.... Everybody needs a dream."

From this dark, dank and claustrophobic opening scene, Young shifts, with a spectacular aerial shot, to spacious skies and amber waves of grain (could there *be* anything more all-American?) as Olmos drives his vintage red Mustang on two-lane roads through the expansive heartland of the nation. This montage sequence (in which the scout times wind sprints and scrutinizes hitters' swings) introduces the viewer more formally to Virgil Sweet (Olmos), an Angels scout searching for talent (literally, "mining for prospects") in the smallest small towns of Idaho state. The last of a dying breed, Virgil, an old-fashioned scout who prefers hand-scribbled notes and stop-watches to computers and bureau reports, loves baseball and life on the road. He scorns the high-tech approach to scouting, mocking the radar gun as a dangerous source of radioactive vibration. He trusts, instead, his own instincts, which tell him, as accurately as any machine can, how fast a fastball really is. What Virgil, and every scout, dreams of finding is the "Phenom": the player with all the tools who comes out of nowhere, who rises, "perfect" in his skills, right out of the earth. Nobody teaches the phenom how to play, how to pitch; he is simply born with the knowledge. Such a prospect, Virgil knows, exists; the hard part is finding him.

But *Talent for the Game* is not just a film about Virgil's love for the game; it's also a film about his love for long-time girlfriend Bobbie (Lorraine Bracco), who does public relations for the California Angels' front office. Bobbie summons Virgil home with a cryptic message that Weaver, special assistant to the A's owner, wants him back in Los Angeles. After 63 days of abstinence on the road, Virgil gladly complies, anticipating a romantic liaison with Bobbie. In her apartment, as he awaits her arrival, he tosses paper wads to her pet cat, who swats at them playfully "in the bottom of the ninth." But once he hears Bobbie open the door, the music (Johnny Rivers' remake of Huey "Piano" Smith's "Rockin' Pneumonia and the Boogie-Woogie Flu") begins, and the feverish pursuit is on. In a hilarious and unexpected gesture, Bobbie empties a bucket of water on Virgil's head; as he chases her around the dining room table, she falls hard on the floor — in what appears to be a totally unscripted moment — but Bracco gamely plays through the scene, giving it additional spontaneity and comic intensity. Bobbie hurries to the second floor bedroom, but, again unexpectedly, Virgil, unable to run, cannot follow her; sizzling with sexual chemistry, the scene, which should have culminated in bed, culminates instead on the stairs. The question — why can't Virgil run? — will be answered in the film's subsequent conversations.

Perhaps more time than is warranted has been spent on *Talent*'s opening sequence (what might be called Part I), but these are lively, energetic, engaging, clever and charming scenes, effectively paced and carefully choreographed, and they establish, for our consideration, a few of the film's main issues: corporate management, professional integrity, individual dreams, and romantic love. At this kind of narrative exposition, Bob Young is especially skillful.

Virgil's first glimpse of baseball's new world order (Part II of the film) occurs in old friend Tim Weaver's office. Young's camera catches Weaver (played nicely by Jamey Sheridan) working his abs, his image reflected upside-down in a mirror which surrounds the office's exercise room; the inverted image suggests an inverted universe, where all things, including baseball things, are topsy-turvy. Weaver has recalled Virgil to give him big news: the Angels have been sold to advertising czar Gil Lawrence (Terry Kinney). Lawrence knows nothing of baseball. A businessman with a billion dollars to spend, he worships the bottom line: it's all, as Weaver explains, "profit and loss." A man with his own ideas, Lawrence has determined that computerized (and inexpensive) Bureau Scouting Reports have made the costly scout in the field obsolete, a dinosaur: unless Virgil can sign a prospect soon, a real franchise player, he will lose his job with the A's organization.

Thus does Young set in motion the film's central conflict, one whose implications will test Virgil's integrity more than he can possibly anticipate. The race is on to find the "Phenom" before time runs out.

Bobbie agrees to join Virgil in his quest for the holy grail of baseball players, a pursuit which takes them to the "middle of no place," a wheatfield outside Pocatello where their car breaks down: "Well, Sweet," says Bobbie, "we got two choices. We can either sit here and sweat, or we can start to walk." After a tantalizing pause, Virgil deadpans a third alternative: "We could dance." And so they dance, to a sizzling salsa tune played on the car's radio, their passionate intensity mirrored by the swiftly surging needle of the Mustang's dashboard thermostat. Temperatures, indeed, are rising. Like earlier unexpected scenes, this one catches the viewer by surprise, unprepared, unawares. It is Young's direction at its best.

The breakdown scene also provides for an epiphany and a coincidence, both of which drive the remainder of *Talent*'s plot. The epiphany belongs to Virgil, triggered, in effect, by Bobbie. When Virgil despairs, here in the middle of nowhere, of finding the phenom, he likewise despairs of holding onto Bobbie who can, in his self-pitying eyes, do so much better for herself than a penniless, nomadic, aging, irrelevant scout like himself. But Bobbie abruptly sets him straight: "You don't get it, Sweet; I don't need that kind of security.... I love that you're a scout and that you get to do what you want to do.... I believe everything happens for a reason — that's why we're out here getting sunstroke. You know what your problem is, Sweet: you got your head so far up your ass feeling sorry for yourself, you can't see that everything you need is standing right here in front of you." Young cuts to the chastened and wizened Sweet, now unceremoniously bent over from the waist, making futile and funny attempts to shove his head up his ass. The scene concludes brilliantly with that comic (if coarse) touch and,

10. "California Dreamin'": *Talent for the Game* (Miller)   183

Lorraine Braco (Bobbie) and Edward James Olmos (Virgil Sweet) in *Talent for the Game*.

providentially (fatalistically?), with the unmistakable sounds of a nearby ball game.

As Bobbie correctly intuits, "We're in this town because we're supposed to be," and things happen for a reason, for here they meet wholesome Sammy Bodeen (Jeff Corbett), star pitcher for the local baseball team, who is busy striking out everybody this afternoon with a fastball of inconceivable velocity. Bodeen, who still says "Yes, ma'am" to his mother, also throws so hard that Virgil hurts his hand when the ball "pops" his glove (aficionados know this sound, the metonymy and onomatopoeia of baseball, much like they know the "swish," the metonymy and onomatopoeia of basketball). But now, having discovered the phenom, Virgil confronts an even more pressing predicament: how, against Sammy's parents' better judgment, to get the kid out of Idaho and into professional baseball. It's a tricky and touchy conundrum, particularly since Reverend Bodeen (Tom Bower) has plans for his son to inherit the ministry at the local church in Genessee, much like his father's father, and his grandfather's father, and his father before him. Virgil wisely appeals on religious grounds: if "sin" (defined for Virgil by an "old Greek") means missing the mark, would it not be "sinful" for someone like

Sammy to waste a God-given talent? Isn't that like "missing the mark?" With help from Ma Bodeen (Janet Carroll), to whom Virgil admits that her son Sammy "is the best [prospect] I've ever seen," Sammy gets his chance for a "wondrous adventure" and Virgil gets his dream, with this proviso: Virgil, in accordance with mom's wishes, will look out for Sammy, still a child in her eyes, and much in need of guidance. (Who better for this job than Virgil, named for the prototypical and archetypal mentor and guide in Dante's *Inferno*?) As Sammy and Virgil leave town (Bobbie has taken the bus home), they drive past the community church, a symbolic leave-taking in which conservative, religious values have presumably been exchanged for liberal, secular ones. Whether Sammy and Virgil can withstand the forthcoming test of their integrity and ideals remains to be seen.

For the classic car lover, the most excruciatingly painful scene in the film happens during the return to Los Angeles. To promote the importance of believing in oneself, to test some quasi-mystical, zen-like theories of pitching, theories of total concentration and hypnosis taught to him by his own coach, a full-blooded Blackfoot Indian, Virgil stops the car — his red 1965 Mustang convertible — and conducts a pitching experiment: he implores Sammy to relax, to visualize his target, close his eyes, and let it go. And let it go Sammy does, twice, throwing glass-shattering fastballs through the windows of this classic Mustang rag-top. (It is a Mustang owner's nightmare which, one can only hope, was a computer generated image). Shortly thereafter, the audience learns the real reason for Virgil's infirmity, what kept him from "The Show": as a minor leaguer, he got beaned so hard that whenever he tries to run, he gets dizzy. And if you can't run, you can't play the game.

In Part III of *Talent for the Game*, Young turns his attention to the issue, of politics, management (or, more properly, ownership), and the villainous new owner of the A's, Gil Lawrence. Lawrence, Mr. Pony-tail Guy, has reluctantly agreed to give Bobbie "five minutes" of his precious businessman's time to observe a new kid discovered by field scout, Virgil Sweet. At the ballpark, Lawrence, who, ironically, "doesn't like games," looks on with skepticism and bemusement as Virgil warms up the kid. At first, Bodeen's control problems elicit the standard wisecracks from the gang gathered around the batting cage. But soon, to everyone's amazement, Bodeen's 98 and 102 mile-per-hour fastballs are whizzing past the A's leading hitter, Dick Bortner (Murphy Sua), whom Virgil calls, in one of the film's few bawdy exchanges, "Dick for Short." After Bortner fails to connect on ten or twelve pitches, Lawrence has seen enough: "Sign him," he tells Virgil. And it would appear that both Virgil and Sammy have gotten their wish.

But be careful what you wish for, as the old saying goes. To promote his phenom, Lawrence stages a press conference at his home in Los Angeles (a place where one "very rich person lives") which resembles, in its architectural splendor and opulence, a cross between the Biltmore House and the Palace of Versailles. In casual clothes, Virgil clearly feels out of place among the "suits" who run the organization and awkward in the presence of such conspicuous consumption. And in no time, Bodeen becomes the object of a publicity stunt arranged by Lawrence and his yes-men. Against the backdrop of piano fanfare, an announcer's voice heralds the arrival of "our newest angel, a gift from *heaven*, Sammy Bodeen." And, suddenly, from on high, Bodeen descends on a trapeze, in a cloud of smoke, to join the astonished onlookers below. Literally, the *deus ex machina*, from the Greek theater of old, has appeared on stage: Bodeen represents the omnipotent and anointed one, destined to rescue the A's from future oblivion.

Young's outrageous, over-the-top machination reminds one of religious and spiritual themes and issues subtly woven into the film. This is, after all, the Angels' organization and Sammy is a gift from heaven, sent by the gods. Bobbie's belief in fate and predestination (everything happens for a reason) brings Sammy and Virgil together. Virgil has learned his art and craft from Iron Jack (not John) Kelly, his mystical Native American coach. Virgil acts as Sammy's guide through an inferno of urban complexities and choices. An old Greek philosopher-shortstop defines for us the concept of "sin." Sammy's dad descends from a long line of preachers who prefer the simplicity and austerity of life in the small town and who want that life for their offspring. The Phenom, by definition "born to play the game," comes mysteriously, magically, out of nowhere, and acts as savior and redeemer. Sammy leaves behind the Church of Genessee for (if we may borrow a phrase from *Bull Durham*) the Church of Baseball.

Additionally, Virgil and Sammy face worldly and fleshly temptations of almost biblical proportions. After his introduction to the media, Sammy dances with a stylishly, seductively dressed lawyer — too tall, too rich, and too sophisticated for this young country boy still ludicrously wearing his baseball cap. As she clutches his face to her bosom, the viewer wonders if he can resist her sultry charms. When Lawrence proclaims that Sammy will start the A's next game against the division-leading Kansas City Royals, Virgil strenuously objects, knowing that it's all happening too soon, that Sammy isn't ready for big league pressure, that this premature notoriety might ruin his career. But Lawrence (Satan?), who wants Virgil "on board" with the plan, authorizes Weaver to offer Virgil the world: a contract as assistant General Manager at an annual salary of $60,000, complete with guarantees, bonuses, a retirement portfolio, and a new wardrobe for the heretofore disheveled scout. Virgil accepts, thinking that this is the kind of status and security he has always desired and that Bobbie deserves. And one worries that Virgil has sold out both the boy and himself.

In a recent interview, Young explained the conflict pretty much in those terms:

> The story really had to be about character and the willingness of Eddie's character to sacrifice the kid for his own career. After all, it's about the scout, too, and his relationship to this kid and his relationship to this woman, and you had to see those relationships and to see the give-and-take in them and to see what the character development of this guy was and how he's threatened by the kid or how he's willing to sacrifice the kid. That's where the nexus of the story had to be. It wasn't just that the kid turns out to be fantastic; it's not just a baseball story [Arnold interview].

The night before the big game, Sammy doubts that he has what it takes: "Am I ready? What if I fail?" he asks Virgil. "You can't think that way, kid," Virgil replies, "you have to believe in yourself. If you want something, sometimes you gotta take the risk, and if you really want something, then you gotta risk everything. It's the scariest thing in the world." Sweet's response, almost clichéd, nonetheless reinforces Young's themes about self-confidence, self-esteem, risk-taking, and the American Dream.

The game itself, which comprises Part IV of *Talent*, generates and sustains suspense through editing and cross-cutting between the players themselves, the announcer in the booth, the owner in the clubhouse, Bodeen's family at home watching it all on TV, and the close-up reactions of Sammy, Virgil, Weaver and Bobbie to the on-field action. Predictably, things at first do not go well for the 20-year-old right-hander with no previous pro experience. Lawrence, smoking his signature fat-cat cigar and feeling pressure from the press corps who suspect Bodeen's a fraud, orders Weaver to call the manager and "get that kid outta there" after Kansas City scores four runs in the first inning. Virgil again protests: "If you take him out, he may never pitch again." To underscore his point, Virgil rips the phone off the wall, thus preventing, at least temporarily, that fateful phone call to the dugout. The gesture costs Virgil his job which, he tells Lawrence, he can "shove where the sun don't shine." Even Weaver—up to this point a company man but also, finally, a baseball man—has second thoughts: he decides, after the A's close out the inning with a double-play, to ignore his boss's decree and allow Bodeen to start the top of the second.

If our credulity has been strained a bit by unlikely plot developments thus far, it is strained a bit more when the A's take the field in the second inning. The catcher approaching the mound is not the real A's catcher but, implausibly, Virgil Sweet incognito, a quick change that no umpire, even the blindest, could possibly miss. Virgil urges his protégé to "remember the first time you threw the ball to me ... to go back there in your mind and

10. "California Dreamin'": *Talent for the Game* (Miller)   187

Robert Young preparing a scene in *Talent for the Game* with Jeff Corbett (Sammy Bodeen) and Edward James Olmos (Virgil Sweet).

throw the way you did that day." That being said, Virgil "hypnotizes" Bodeen with a snap of the fingers and the kid throws nine fastballs to strike out the other side, the last pitch bruising Virgil's hand, which he pumps vigorously in the air, his fist clenched in ecstatic victory. Sammy has proved himself the Phenom, and Virgil has played, if only for an inning, in "The Show." Both, apparently, have realized their dreams.

But *Talent for the Game* ends not with a dramatic bang, but with a kind of ethical whimper. In a curious coda or epilogue (Part V for more traditional structuralists), Young takes the viewer into Lawrence's office, where Sammy the Phenom negotiates his contract. The boy hero has learned quickly the mercenary ways of the baseball world: "I want a $1 million signing bonus, I want $1 million per year for six years, I want to be paid if I'm injured, and, incidentally, I won't play on artificial turf." All the dejected Lawrence can do is accede to the boy's demands. One wonders what happened to the bright-eyed, wholesome, innocent farm boy whose benign countenance both men and women could so readily identify with. Has Sammy's heart, so pure and righteous, been so easily corrupted by the blandishments of professional baseball?

But the closing shot is reserved for Virgil and Bobbie, who has graciously "fired herself" in sympathetic solidarity with Virgil's dismissal from the front office. Now unemployed, the two, facing an uncertain future together, drive off into the sunset playfully spitting sunflower seeds at one another in the Mustang convertible whose smashed windows, one can only hope, have been respectfully repaired. "Rockin' Pneumonia" blares as the credits roll. Unlike Benjamin and Elaine, who sit befuddled in the back of the bus at the end of *The Graduate*, Virgil and Bobbie are grown-ups who know who they are and what they've done and how to find their way, though their future is certainly left in doubt. What matters is that the two have emerged with integrity intact: both have refused to compromise their principles, and both have said "no" to corrupt power and authority. And they are hopelessly in love, unfettered, and free to roam, seeking a new beginning and, perhaps, a destiny that will reveal itself when the time is right, when, as Bobbie might wistfully say, it's "supposed to happen."

It is, in fact, this sexual chemistry between Bracco and Olmos that makes the film work, that carries it for at least the first thirty or forty minutes. The viewer likes these two characters immensely: they're smart, funny, attractive and engaging. Their connection — their affection for one another — feels authentic. And the baseball feels real also: Olmos can catch (he has all the right moves, throwing decisively from the squatting position, one hand strategically placed behind his back) and Corbett can pitch (the fluid motion, the high leg kick, the push off the rubber, the right knee nearly brushing the mound — these are tough moves to fake). Clearly, these guys can play, and Young surrounds them with ex-players (in supporting roles) who move, talk and act like real jocks. The practice and game sequences look professional, not amateur. This point about verisimilitude should be underscored because similar claims, unfortunately, cannot always be made about baseball movies in general (John Goodman can't swing like the Babe, and Brendan Fraser looks downright uncomfortable on the mound in Albert Brooks' *The Scout*).

What does *not* feel quite real or right is Young's treatment of the A's owner, Gil Lawrence, and *Talent* loses some of its zip and rhythm — maybe even its focus and its sweet, charming tone — from the moment he appears on screen. Lawrence, surrounded by sycophants, comes off not so much as an owner as a grotesque caricature of an owner (In the mansion scene, Virgil quips that the whole staged event resembles a "cartoon," and he's right). Imperious and unassailable, petulant and mean-spirited, Lawrence rules the club like a spoiled despot (is there any other kind?); the players know he cares nothing for them, as the audience cares nothing for him. Lacking even the semblance of socially redeeming qualities, Lawrence epitomizes the ogre, and not the *Shrek* variety. As a consequence, plot and character relationships suffer, tone shifts from sentimental to satiric, and what might have been a more complex drama of moral choices and considerations devolves, instead, into simpler farce in black and white terms.

To some extent, such problems may ultimately have to do with editing: entire chunks of exposition in *Talent* appear to be missing. Where, for example, is the scene in the Bodeen home when Sammy's future is debated by the family? Where are scenes between Weaver and Sweet which might explain their mutual respect, and mistrust, of one another? Where are scenes with Lawrence which might soften and mitigate his Snidely Whiplash impersonation? Why and how did Virgil and Bobbie, such different people, become lovers? Why does Sammy morph so quickly into Donald Trump enacting the art of the deal?

As is often the case with a Hollywood film, *Talent*'s difficulties with focus, continuity and direction on-screen may be attributable to power-struggles off-screen, where powerful egos and personalities clash and where corporate and artistic visions collide. Disagreements about plot and narrative direction in *Talent* were apparently never fully resolved. Olmos (co-producer) and Young (director) had strong views about where the film should go; so did producer, Marty Elfand; so did Paramount studio head David Kirkpatrick; so did writers David Himmelstein, Thomas Michael Donnelly, and Larry Ferguson. At the center of the debate remained a persistent question: Was this a baseball film with a romantic subplot or a romantic film with a baseball subplot? Young spoke to this quandary in a recent email message:

> It wasn't that we wanted romance in the film — although that is never bad — it's that we felt that the development of Virgil's story had to go much deeper than finding a young phenom, who obviously gets to win the game. We thought that Virgil's character could be seen in how he interacted with both the kid and his woman. We thought that the baseball story part of it — find phenom, teach him, he wins — was sort of simplistic and expected ... and we wanted to do much more [personal email from Robert Young to author, 11/17/2003].

Though he disagreed with studio head Kirkpatrick, who wanted a straightforward (and necessarily formulaic) baseball film, Young, wanting to be "the nice guy ... cut it his [Kirkpatrick's] way, like an idiot. And then, without letting me do anything more, they [Paramount] screen it for a paid audience ... and it does poorly, as it should" (Arnold interview). Young felt so strongly about re-cutting the film, about making it more consistent with his and Olmos' vision, that he offered to forego the remainder of his salary and, at his own expense, to shoot six additional scenes on video, transfer the video to 35 mm, re-edit the alternate version, and pay for a second audience screening. And, recalls Young, this version proved successful: "It scores at least fifteen points higher and you could tell the audience loves the film" (Arnold interview). But Paramount, feeling insulted and perhaps threatened by Young's independent spirit, refused to screen the finished product: "*They wouldn't look at it.* It was written off for them. And they were hurt, angry that I had done this, because now I'm challenging the egos" (Arnold interview). With characteristic honesty, Young offers this final appraisal of *Talent for the Game*: "I felt it was very flawed. And, sure, I felt very hurt and put upon to not be able to take it to where I thought it ought to go. And I feel bad for Marty Elfand. He didn't get what he wanted, and I didn't get what I wanted, and Eddie didn't [get what he wanted]. None of us got what we really wanted ... I think that's what happens on lots of films" (Arnold interview).

In the final analysis, however, *Talent for the Game*, aside from its commentary on baseball and romance, may be seen as a kind of parable and allegory for Robert Young's own career, for the kid's story is Young's story too: the story of the talented and independent filmmaker, the determined and single-minded artist, struggling for recognition, self-determination, self-esteem and success against a monolithic system which abjures integrity and co-opts all but the most principled and self-reliant individuals. *Talent for the Game* may never compare with *The Natural*, *Bull Durham*, or *Field of Dreams*. But it's a satisfying film, better than most have given it credit for. Though he's not, by his own admission, a baseball fan or a baseball guy, Young has, in *Talent* and in all of his films, taken as axiomatic some timeless baseball advice: to follow through on your swing. Such "follow through" undergirds the career of Robert Young, himself a talented player in the filmmaker's game.

Works Cited

Arnold, Edwin T. Interview with Robert M. Young. In this volume.
Young, Robert. Email to author. 11/17/2003.

11. Stereotypes Collide: Machismo and Marianismo in *Roosters*

Holly E. Martin

In the beginning, painted skulls dance eerily across a black background. A confused flurry of feathers and wings follows as roosters attack, fight, and draw blood with the razors attached to their already sharp talons. A man of Mexican descent, holding a thrashing black rooster, calls out the name "Zapata"[1] and pulls out a knife as if to sacrifice the bird. The bird flies away, and the man chases after it. The focus switches to a young teenage girl, wearing a white angel costume, standing trapped behind bars in what appears to be a combination of a bird cage and a church altar. She calls out, "Papi! Let me out! I can fly; I'll show you."

The viewer at this point, confused yet attentive, concludes this must be a dream, a nightmare, or perhaps the beginning of a film in the mode of magical realism. But if it is a dream, who is the dreamer? The viewer will never know, but the meaning of this opening scene will become all too apparent by the film's end as this surreal beginning foretells what sacrifices are to come. As for magical realism, there is plenty of reality in this film, but no magical happenings. Magic would leave open a doorway of hope made possible through a connection with another realm, but the characters in this film, as we shall see, simply do not have that kind of optimistic luck.

After the brief, impressionistic opening, the scene switches to a funeral, and the film takes on the kind of ordinary sequencing of events one is accustomed to in everyday life. Indeed, most of the film occurs in the time period of one day, with some use of flashbacks that often occur with a surreal quality that harkens back to the opening of the film. The girl from the film's beginning who was trapped in the cage/altar (Angela Morales, played by Sarah Lassez), now perches, bird-like, in a tree, watching the ceremony for her grandfather's funeral. During the ceremony a young man (her older brother Hector Morales, played by Danny Nucci) receives a rooster in a cage, an inheritance from his grandfather. And so starts a wrenching and unexpected film that on the surface appears to be about cockfighting, but actually is a portrayal of the violent outcome that occurs when gender roles, as traditionally conceived in Mexican and Mexican-American culture, are taken to their extremes. The film explores several male and female stereotypical behaviors, but in particular, *machismo* and *Marianismo*. The volatile combination of these two stereotypes, and their interactions with others, proves lethal for at least one member of the Morales family.

Machismo (popularly known by its adjectival form "macho") is the expected stereotypical behavior of Mexican or Mexican American males. Evelyn P. Stevens, in "Marianismo: The Other Face of Machismo in Latin America," defines machismo as "...the cult of virility. The chief characteristics of this cult are exaggerated aggressiveness and intransigence in male-to-male interpersonal relationships and arrogance and sexual aggression in male-to-female relationships" (90). The macho man is strong, virile, sexually aggressive with women, brave, and easily roused to anger or violence. Although the macho male is meant to protect the female members of his family, he often views his role as a protector primarily against threats coming from outside the family. Within the family, he can be violent toward the female members without arousing much censure from others within his community. In the film, the rooster symbolizes the epitome of macho behavior, fighting, often until death, from a natural impulse that comes from deep within the bird's very nature.[2]

In *Roosters*, as one might gather from the title, the rooster symbolizes machismo and is a totem for the main character, Gallo Morales (played by Edward James Olmos), father of Hector and Angela. Gallo is the personification of machismo. Even the word *gallo* means rooster in Spanish, and Olmos plays the macho stereotype to the hilt with every stance, look, and utterance. There is nothing soft in this character, yet he has a romantic allure as a true macho man should. His speech, when talking to his wife or daughter, is fluent and poetic (overly so, according to some film critics[3]), but the suave charm and silver-coated tongue are part of the Don Juan image, also a necessary attribute for the macho man. Gallo's charm adds to his danger, because with it he disarms his wife Juana (Sonia Braga), his daughter Angela, and even his sister Chata (Maria Conchita Alonso) who lives with the family.

After the funeral scene, which seems to have occurred in the recent past, the present time of the film begins. Gallo prepares to leave his prison cell and to begin his journey home to his wife, sister, son and daughter. We find out that he has been in prison for seven years for manslaughter. He killed a man, a Filipino, over a rooster. Just as there have been three generations of men who have raised roosters for cockfighting in the Morales family (Gallo's father, Gallo, and now Hector), there have also been three parallel generations in the Filipino family (the grandfather; his son (the one killed by Gallo); and the dead man's son, referred to in the film as "the Filipino's son"). The Filipinos raise champion fighting roosters, and once, in the past, Gallo put one of his hens in a cage with the Filipino's prize rooster. The result was a champion fighting cock that both families claimed. At a cockfight involving this particular rooster, a fight occurred and Gallo stabbed and killed the middle-generation Filipino.

Edward James Olmos in *Roosters*.

As Gallo heads homeward from prison, the family prepares for his arrival. His wife, Juana, worries that he has not arrived home yet. Gallo's sister, Chata, explains that he is a "man" and therefore probably has to sleep around before coming home. We see Angela, Gallo's daughter, wearing a costume of cowboy boots, a white dress, and white angel wings. She sleeps under the house in a niche she has created for herself decorated with statues of the saints and many glowing candles. When her brother Hector teases her and claims that, in spite of aspiring to sainthood, she masturbates in bed, Angela prays furiously that she be kept from "low companions" and "stupid rooster fighters" like her brother.

Angela's role perplexes most reviewers of the film. Rob Lurie writes in

Los Angeles Magazine that when Gallo comes home, he finds that "his daughter has become a Jesus freak" (106). Joe Baltake, *Sacramento Bee* Movie Critic, writes of Angela, "...she's less touching than she should have been as she takes her religious fanaticism to such heights that she dons paper wings and tries to fly.... Angela thinks she's an angel, see? (Get it? Angela ... angel)" (*Sacramento Bee's* Movie Club). While it is not difficult to get the Angela/Angel connection, the critics have missed that Angela represents yet another gender stereotype, one that is as pervasive, if less known in the United States, as the macho male. Angela is a *Mariana*, a young, virginal girl who desires to model her life after the Virgin Mary. *Marianismo* is the female counterpart to *machismo*. Evelyn P. Stevens writes, "*Marianismo* is just as present as *machismo* but it is less understood by Latin Americans themselves and almost unknown to foreigners. It is the cult of feminine spiritual superiority, which teaches that women are semi-divine, morally superior to and spiritually stronger than men" (91). Stevens continues to explain that the stereotype of the *Mariana* can be found in all social classes, and that "There is a near universal agreement on what a 'real woman' is like and how she should act" (94). Coupled with the semi-divinity and spiritual superiority, according to Stevens, is submission to the male members of the family and "an infinite capacity for humility and sacrifice" (94). In other words, the *Mariana* is the perfect compliment for the macho man. He embodies dominance and aggression; she reacts with submission and sacrifice.

When taken to extremes, as in *Roosters*, the interaction of these two stereotypes can end in the woman's complete effacement or even annihilation. While the two stereotypes may seem to compliment each other, the counterbalance leads to a sick combination–like pairing an extreme sadist with an extreme masochist. Nevertheless, *Marianismo* presents a life option for women throughout Latin America and within the Mexican-American culture that some women do indeed adopt. Angela does not don her lifestyle in a cultural vacuum, nor is it some crazy make-believe fantasy created in her own mind, there is cultural precedent and support for Angela's behavior no matter how unique, odd and artificial it may appear to viewers of the film who are not familiar with *Marianismo*.

Both *machismo* and *Marianismo* are believed to have originated in Europe, particularly in Spain. But although the stereotypes are no longer as prevalent in Spain, they still have a strong hold within Latin America and within the Mexican-American community. Several authors who have studied the phenomenon believe both gender stereotypes arrived with the conquistadors (see Stevens, 91, and Bocchi, "The Meaning of Marianismo in Mexico"). The conquistadors of fifteenth and sixteenth century Spain traveled to America to seek adventure, fortune and fame. They were perceived by the indigenous peoples to be fierce, aggressive and frightening — in other words, macho. As the Spanish and Indian races mixed and the population in Mexico became *mestizo* (mixed Spanish and Indian), the stereotype of the macho man persisted. *Marianismo* arrived with the Spanish as well by means of Christianity. The reverence for Mary as a role model, already prevalent in Spain, received a boost in Mexico from the appearance of the Virgin of Guadalupe on the hillside of Tepeyac, near what is now Mexico City. The legend centers on a newly baptized Indian man, Juan Diego, who saw the apparition of the Virgin Mary on the hill. What was unique about this particular appearance of Mary is that her skin was dark, like the Indians, and she spoke in Nahuatl, the language of the Aztecs. Her appearance helped to rapidly spread Christianity among the Indians, since it was believed that in at least this incarnation, Mary was indigenous to the Americas. In 1756, Pope Benedict XIV declared the Virgin of Guadalupe, the name by which she became known, to be the patroness of Mexico (then New Spain). The Virgin of Guadalupe still today remains immensely popular throughout Mexico and the Mexican American communities in the United States.

In keeping with her embracing of *Marianismo*, Angela tries to ward off her own sexual impulses. She is fifteen and has celebrated her *quinceañera*, the birthday that marks a girl's transition into a woman. Biologically, Angela is on the brink of puberty. Dismayed at the changes she notes in her body, she longs to be little again and abhors especially the blooming of her "big butt." Yet her sexuality emerges in spite of herself. Hector's accusation that she masturbates in bed seems not so far fetched, given Angela's outraged response to his teasing. Like many adolescent girls, Angela worries that she is not pretty. She fears that her returning father won't like her, and she desires to be beautiful so he will notice and love her. Angela also shows her interest in sexuality when she is amused by her Aunt Chata's off-color advice on how to get a man.

Fearing that her spirituality may be waning as she develops physically, Angela seeks a sign that will strengthen her faith. She wants to fly like an angel and throws herself off of the chicken coop in her attempts to be airborne. She fails, however, and falls to the ground with a thump. Angela declares herself to be the angel of her yard and lies down in the dirt to await a spiritual sign; the sign does not come. Instead, the Filipino's son drives into the yard with some of his companions. They leer at Angela in a menacing manner and drive off.

Traditionally, women in Mexican and Mexican-American culture have been restricted to two lifestyle choices: the virgin or the whore. Luis Leal in "Female Archetypes in Mexican Literature" writes, "The characterization of women throughout Mexican literature has been profoundly influenced by two archetypes present in the Mexican psyche: that of a woman who has kept her virginity and that of the one who has lost it" (227). We have explored the archetype of the virgin and how Angela portrays this stereotype, now we turn to the opposite, the *puta* (the whore). Stevens also writes about this alternative: "The same culture provides an alternative model in the image of the 'bad woman' who flaunts custom and persists in enjoying herself. Interestingly enough, this kind of individual is thought not to be a 'real woman'" (Stevens 96). Gallo's sister Chata represents this archetype. Her first comments in the film suggest that Gallo is probably sleeping around before coming home as an explanation for his being late. Then in the kitchen while Juana bakes and listens in amusement and Angela eavesdrops from under the table, Chata entertains her listeners with the advice her grandmother gave her on how to capture a man. Chata grabs and molds a handful of bread dough and then sensuously rolls it on the inside of her bare thigh to warm it. Then, she declares, bake the dough and give it to the man; he will not be able to resist. As the film progresses we see more and more that Chata represents the stereotype of the whore. She evidently had many lovers in the past who referred to her as "the encyclopedia of love." At one point in the film, after Gallo's return, Hector in anger demands to know if Chata has even slept with his father, who is, of course, Chata's brother. "Did you sleep with my father? Did he yearn for you? Has he slept in your little, white, narrow bed? Did he steal you while you were dreaming?" Hector, it seems, has also done some of his own yearning for Chata. To put him in his place, Chata reminds Hector that she has caught him watching her through the keyhole while she dresses.

The stereotype/archetype of the whore can also be traced back to the time of the conquistadors. During the conquest of Mexico, Hernán Cortés wrote letters back to Spain relating the details of the conquest. In the second letter (July 16, 1519), he mentions an Indian woman who serves him as an interpreter (Cortés 48–49). Although Cortés does not mention her name, a historian traveling with Cortés, Bernal Diaz del Castillo, lets us know in his history of the conquest that she is called doña Marina by the Spanish conquistadors and del Castillo discusses her invaluable assistance in the defeat of Montezuma and the taking of Tenochtitlán (see del Castillo *capitulo* LXXXIII). Doña Marina not only spoke several Indian languages, but could converse in Spanish and was knowledgeable about local politics. Without her linguistic abilities and her talents for forming allegiances, the conquest of Mexico would have been much more difficult, if not impossible. Doña Marina became Cortés' mistress, and they had a child, often referred to as the first *mestizo*. Although their child was probably not, in actuality, the first *mestizo*, legend proclaims it to be so.

Because of the aid doña Marina gave to Cortés, and because she became his mistress, history later vilified her, claiming her to be a traitor against her own people. She, however, was not Aztec, she was Mayan, and many indigenous tribes united with Cortés to bring down the Aztecs. The Aztecs evidently were not well liked by the surrounding population because of their penchant for human blood sacrifices. Nevertheless, the blame for Cortés' victory fell on doña Marina. She became known as *la Malinche* (the traitor) or *la chingada* (literally, the fucked one). Even Octavio Paz in *The Labyrinth of Solitude* refers to Mexicans as the Sons of Malinche, and as *hijos de la chingada* (Gutierrez 51). This debased image of doña Marina still persists in Mexican and Mexican-American culture to the point that women who do not adhere to *Marianismo* are usually relegated to the role of *la chingada*.

There exists, however, one alternative beyond the Marianismo/whore dichotomy, and this is the "mother." Gallo's wife, Juana, portrays the stereotypical mother with some variation. As a wife, the mother can have sex within the bounds of marriage, though ideally, only for the purpose of having children. Her life centers on her husband and her children, and she suffers, uncomplaining, on their behalf. When Gallo sees Juana standing in the doorway awaiting his return from prison, he sums up her character as the long-suffering, resilient mother and wife. "*Mujer de piedra*, my rock woman, still enduring. You must be made of the hard parts of the earth: minerals, bits of glass, ground up shells, small stones, brittle bones of dead animals. I'm home." Although romance may seem to be lacking in this greeting, Gallo's delivery of these lines is definitely sexy, and Juana melts. There is an obvious passion between the two, a passion aroused in Juana by Gallo's unmistakable *machismo*. But Juana has spent seven years without Gallo, raising two children, and she has developed some ideas of her own. She also is experiencing menopause. She realizes her possibilities of bearing more children are nearing the end, and therefore, so is her usefulness as her society defines it. Consequently, she begins to assert herself outside of the stereotype of a mother. She keeps up the appearances of submissiveness, but she obviously resents Gallo's attempts to run the family immediately upon his return when she has been doing it on her own for seven years. Soon after Gallo's arrival and their brief time lovemaking, the conflicts begin as Gallo and Juana discover that their plans for their children, particularly Hector, are not the same.

While Gallo has been gone, Juana has encouraged Hector to work in the fields to help support the family. Although Hector hates the backbreaking work, his mother insists that hard work never hurt anyone. Gallo, however, is incensed that she has allowed Hector to work in such a degrading job. A macho man does not work in the fields under the authority of someone else. Such a fieldworker, a *campesino*, in Gallo's view, is the opposite of a real man. Thus the film presents a stereotype for male behavior that is opposite from the macho man. A *campesino* is docile, passive, a coward who readily submits to authority and is undeserving of respect. However, as we see in the character of Hector's friend, Aden (Valente Rodriguez), a *campesino* also possesses kindness and sensitivity. When Gallo and Aden first meet, Gallo immediately asserts his violent superiority over Aden, even though Aden is his son's friend. Aden has a pet rooster, and like Aden, the rooster exhibits a mild manner with no desire to fight. Aden treats the rooster with kindness as his pet. Gallo claims that Aden's rooster will fight if forced, and he verbally bullies Aden into allowing his rooster to fight one of Gallo's birds. Aden's rooster, out of condition and without the fighting temperament usually associated with roosters, dies a predictably prompt and bloody death.[4] Aden fights back tears for his lost pet, not wanting Hector or Gallo to see how the loss hurts him.

Gallo need not worry that Hector has the same passive nature as Aden, despite working in the fields. Hector is the one character in the film who seems to elude stereotypes altogether. He represents the hope for the future, the young man who desperately wants to get out of his present situation. Hector is eager to fight the rooster that he inherited from his grandfather, but not as a sign of his *machismo*. The money Hector can win from cockfighting is his way out of his present situation. Hector wants to escape, to "fly over the mountains," and leave the restrictive valley forever. He wants more options than the narrow cockfighter/fieldworker choice that faces him if he stays in the valley. Hector harbors a deep resentment toward his father for committing a murder that took him away from his family for seven years. In the meantime, Hector has felt responsible for his mother, his aunt, and his sister and has had to shoulder much of the burden of supporting the family. He also resents the way his father takes over the rooster, Zapata, immediately upon his return, ignoring Hector's ownership of the bird and making his own plans concerning it. He talks with Hector about the bird's care, but clearly plans to take over the bird's training for fighting. As Gallo holds the rooster, he murmurs to it, kisses it and strokes it with his lips in a sensual greeting. Clearly Gallo's affection for the rooster outweighs any he holds for his family.

Sensing her father's passionate affection for the rooster, Angela, who has hidden from her father since his return earlier in the day, takes the rooster and puts it in her hideaway under the house. She wants her father to notice her, and she also hopes to quell the violent side she sees as inherent in the rooster. She is aware that like the rooster, Gallo is also capable of violence.

She discovers this when Gallo first returns and is in the house making love to Juana. Angela takes his suitcase into her hideaway, opens it, and lovingly smells his clothes; but then, she discovers a knife. In a conversation with Hector, Angela displays her distress over the rooster's violence, especially its habit of killing its own chicks. "How could he do it?" she asks, "He's their Papa."

Gallo guesses that Angela is hiding the rooster, and he crawls into her hideaway, pretending he has come to see her. He smooth-talks Angela, wooing her by reminiscing about how he loved her as a baby. He strokes her feet, talking about how little and precious she was. He says he will take her to the ocean, just her alone, and teach her to swim. The macho man shows his charm and the verbal seduction works. Angela reveals the hidden rooster.

In the meantime, the Filipino's son has been riding around the valley making threats against Gallo. When Hector realizes that the Filipino's son plans to harm his father and perhaps other members of his family, Hector shows a courage that goes well beyond the bravado of *machismo*. He abandons his hope of fighting the rooster and using the winnings to leave the valley. Instead, he works a deal with the old Filipino to give him the rooster in exchange for peace between the two families.

Gallo also discovers the Filipino's son's plans for revenge and decides to take the rooster and once again leave his family. There remains only one problem, he no longer has the rooster. Gallo knows Hector has taken the rooster, and when Hector returns Gallo and Hector fight, viciously, physically, like roosters. Gallo pulls out a knife and fully intends to slit Hector's throat (a connection back to the opening scene in which Gallo attempts to cut the rooster's throat). Gallo is willing to sacrifice his son for the rooster, but before he can, the family, beginning with Hector, notices Angela.

During the fighting, Angela has been hiding under the house. Earlier, seeing that her father intended to leave again, she had packed a bag and was eager to go with him, thinking he intended to take her to the ocean. Gallo dismissed her abruptly, however, and realizing he had callously lied to her, Angela fled to her hideout. Under the house, Angela again questions her religious faith and asks for a sign. She discovers she has started to menstruate, and she takes that as a sign that she is spiritually unworthy to be an angel. She becomes aware of the disturbance in the yard and leaves her hideout. Reflecting back to the beginning of the film, Angela hopes to prevent Hector's sacrifice by showing her father she can fly. She slowly climbs to the top of a high windmill tower located in the yard. She stands boldly at the top with her arms outstretched for flight. As Hector, Juana and Gallo become aware that Angela intends to jump from the windmill tower, we see close-ups of their faces. Hector is the first to realize what is happening, and we see the look of anguished realization on his face as he begins to run toward the tower. Juana has a similar look as she too starts to run toward Angela. Then we see Gallo, still lying on the ground. Even though he sees Angela about to jump, his look indicates that he is more confused about why she is jumping rather than distraught that she is about to die. Angela leans, falls forward, passes the balance point at which she can stop herself, and goes into a free fall as the movie ends.

The viewer never sees Angela hit the ground, and because of that, some reviewers have suggested that it is up to the audience to decide if she flies or not.[5] Anyone who thinks Angela flies at the end of this film, however, has not been paying attention. Although Angela desperately wishes otherwise, there is no magic, no indication that there will be a sign from God anywhere to be found. At the end, Gallo's look implies that he will not even realize his part in her death and will never change in spite of Angela's sacrifice. It is a pessimistic and depressing end, because Angela not only does not fly, but her sacrifice will not be understood by the one person who needs to change. Her death will have no purpose. The sacrifice makes the audience aware of the destructiveness of extreme *machismo*, but it does not have that affect on Gallo. Yet as the film's director Robert Young states, "I felt that a real sacrifice had to be made. That the father's machismo took a toll and that they could not end up like middle-class Americans driving a car and relaxing on the beach. I thought the film required a sacrifice ... a blood price had to be paid."[6]

The reference to driving a car and relaxing on the beach refers to the end of the film as it was intended in the screen play. The screen play was written by Milcha Sanchez-Scott, adapted from her original play for the theater written in 1984. Unlike the final version of the film, the screen play had instances of magical realism which may have worked in the original play, but appeared unconvincing during the filming. Another director had originally begun the filming of *Roosters*, but after eight days of shooting, Lindsey Law, the Executive Producer of PBS's *American Playhouse*, fired the director, the producer and the cinematographer and asked Robert Young to step in. Young at first declined the offer, but his friend Eddie Olmos, playing Gallo, convinced him to come to Tucson and take over directing the film. Young read the script on the way to Tucson, and arrived at the airport just as the fired personnel were leaving the state–an embarrassing encounter.[7] Young eliminated the magical realism aspects of the film and concentrated on creating a psychological realism that would ring true with the viewer. The actors, under the original director's guidance, had been acting in ways that seemed extreme and inappropriate for the content of the film because they were attempting, unsuccessfully, to create a work of magical realism.

The results, however, ended up seeming artificial and unbelievable, not because of the actors, all of whom Young praises for their talents, but because of the acting style that was imposed upon them. Since much of the budget was already spent, Young had to start filming the day after he arrived, not leaving him much time for changes in the script.

In addition to the imposed, unnatural, magical real acting style the cast had been asked to adopt, Young found other aspects of the film that seemed out of sync with the serious theme of the destruction of a family caused by a father's extreme *machismo*. The end, for instance, had to be changed. At the end of the screen play, Angela jumps off the chicken coop for the second time and whether or not she survives is left ambiguous (although since she safely jumped off of the chicken coop earlier, it seems likely that she will survive a second time–the chicken coop is not that high). In any case, in the screen play, Angela ends up driving on the beach with Hector while her father relaxes on the sand in a beach chair. Such an ending is not only artificially unrealistic given the nature of the story line, but also does not connect with Angela's dire prediction that roosters kill their children.

Young also made changes in some physical aspects of the set. One was in the appearance of Angela's cemetery: "...one of the things that I did was to change the cemetery that had been constructed–it was an Anglo type of cemetery with Barbie dolls, etc. I had it made into a Mexican style cemetery and I had fetish-type dolls made to make a connection with their Indian roots."[8] In the film, Angela has created a cemetery for pets and small animals. She has a sign that names it the Chino Valley Cemetery, "Final resting place of the stars. Pets and small animals accepted." In accordance with the Day of the Dead tradition of writing *calaveras*, obituaries (often humorous) that are written about people who are still alive, Angela has made headstones and written epitaphs for members of her family. "Here lies horrible Hector Morales. Died at age twenty in great agony for tormenting his little sister." One for Juana reads, "Juana Morales died of acute identity crisis sustained during the menopause." And finally one for herself states, "Angela Ester Morales died of acute neglect. Although she'll be mourned by many, she goes to a far, far better place where they have better food."

The connection of the cemetery with a Day of the Dead tradition is not arbitrary. In the opening surrealistic scene with Gallo attempting to sacrifice Zapata and with Angela in a cage shaped like an altar, the skulls indicate a Day of the Dead celebration. The Day of the Dead occurs on November 2 and is also known as All Souls Day. It is a day for honoring the dead and its roots trace back to Spanish, Catholic traditions as well as to the Aztecs, who held a great feast for the dead as part of their ritual calendar. It is common on the Day of the Dead for people to wear skull masks and for children to delight in eating small, colorful skulls molded out of sugar. People decorate the graves of their departed family members much like Angela has done with her cemetery. Hector's first cockfight that he attended with his grandfather when he was a little boy, shown in a surrealistic flashback, was also held on the Day of the Dead. Hector was terrified by the masks and the bloody fighting of the roosters, but his fear changed to delight when his father's rooster won. The skull masks and fighting cocks foretell the violence and death that will result from the family's involvement in cockfighting, so Hector had good reason to be frightened; but, even as a little boy, Hector already showed some fascination for the fights.

Connections with the Aztec past of Mexican-Americans extend to the windmill from which Angela jumps. Young writes, "I also had the windmill constructed next to the cemetery. That was not in the original film or script. I was familiar with the fact that in the Aztec culture they sometimes performed sacrifices before a tall stripped tree that had 'wings' attached across the top–reminding me of the windmills that dotted the Arizona landscape that pumped up water. When I thought of that Aztec image, I just knew that the windmill tower had to be by the cemetery."[9] The tree or pole that Young refers to was used by the Aztecs in a ritual for young warriors:

> In the month preceding the season of war, when the young men were restless, they went out in a thronging mass to find, fell, and drag back to the city a fine tall tree. Arrived at the main temple precinct, amid much shouting and instructions from the overseer, the young men "expended their strength" to haul the tree upright.... So it remained, unadorned, for twenty days, and was then lowered, and on the day of the feast smoothed, strengthened and hauled upright again, braced and laced with great ropes, decorated with sacred paper, and the *Xocotl*– a little moulded seed-dough figure decked with paper regalia–placed at the top. Then, after the main business of the festival [the slow killing by fire of warrior captives in the dawn] at midday all the men and youths ... first arranged themselves into the "serpent dance," ... and then swept to the great tree for the assault on the Xocotl. Tough warriors ... had been set to guard it, so the wave of men had to break through their whirling pine staves, taking the blows as they fell. Then, clawing and kicking and holding each other back, they clambered up the ropes–perhaps as many as twenty men festooning each one–until the swiftest climber, feet in the faces of those below, managed to reach the little figure, seize it, break it, and send the fragments scattering to the crowd below, who in turn brawled enthusiastically for even the smallest piece [Clendinnen 126–27].

As Angela climbs the windmill, she becomes the sacrificial doll, the *Xocotl*. Although no one climbs the tower to throw her off, her father and brother struggle just below her in the yard with intentions of fighting to the death.

Angela leaps from the tower, hoping to fly and thereby stop their fighting. Instead, she becomes a blood sacrifice to Gallo's violent *machismo*.

There were aspects of the set that Young chose to retain from the first film director's design, including the house and the desert setting. The house is a modest adobe and sits isolated in a natural desert setting. This particular stretch of desert (near Tucson, although the story is meant to be set in Nogales) offers an abundance of cholla cactus. The sunlight glints off the cholla's spiny appendages with a glowing, translucent yellow, making apparent both the beauty and the harshness of the long, barbed spines. The house seems a protected space in contrast to the dry and rocky desert. The men in the film walk effortlessly through the desert terrain, a reflection of their tough exteriors, but when Angela and Chata walk out into the landscape, they appear vulnerable. While everyone awaits Gallo's return, Chata leaves the house to go to the beauty parlor and Angela follows. Chata walks unsteadily in her high heels over the rocky ground, looking out of place. Angela, with her light, airy wings attached to her back, seems especially vulnerable to the stark tree branches and cactus thorns that could tear her delicate wings. Both leave the house in a quest for beauty — Chata on her way to the beauty parlor and Angela wishing she too could do something to become more beautiful. Both, already attractive, want to look especially beautiful for Gallo's return.

No one escapes the destructive results of Gallo's extreme machismo. The Filipino of Gallo's generation is killed. The old Filipino loses his son, and the youngest Filipino lives without his father. Gallo spends seven years in prison, leaving Juana to survive and care for the family alone until her youth is all used up. Chata lives in the shadow of her brother, having spent her youth as a prostitute, longing for someone who, like Gallo, is so handsome he can make her "teeth ache." Aden, Hector's friend, loses his pet rooster to a violent death. Hector loses his chance to escape the valley by exchanging the champion rooster for his father's life, and he almost loses his own life when his father tries to cut his throat. And then there is Angela, the young *Mariana*, who with a limitless capacity for sacrifice becomes the perfect victim of her father's *machismo*. Unfortunately, as we see by Gallo's expression at the end of the film, he will never understand the sacrifice Angela has made nor his role in her death. As Angela warns, the rooster does indeed kill his children.

Notes

1. Zapata is the last name of Emiliano Zapata, a Mexican Revolutionary leader who fought with Pancho Villa. During the Mexican Revolution Zapata championed a land

distribution program to take land away from the wealthy and to redistribute it among the poor. His rallying cry was "*Tierra y Libertad*," "Land and Liberty."

2. That roosters are inherently violent is a view expressed by those who defend cockfighting against those who claim it is an instance of cruelty to animals. In November 1998, when the voters of Arizona passed Proposition 201 in order to, among other things, make cockfighting a felony, the arguments against the proposition centered on the conviction that roosters are naturally violent, and that to prevent them from fighting was even more cruel than allowing them to fight.

3. Joe Baltake of the *Sacramento Bee* writes, "The movie is a filmed play through and through, replete with self-conscious, near-poetic dialogue and stagey devices — all of which come across as wildly artificial when acted out in a natural setting with the camera up close." In "'Roosters' is a flight of fancy." (*Sacramento Bee*, August 18, 1995. The *Sacramento Bee's* Movie Club. <http://www.movieclub.com/reviews/archives/95roosters/roosters.html>.) James Berardinelli also criticizes the dialogue saying, "If *Roosters* has an obvious flaw, it lies in the dialogue, which is often too flowery or intellectual. The author is taking poetic license to get across her higher meaning, but, on more than one occasion, a line is jarringly inappropriate for the speaker or the circumstances in which it is spoken" (2). (In "*Roosters*: A Film Review by James Berardinelli," Summer 1994. <http://movie-reviews.colossus.net/movies/r/roosters.html>.)

4. The mild mannered nature of Aden's rooster calls into question the assumption that all roosters are vicious by nature. Aden's rooster shows us that the violence may come about as a result of training the rooster to fight, just as the violence in macho men may simply be a result of how they are socialized rather than the result of a natural tendency.

5. James Berardinelli writes, "Little has been resolved as the final credits roll, and it's up to the viewer to decide exactly what happened, and what will come next" (2). (In "*Roosters*: A Film Review by James Berardinelli," Summer 1994. <http://movie-reviews.colossus.net/movies/r/roosters.html>.)

6. E-mail correspondence from Robert Young to Holly Martin. Tuesday, October 7, 2003.

7. For more details, see interview with Robert Young by Edwin Arnold in this volume.

8. E-mail correspondence from Robert Young to Holly Martin. Tuesday, October 7, 2003.

9. E-mail correspondence from Robert Young to Holly Martin. Tuesday, October 7, 2003.

Works Cited

Baltake, Joe. "'Roosters' is a flight of fancy." Review of *Roosters*, dir. Robert Young. *Sacramento Bee* 18 August 1995. The *Sacramento Bee*'s Movie Club. <http://www.movieclub.com/reviews/archives/95roosters/roosters.html>.

Berardinelli, James. "*Roosters*: A Film Review by James Berardinelli." Review of *Roosters*, dir. Robert Young. Summer 1994. <http://movie-reviews.colossus.net/movies/r/roosters.html>.

Bocchi, Steven. "The Meaning of Marianismo in Mexico." 9 October 2003 <http://www.lclark.edu/~woodrich/Bocchi_marianismo.html>.

Clendinnen, Inga. *Aztecs: An Interpretation*. Cambridge: Cambridge University Press, 1991.

Cortés, Hernán. *Cartas de Relación de la Conquista de México*. Reimpresión. Pitágoras, 1139: Espasa-Calpe Mexicana, S. A., 1995.

del Castillo, Bernal Diaz. *Historia verdadera de la conquista de la Nueva España*. Edición de Miguel León-Portilla. Tomo A. Madrid: Historia 16, 1984.

Gutierrez, Ramon A. "Community, Patriarchy and Individualism: The Politics of Chicano History and the Dream of Equality." *American Quarterly* 45.1 (March 1993): 44–72.

Leal, Luis. "Female Archetypes in Mexican Literature." *Women in Hispanic Literature: Icons and Fallen Idols*. Ed. Beth Miller. Berkeley: University of California Press, 1983. 227–242.

Lurie, Rod. "Roosters." Review of *Roosters*, dir. Robert Young. *Los Angeles Magazine* 40.7 (July 1995): 106.

Roosters. Dir. Robert Young. Perf. Edward James Olmos, Sonia Braga, Maria Conchita Alonso, Danny Nucci, Sarah Lassez and Valente Rodriguez. American Playhouse Theatrical Films and WMG, 1993.

Stevens, Evelyn P. "Marianismo: The Other Face of Machismo in Latin America." *Female and Male in Latin America: Essays*. Ed. Ann Pescatello. Pittsburgh: University of Pittsburgh Press, 1973. 89–101.

Young, Robert. "Re: *Roosters*." E-mail to Holly E. Martin. 7 October 2003.

12. Space and Sexuality in *Caught*
Thomas McLaughlin

As its title tells us, *Caught* is a film about entrapment. The characters don't have a chance. They are trapped by their own histories, by their needs and desires, by the inescapable consequences of their actions, and by the plot itself. From the very beginning of the film it's clear to the audience — if not to the characters — that the story will end in tragedy. The unfolding of the plot is almost unbearable. Robert M. Young and his fine actors induce us to identify and sympathize with these characters, then force us to watch them move step by step toward disaster. This sense of entrapment is enhanced by the physical spaces in which Young contains the action. Almost all the film takes place either in the busy fish store that Joe operates or in the cramped apartment where Betty fulfills her erotic desires. These tight quarters increase the heat and emotional intensity. Of course not all of the action takes place in these interiors — there are scenes in parks, bars, markets, riverfronts, and other public spaces. But most of the film takes place either in the workplace or in the domestic space, and the characters cannot be understood outside these intimate, personal environments. These spaces both determine and express character, and they also serve as symbolic elements in the film's political critique of this personal tragedy.

Caught is the story of a marriage. Joe and Betty married when they were young, and raised a son. Now, they work together in their fish market. The film begins by following a young homeless man, Nick, who stumbles into their store and into their lives, on the run from the police after a street hassle. Almost instantly, Joe and Betty take Nick in, giving him a job in the market and a room in their apartment, drawing him into the dynamic of their marriage and their emotional history. Nick takes over the role of the missing son, becoming Joe's apprentice and Betty's project, the object of her maternal instincts and eventually her sexual desires. As in all stories about

12. Space and Sexuality in *Caught* (McLaughlin)   207

Maria Conchita Alonso (Betty), Arie Verveen (Nick) and Edward James Olmos (Joe) in the fish shop in *Caught*.

erotic triangles, this tense structure of emotions cannot be maintained, especially in the claustrophobic spaces of the shop and the home. Nick and Betty engage in a passionate, high risk affair, just outside Joe's awareness, in that claustrophobic home, in fact in its most enclosed spaces — the closet in the son's bedroom, the shower, the narrow hallway of the apartment. Their affair is discovered by the son, Danny, a cynical and world-weary comedian who returns to the home because of his failure in the entertainment business, and who *instantly* sees all the evidence that Joe is too trusting to notice. In an act of jealousy and revenge, Danny exposes the affair to Joe, whose weak heart gives out at the news. In the end, Danny avenges his father's death by slitting Nick's throat. All the characters are, in one way or another, destroyed by their own actions and by what seems an inexorable fate. They are *caught* in the nets of their own desires, just as they are trapped in the suffocating physical spaces of the film.

Of course, this brief summary of the plot does not do the film justice. In this outline form *Caught* sounds like a replay of *The Postman Always Rings Twice* or a thousand other film noir plots. Many reviewers noted this resemblance, but almost all realized that *Caught* should not and cannot be reduced to a generic formula.[1] What lifts the film above the bare bones of its plot is the intensity of the actors' performances and the passion of Young's filmmaking. Seen from the outside, in the abstract, Joe would appear as a gullible fool, Betty a selfish betrayer, Nick a calculating ingrate, and Danny a spoiled and vicious infant. But the actors never allow the audience that external, judgmental perspective. Edward James Olmos, who plays Joe, and Maria Conchita Alonso, who plays Betty, give their characters a human dignity that makes their weaknesses seem like tragic flaws rather than venal indulgences. Arie Vereen, who plays Nick, is much less imposing as an actor, but his relative blankness works to the benefit of the story, establishing Nick as an empty screen on which Joe and Betty can project their desires. And Steven Schub, who plays Danny, creates a character who is both pathological and vulnerable — the spoiled baby *and* the avenging angel. As a result of these rich performances, the characters in *Caught* can be judged and found morally wanting, but they cannot be dismissed or reduced to their weaknesses.

Young never simply uses the characters as figures in the plot. We often see them in intimate close-ups that reveal their emotional complexity. We see Joe's love of his work as well as his blindness, and Betty's desperate need for an emotional outlet as well as her self-indulgence. Young also frames these complex characters in the texture of city life. If their lives are a melodrama, it is a believable proletarian melodrama, set in the busy streets and in the complex economic realities of the city. Betty and Joe, Nick and Danny are much more than counters in a predetermined plot. Young constantly reminds us that they live recognizable and complex lives. They seem like people we might know from the neighborhood, people struggling with daily survival, people we would never expect to be entangled in a plot that seems right out of the movies.

One of Young's most useful strategies for characterization is his careful arrangement and exploration of physical and psychological space. Young says in an interview: "I try to give each character their psychological space, without making any kind of rationalization for their behavior. I want to give them the room to have freedom of action. I don't want to be making apologies for Nick or Danny or Betty or Joe. But I do bring the camera into their psychological space so that you can understand Betty and her needs, and you can understand Danny's feelings of displacement and his craziness."[2] The film moves back and forth between the shop, the domain of work and commerce, Joe's domain, and the home, where Betty rules, suffusing the space with her erotic energy. In the shop, Joe is the expert and Betty is "Mrs. Joe." At home, Joe is either asleep or in front of the TV, in a space organized around Betty's desires. These oppositions — work, the public sphere, and masculinity VS sexuality, the private sphere, and femininity — are not novel, of course; they are the familiar conventions that define physical space in a patriarchal culture. What is remarkable about *Caught* is that these oppositions and the restrictions that go with them are revealed to be the very nets in which the characters are caught.

Joe's Fish Market

Joe defines himself as a person by the work he does — he is a "fish man." And he has created in his store a space designed precisely for the exercise of his skill and the display of his products. Young takes the camera into this space, moving responsively with Joe and Nick and Betty as they work and interact. Joe moves fluidly and unselfconsciously through the space, as any practiced and skilled worker moves through a space designed effectively for the work. He *belongs* in the space of the market, cleaning the fish, preparing them for sale, dealing with customers, managing the operation. He is the master of every aspect of the work, and he is proud of his skills. The work is satisfying to him, not just as a way to make money, but as a task worthy of attention in and for itself, a source of pleasure in a job well done.

Joe's market is the space where he can pursue his "practice," to borrow a term from the ethical philosopher Alisdair MacIntyre and the social theorist Pierre Bourdieu.[3] MacIntyre defines practices as activities that generate their own ethical codes, requiring of practitioners the virtues necessary for the task. These virtues can flourish only when the practitioner is dedicated to the task itself and the goods proper to it, rather than to the economic rewards that might come from it. Only then will the virtues promoted by the practice become part of the fabric of the practitioner's ethical life. For MacIntyre, practices are important because they encourage a coherent ethical life in which moral behavior is connected organically to the tasks of everyday life. For Bourdieu, practices are important because they shape the very identity of their practitioners. Each practice develops what Bourdieu calls a *habitus*, a set of habits and dispositions, an unconscious mode of operation that guides the practitioner in the daily work of the practice. Over time, these habits and dispositions become internalized and embodied, seeping into the unconscious lives of practitioners. The *habitus* becomes what can be taken for granted, what one knows instantly and without reflection, simply by virtue of being immersed over time in the practical requirements of the evolving task. Both MacIntyre and Bourdieu emphasize the power of practical, everyday experience. Repetition produces identity. The requirements of the practice become the character traits of its practitioners.

For Joe, running the store, preparing and selling the fish, is the central practice of his life. So when Young takes us into the market, he shows us what *matters* to Joe, the daily tasks that make him what he is. When Nick first comes to work in the store, Joe initiates him into the business by teaching him how to lay out the fish in the shop window. Even in this "mundane" task, we find that there is a knack to it, a skillful and cunning way of laying out the fish to appeal to the customers and to maximize profit. Mix the fresh fish in with yesterday's fish, Joe tells Nick. The discerning customer will know which is which, and the non-discerning customer won't ever notice. The task is worth doing well, as an expression of knowledge gained over years in the practice. And it is justified by a practice-specific ethic—fairness to the customer, but only on the condition that the customer is as smart as the storekeeper. In this one gesture from within the day's work we see Joe's character, his dedication to practical intelligence and skill, his sense of fairness and responsibility.

When we are in the market, we are in a space that Joe has designed for the efficient pursuit of his practice. The tools of the trade—the knives, the chopping blocks, the ice, the coolers—are all within easy reach. The store is crowded but not cluttered, so that Joe can move with perfect practical confidence. In several scenes, the camera moves around in the space with Joe, allowing the audience to feel his comfort. And then, in an intense later scene, when Nick, Betty, Danny, and the camera all bustle around in Joe's space, the tension rises as the traffic in the space increases. Movement becomes unnatural in the crowded space, and Betty and Danny are clearly identified as the disruptive elements, getting in the way of efficient movement, forcing the entanglements of the home on to the work environment.[4] Throughout the film, Betty never looks comfortable in the space, even though we know she has worked there for years. She is physically present but spiritually aloof. This practice is not hers. For Betty, the store is only a source of income. She invests nothing of herself into the practice, and she therefore gets nothing out of it. Joe and Nick belong in the space because they engage in the practice for which the space is designed.

As a result, the store is not just a place of work for Joe, it is a place of pleasure and physical comfort. Joe dances as he works, taking pleasure in his skill and in the energy of the work. It's not an exaggeration to call it a sexualized space. Joe takes physical pleasure in the fleshiness of the fish and even in their pervasive smell. In the most remarkable visual images of the film, Young shows us Joe boning the shad, a task that requires delicate touch and years of experience. The challenge is to remove from the fish all the bones in its complex and tiny skeleton. To test his success, Joe moves his fingers through the flesh of the shad, in an image that recalls the movements of fingers through labial folds. This startling Georgia O'Keeffe moment provides perhaps one of the oddest sexual images ever seen on film, and makes it clear that Joe's practice is infused with erotic energy, that his work is his sexuality. We know that he has only the most routine sexual interest in Betty, and that all his vital energy goes into the store. Danny turns the tragedy into a smutty joke; he can't stop repeating the inevitable "boning the shad" jokes, overselling the obvious innuendoes but nevertheless hitting the nail right on the head.

The distance between Joe and Betty is manifest in their inability to move and work together in the space of the store. In one wonderful scene, Joe is dancing to Latin music on the radio, turning work into play. Betty barges into the space and changes the radio to a pop station. Joe, still full of energy, changes it right back. She retaliates. Then Nick, playing off Joe's energy and asserting himself, finds a hard rock station. Joe laughs and dances on, claiming a victory and control over the space, marginalizing Betty and claiming Nick's allegiance. The whole triangular relationship is on display. We see Joe win Nick in the work space, though we know that Nick belongs to Betty in the erotic space of the home. Joe does not know what we know, and we can see, in the tensions of this scene, the explosion that will follow when he does.

Given the intensity of Joe's commitment to his workplace, it seems inevitable that his death will take place in the store, that his life will end where it was spent. Joe's death occurs because he has invested his erotic energy in his work and not in his marriage. In an inevitable return, the erotic life that he has denied in his marriage invades his space and destroys him. Danny calls Joe at the market and taunts him with his wife's betrayal and with the complicity of his surrogate son. In an almost unbearable scene, Joe attacks Nick and then collapses under the strain on his weak heart. His immersion in the life of his work and his emotional absence from his home and his family have made him blind to Betty's erotic needs and to her torrid affair. Joe is so blind, in fact, that it strains credulity. We in the audience know so much about the affair that we can hardly believe that a man as bright as Joe knows nothing. But the affair happens in the home, and Joe is not alive at home, only in the store.

When we see Joe at home, he is watching TV, eating, drinking beer, sleeping, ignoring his wife, operating at minimum energy. In the masculine workplace he is alive, but he is near dead at home. In this pattern, of course, Joe is not unique. To see Joe at home is to see the millions of men in our culture who invest so much in their work that they are zombies at home. One of the costs of having a practice that matters is that life outside that practice can seem unimportant, indistinct. Joe and Betty's marriage fits a familiar and dangerous pattern. As a man, Joe's identity comes from his work; as a woman, Betty's identity comes from her domestic role as mother and housekeeper. Both are, therefore, radically incomplete. Joe's erotic energy is entirely directed toward his work, abandoning Betty at a crucial time in her life, now that her son is grown and gone from the home. Joe is caught in a powerful cultural pattern, a regime of gender that divides him from his own emotional, erotic life. While he is in the store he can survive by redirecting his energy into his practice, but at home he can only escape by reducing his consciousness and ignoring the obvious. And when the repressed returns and invades the workplace, his heart cannot survive. He dies what we have to see in our culture as a *man's* death, a victim of a fatal self-division.

This is not to say that Joe is presented by the film as a sociological case study. There is no hint in the film that Young and his collaborators had an abstract political point to make and then fabricated a story which would exemplify it. Joe's tragedy cannot be reduced to sexual and cultural politics. One of the strengths of the film is that Joe and the other characters are too complex to be useful in such a project. Olmos makes Joe feel lived in, with a complex personal history and inner life. We know, for example, that for all his commitment to the practice of running the store, Joe really wanted a different life, working as a fisherman on his own boat out on the open water. In fact, the intensity of his work life is a function of this disappointment, as though he has chosen to dedicate himself obsessively to the very task that keeps him from his true self. *Caught* is distinctive because it allows all of its characters to emerge from this kind of implied personal history, not from a stock sociology. The gender politics of the film are tangled up in those personal complexities. Joe may be caught in a typical male trap, but the texture of his experience, fully realized in the film, keeps the political point implicit. Joe's life and death are too messy and human to be explained fully by a political analysis, but neither can they be understood outside sexual politics. Such politics *always* operate in the messy, human events of everyday life. In its rich characterization, therefore, *Caught* provides a more devastating political critique, because we see the crippling effects of a powerful regime of gender, not in the abstract, but in the compelling lives of believable individuals.

Domestic Sexuality

The other important space in which the plot of *Caught* unfolds is Joe and Betty's apartment. Here, Joe is subordinate and Betty is truly at home. When we see her in the store, she seems detached, going through the motions, but when we see her in the apartment, she is in *her* space, and she comes to life. Her energy in this space is not in the tasks of the housewife, the practices of everyday domestic life, but in the erotic life with which she has suffused the entire space. Young provides us with compelling scenes of Betty's narcissistic and autoerotic sexuality. We see her repeatedly in the mirror as she tends the needs of her body and her vanity, and we watch her take erotic baths in the candlelit bathroom. If Joe suffers from his denial of sexuality and his over-identification with his work, Betty suffers from a sexual energy that has no external outlet. She is routinely neglected by Joe, and she has no practice, no task into which she can sublimate her erotic energy. The space of the home therefore becomes her erotic space, redolent with her life history and its complex emotion.

Betty moves around in this space with the confidence that we see in Joe when he is in the store. Maria Conchita Alonso convinces us that she *belongs* in the space, and Young moves the camera around with her so comfortably that we share the space with her. In this apartment, Betty is living in a shrine dedicated to the history of her relationship with her son. She moves in and out of Danny's room as though it were her own, and she keeps Danny's history everywhere around her. She is always ready to pop one of his videotaped performances into the VCR or to find an artifact of his childhood history. They are as ready to hand in this space as Joe's knives are in the fish store. The home constantly reminds us that Betty did once have a practice that defined her — the task of raising her beloved son and encouraging his talents. But if that is where her energy was once directed, now there is nothing for her but her own narcissism. The space of the home is charged with her frustrated sexual desire, and in that space Joe is a cipher.

Caught is very good at evoking a history it never directly shows — the time when Betty invested all of her energy in Danny and his talents. Betty tells Nick with great enthusiasm about the act that she and Danny developed when he was a boy. They sang and danced and did comedy skits, and their audiences loved them. At times the grown-up Danny and Betty break into a bit of the old routine. Young leaves it to us to imagine how the energy of creating that act must have suffused this small apartment with costumes and music and lively movement. And we can see in Joe's response to the old routines that he must have been marginalized in that space, always in the way or made to sit and watch. What Betty and Danny would have put on display for Joe was a thinly veiled version of their own incestuous relationship. We can see in their current interactions that there is too much touching which is too intimate, just sexual enough to make us uncomfortable. It's easy then to extrapolate back into that past, when Betty, already alienated from Joe, invested all her sexual energy in her son, with no other task that mattered to her but creating a son who would exceed the father, become a celebrity, and make it big. The residue of that energy is all that remains in the space — videos, posters, snapshots. Now Betty's home is a shrine to those erotic memories and a constant reminder of the life she no longer enjoys.

With Danny gone and Joe lost and no work that matters to her, Betty falls back on a desperate narcissism. The only remaining outlet for her sexual energy is herself, her pampering and satisfaction of her own body. Young shows her repeatedly before the mirror, in what is clearly her daily ritual, taking elaborate care of her face and skin. In all of these scenes, there is little sense of pleasure. She seems sad, even despairing, watching her beauty fade, regretting the past. Hers is a *desperate* narcissism, not a healthy self love. She has turned her energy on herself only because there is no place else for it to go. The erotic bath scenes have a similar feel. They are candlelit and sensual, but they only remind us that this is the full extent of Betty's sexual life. Because of these erotic habits, the home then becomes Betty's sexual space, even before Nick enters the picture.

When Nick moves in, the home becomes an entirely sexualized space. Much of the emotional intensity of the film comes from the fact that Nick and Betty are always ready to catch a sexual moment, anywhere in the apartment. Kitchen, hallway, bedroom, bathroom, anyplace where Joe cannot see, has the potential for sexual contact. Betty and Nick have no sexual experience outside this space. They never go to a hotel or seek their own space. Their sexuality is thus woven into the emotional life of the home. Clearly, Nick becomes the substitute for the missing son, allowing a sexual release that mother and son were not quite allowed, and he becomes the fulfillment of her narcissistic fantasies, a man who recognizes the sexual energy that Joe ignores. Two of the most intense sexual scenes in the film reinforce these connections. In one scene, Nick and Betty have sex in Danny's closet, surrounded by all his adolescent gear, his clothes and toys and decorations. The energy of Betty's sexual release is a function of all the sexual history of the space, all the times that Betty just barely sublimated her incestuous desires into entertainment and performance. In another scene, Betty and Nick make love in the shower, in the space where we have seen Betty's autoerotic sexuality, perhaps playing out a scene already imagined there. Just to show us how dead to life Joe is in the domestic space, Young has Joe stagger into the bathroom, take a piss, and stagger back to bed, oblivious to the lovers standing literally inches from him. He assumes, possibly, that Betty is taking one of her "long showers"—nothing remarkable there. Nick and Betty take advantage of Joe's diminished awareness; they can play with their sexuality anywhere they want.

Joe's blindness to the affair, especially in that shower scene, is a difficulty for the film. How can a man who is as smart as Joe shows himself to be in the store be so ignorant about facts that seem so obvious to us? Young risks losing audience sympathy for Joe, making him seem culpably ignorant, and therefore too dense to care about. But perhaps Young takes this risk in order to make a powerful point about the fatal divisions in this marriage and, by extension, in our culture. Joe is alive only at work; his domestic life is just a routine. Betty is alive only in her sexuality; everything else is just a routine. Of course Joe cannot see what's happening all around him in that apartment. He has for a long time trained himself not to see the sexuality in the home. First marginalized by Betty and Danny, now toyed with by Betty and Nick, Joe turns himself off when he enters the sexualized domestic space.

A husband who lives only for his work, a wife who has nothing to live for now that she is no longer the nurturing mother — Young presents us with a pattern all too familiar in our culture's gender environment. Just as Joe is trapped in a typical male role, Betty operates inside a common self-defeating pattern for women. If you invest all your energy in your children, with no other practice that matters, what happens when the children grow up? Where does the energy go, especially if it's enclosed in the tight confines of the home? It takes only a figure like Nick, a reminder of what she has lost, to force that energy out of control. But what if Betty had a task that mattered to her as much as the fish store matters to Joe? Would that not provide a healthy and satisfying outlet for her energy? Perhaps in that utopian circumstance the divisions between Joe and Betty would be healed. Both would have a source of self-esteem outside the other and they could then turn to one another for mutual support and affection. But the fact that they, like many couples, live in mutually exclusive spaces — the man in his workplace and the woman in the domestic space — leaves them no common ground, no shared experience. Both characters are *caught* in the nets of gender definitions that fatally limit their choices. And the fact that Young and Olmos and Alonso infuse these characters with a complex individuality, a sense of *particular* lives lived in a complex mutual history, only deepens the political point.

Open Spaces

One powerful element in the tragedy of *Caught* is that the characters can see the prospect of a different life, a less restrictive life, even as they head toward their doom. The chance for a new life comes in the form of an offer from a real estate developer to buy the store, anticipating the yuppification of the neighborhood. Betty instantly sees this offer as a salvation, a chance to live the bigger life she has always desired. Joe, on the other hand, at first rejects the offer because he sees it as some rich guy trying to buy him out of the independence and self-esteem that comes with a job well done. He is so committed to the work, so immersed in his daily practice in the store, that this opportunity seems to him to be an insult, an offer of money in exchange for the intrinsic satisfactions of his practice.

Joe changes his mind after Nick, following Betty's encouragement, convinces Joe that the money will allow him to return to his first love. He will now be able to buy that fishing boat he has always wanted, to live his life in the open space of the ocean rather than in the confined space of the store. Nick helps him to realize that he has embraced the identity of the "fish man," taking pride in his ability to bone the shad, only as a weak substitute for the larger dream that he has abandoned. Significantly, this recognition scene happens *outside* the confining spaces of the store and the home. Joe and Nick have the conversation while they are standing on the waterfront, looking out on the open water and on the distant skyline of Manhattan. It is only outside the spaces that dominate the film that it is possible for Joe to have a thought outside the stifling patterns that dominate his life. Joe first tells Nick about his sense of entrapment in his job and in his marriage in a similar scene, as he and Nick go for a run on a riverside pathway, again outside the enclosures of work and home. And in a similar vein, we see all of the characters celebrate their new freedom outside in a public park and on a fishing boat which Joe is thinking about buying with his newfound wealth. Tragically, these visions of alternative lives are never realized. The characters are caught too deeply in their old patterns to be able to break through to an imagined alternative.

The other significant scene that takes place in these open spaces is the scene of Nick's murder. After Joe dies in the store, we no longer see any of the characters in the two dominant spaces of the film. When Joe dies, the old life with its rigid dichotomies is gone, and none of the characters belong symbolically in those familiar spaces. Danny kills Nick out in public, again down by the waterfront. But unlike the earlier scenes which emphasize the broader horizons available in the open, public space, in Nick's death scene the outdoors seems as confining as the workplace or the home. The scene is shot at night, in a pouring rain, with tight camera work that cuts off any broader visibility. It's as though the violence and horror that have built up in these enclosed interiors finally escapes into the open spaces of the world, which had previously served as a way out, a place where new lives could be imagined. In the spatial symbology of the film, the tragedy of the story cannot be contained in the little world where it began. The whole world is implicated and tainted with blood, and violence seems inescapable. The ending suggests that Joe and Betty are not just individuals living through a personal tragedy. Their entrapment is our entrapment, and there seems to be no neutral space into which one can escape.

Conclusion

Caught is an uncomfortable and unsettling film. It transforms the ordinary spaces of our lives into self-created prisons that limit our choices and divide us from those we love and from our own possible selves. Joe cannot survive outside his store. Betty has no life outside her home. The store robs him of his erotic life. The home robs her of anything but an erotic life. In this film, Young suggests that we are trapped by our histories and choices, within the spaces that embody them. It takes filmmaking courage to restrict a film so carefully to these two small, everyday spaces. It runs the danger of making the audience feel claustrophobic and bored, captured by the film just as Joe and Betty are captured by their lives. But in *Caught* the risk pays off. The powerful drama of love and death is made more powerful by restricting the intense emotional energy of the story to these physical and emotional enclosures. In the hothouse atmosphere created by spatial confinement, the passions of the characters have no alternative but to explode. *Caught* should make us all wonder about the limits we place on ourselves and the social codes in which we can be caught.

Notes

1. Some of the most interesting reviews of *Caught* include John Anderson, *LA Times*, 9/27/96; Joe Baltake, *The Sacramento Bee*, 10/18/96; Godfrey Cheshire, *New York Press*,

9/25/96; Donald Munro, *The Fresno Bee,* 10/25/96; Rex Reed, *New York Observer,* 10/7/96; George-Ann Silverman, *Denver Post,* 2/4/96.

2. This interview is available on line at the Sony Pictures Classics site (http://www.sonyclassics.com/caught/misc/interview.html).

3. See Alisdair MacIntyre, *After Virtue* (University of Notre Dame Press, 1991) and Pierre Bourdieu, *Outline of a Theory of Practice* (Cambridge University Press, 1977).

4. For an interesting analysis of the improvisatory process of creating this scene, see "Celluloid and Synchrony," a *Harvard Magazine* (January–February, 1996) profile of Robert M. Young ('49) by Bill Shebar.

13. From Script to Screen: Adaptation of Richard Dresser's *Below the Belt*

Dennis Bohr

When I first heard that Richard Dresser's *Below the Belt* was being made into a film, I reread the play and was bewildered about how anyone could turn such a bizarre play with only three characters into a full-length film. Maybe it was failure of imagination on my part since I am a playwright, not a director. I was intrigued by the idea, and when Bob Young's film of the play (retitled *Human Error*) was to be shown, I was anxious to see it. What I saw confused and enthralled me. It was the same play with the same words and characters, but it was also something new — something beyond the words on the page.

The keen dialogue of *Below the Belt* first grabbed my attention — the word games the men with the power play and the absurdities of their paranoid universe. Hanrahan and Merkin manipulate a newcomer named Dobbitt into playing their games. Dobbitt is forced to compete with Hanrahan over ownership of the one chair in Merkin's office, the number of beeps that will summon them to Merkin, and even the view of the river at the compound where they work. Merkin and Hanrahan have rules that do not apply to ordinary daily transactions, and Dobbitt has to learn the rules in order to play and to survive. In hilarious, surreal dialogue Hanrahan challenges Dobbitt about every innocuous thing he says. Even when Dobbitt thanks Hanrahan, an act most people accept graciously, Hanrahan questions Dobbitt's ulterior motives, demanding to know why he is being thanked.

A director's vision contrasts with, and at the best of times complements, the playwright's vision. The audience sees what they see filtered through their own lenses of vision, through their own experiences. People who want life to make absolute sense and go out of their way to make sure it does will avoid *Human Error*. People who see the absurdities of life daily will identify with the dialogue that turns them left and right and then back again until they reel with the contradictions involved. As with several of our current institutions (religion, the military, politics), logic doesn't enter into the equation.

Bob Young's *Human Error*, the film version of Richard Dresser's play *Below the Belt*, is a collaboration that has worked, created a new version of the play, and transformed it into a different work of art. Young and Dresser showed the film at Sundance in January 2004 where it competed with five other films in the "Frontier" section — that is, experimental, "cutting edge" films. The film opened the new Vail Film Festival in Colorado and played at the USA Festival in Dallas. Young hoped to take it to Toronto and would like to enter it in the New York Film Festival as well. The film is definitely experimental as Young shot his actors on a blue screen and created the background setting with computer graphics. Adding the computer graphics was a slow, painstaking process. Young said it took an hour to create one frame of film by computer, and he and his crew calculated that it would have taken twelve years to finish the film using only one computer. (They employed 75 computers to finish the film.)

The original play is set in a remote manufacturing plant far away. In the opening darkness, the audience hears Hanrahan attempting to type, something he does not do well but is sensitive about. (Hanrahan is overly sensitive about a great deal, we find out later, so the opening is a precursor of Hanrahan's tetchy personality.) The lights rise and Dobbitt enters into a universe he is not well equipped to deal with. He attempts to make cordial small talk, the common greetings between two people who will be working together:

> DOBBITT: I'm Dobbitt. You must be Hanrahan.
>
> HANRAHAN: I *must* be Hanrahan? I don't have a choice?
>
> DOBBITT: Are you Hanrahan?
>
> HANRAHAN: Who are you to barge into my room and tell me who I must be?
>
> DOBBITT: You're not Hanrahan?
>
> HANRAHAN: As it turns out, I *am* Hanrahan, but not because it happens to suit your purposes.[1]

The dialogue continues in similar surreal fashion, letting us know that this is not exactly the real world. Dobbitt attempts the societal game of empty platitudes and "go-along-to-get-along" that encompasses much of our daily lives. Hanrahan plays a different game, one whose rules only he and Merkin seem to grasp. Two other topics of conversation illustrate that this play is not founded on the usual platitudes: which bed Dobbitt will sleep in (the one that gets the icy wind or the "sweatbox" next to the radiator) and whether he would like a cup of coffee (he would but not if it's any bother, which to Hanrahan, of course, it is). Further evidence of the absurdist nature of the play occurs when a beep from an intercom sounds, and Hanrahan responds, "That's Merkin. And he sounds upset."[2]

We meet Merkin in the next scene, and Dobbitt is subjected to more charades-with-words, in which he has to guess what he should say and do. Merkin explains the system to Dobbitt: while Hanrahan checks, Dobbitt will type reports and vice versa. What they are checking is never made clear, but they will produce 2911 units a day, 125,466 units a week. Dobbitt at first has no question but is harangued by Merkin into asking one, so he asks what the "units" are.

He is not told, nor is his offer to help Hanrahan with his typing well received. After Hanrahan stalks off, Merkin wants to know what Hanrahan has said about him. And the games continue.

In the next scene, Dobbitt interferes with Hanrahan's view of the polluted river. This is the first time the stage directions mention "*several pairs of dim yellow eyes in the darkness.*"[3] These eyes are outsiders (as Dobbitt is), and we never really find out what they are, though they are outside the fence of the compound and therefore not to be worried about.

Act Two begins with a party scene which isolates the three Checkers from the rest of the workers. The Regional Director (unseen in the play) is throwing a "holiday gala" to celebrate Economic Recovery and Realignment Day. There will be fireworks, gambling, and performances, but the Checkers are invited to attend the party for only 45 minutes, well before the "buffet dinner with sing-along." They decide (for once acting in unison) to boycott the official party and have their very own Checkers party. The first thing we see is the threesome looking out the window at the other exuberant party. Dressed for the occasion, drinking punch and eating cookies, they disparage the official party because "something's missing. Like the heart and soul of this compound."[4]

Which, according to the Checkers, *is them*. As Merkin says, "You don't choose checking, checking chooses you. My daddy was a Checker and his daddy checked before him. He'd say, 'Any man can work, it takes an extraordinary man to check work.'"[5] We still don't know *what* they check, nor are we convinced that they themselves do.

The Checkers have their own party and eat sour grapes while creating an elaborate artifice that masks (at least temporarily) their intense dislike of and paranoia about each other. They are for once aligned against outside forces, yet at the same time they compete in telling stories of whose life has been hardest, topped by Merkin's boast that his wife died giving birth. She was revived, however, and wasn't much changed "except she sang differently."[6]

Then the river catches on fire. Because of all the toxic waste the company has dumped into it, a stray firecracker from the party ignites the surface. Merkin does not know what to do; the only water he is authorized to use is the polluted river water. If he does nothing, management will see him as failing to deal with conflict. But if he uses the water from the river, it could simply add fuel to the flames. Dobbitt suggests "some middle ground.... Couldn't you issue a strong statement condemning the fire?"[7]

More creatures with "sharp little teeth and insolent yellow eyes"[8] appear in the next scene, and Dobbitt perceives them as being closer and in greater numbers than before. Dobbitt suggests the path that is played out in many films about alien cultures: "Catch one and study it in a laboratory and find out what it is, for God sakes!"[9] Hanrahan speculates that they may be coworkers who fell into the river. Merkin is apprised of the eyes, but says that the creatures are outside the fence until some higher-up informs him otherwise. As Groucho Marx once said, "Who are you going to believe: me or your own eyes?"

Hanrahan and Dobbitt discuss their marriages, with Hanrahan making cryptic comments that suggest he knew Dobbitt's wife, Catherine, before Dobbitt did. This causes Dobbitt anxiety about his wife and creates the first scene in which Dobbitt acts decisively, holding a knife to Hanrahan's throat. Oddly enough this scene enables Dobbitt and Hanrahan to bond (perhaps suggesting that men can only connect through violence). Dobbitt and Catherine "both love to be at home. Just not at the same time,"[10] while Hanrahan feels his absence is causing him and his wife to drift apart.

In the next scene, Merkin uses information he has gleaned from reading Hanrahan's mail to reveal to Dobbitt that Hanrahan's wife has left him and moved to a convent. Under the guise of "protecting" Hanrahan and his place in the company (as well as his own), Merkin persuades or blackmails Dobbitt into writing letters to Hanrahan, pretending to be Jacqueline Hanrahan. Dobbitt is fully ensconced in the game by now, and he accedes to the "request" despite some misgivings that he would be betraying Hanrahan — which of course he is.

Complications arise, and Hanrahan eventually discovers that Dobbitt has been writing the letters when Dobbitt inadvertently quotes from one of them. Hanrahan decides to leave the company to reconnect with his wife, while Dobbitt has signed on for another tour of duty — tricked into it by

Merkin. Dobbitt attempts to apologize because he and Hanrahan had agreed to always tell each other the truth. He then utilizes the play's twisted logic to rationalize his betrayal, claiming that he surrendered his honesty for Hanrahan's sake. He manages to make honesty look like selfishness, and finishes with a plea:

> DOBBITT: Tell me you'd lie to me, Hanrahan.
>
> HANRAHAN: All right, I'd lie to you. I'm lying right now.
>
> DOBBITT: Thank you. That means a lot.... Hanrahan? These were the most wonderful days of my life.
>
> HANRAHAN: Yes. They became wonderful as soon as they were over.[11]

More male bonding and the typical "purgation" scene of Hollywood films is parodied for its most ridiculous elements. Then Hanrahan leaves for an in-country assignment, and Dobbitt remains, as the mysterious yellow eyes creep closer. Merkin assures Dobbitt that the eyes are no longer a problem. His bosses have declared that the creatures are now *inside* the compound — that "they have, in effect, been captured."[12]

The first obvious difference between Dresser's play and Bob Young's film is the title. At Sundance, Young and Dresser were told by a crew member that "Below the Belt" is a reference to gay pornography, and one of Dresser's friends gave him a book titled *Writing Below the Belt* which contained interviews by writers of pornography. That, Dresser said in an email, "was very convincing in considering a title change. *Human Error* sounds like a comedy and ... is Merkin's explanation for everything that goes wrong."[13] When Merkin cites the wrong date for the completion of production and Hanrahan corrects him by pointing out that he had forgotten the holiday, Merkin replies, "Quite right. Human error."[14]

Another difference between Young's film and Dresser's play is that they are, of course, different media. The play and film contain the same story about relationships between men in the work force, but the film provides us with new pictures: workers in overalls and gas masks cleaning up green, radioactive waste; random, unexplained explosions; Dobbitt speeding up workers with the flip of a strobe light; Merkin's suggestion box and his rubber stamp of "VOID"; Dobbitt's series of night- and daymares; and a backdrop of green (toxic-colored) water contrasting with a beautiful but not-quite-normal yellow-and-green sky. These images (and other computer-generated elements) heighten the absurdity of the original play. Dresser, who wrote the screenplay for *Human Error*, says, "The paranoid universe of the play is made specific in the film.... [The film] is absolutely true to what the play is all about.... We viscerally experience what we might have imagined in seeing the play."

Dresser and Young worked closely on the film and are good examples of the interconnectedness that is vital between artists. As Dresser said in an e-mail:

> I had — and am continuing to have — an unusually close and enlivening collaboration with Bob. I was a part of every decision and he made it clear to everyone where the film came from. He has a sense of respect and collaboration for those with whom he works that is beyond anything I had experienced.... He is secure enough as an artist to value what everyone involved with the project had to say. But he is also enough of an artist to make the film he wanted to make. So this was a highly unusual experience and I recognize that it is quite different from most writers' experiences on a movie, where they are not welcome on set and are often replaced by another writer. But that's Hollywood and this is something quite different.

Young said similar things about Dresser:

> I must say that working with Rick Dresser was always a pleasure. He is so smart and so open and so permissive. I had great respect for the writing and tended to put him on a pedestal, but he was always down to earth, never precious or protective about his words. And he was open to my thoughts and feelings which have developed during the course of making the film.[15]

When asked why he chose to film *Below the Belt*, Young responded:

> When I read *Below the Belt*, I laughed a lot and thought that it was beautifully written. I thought that the situations and characters, though pushed to extremes, were deeply true; that is, they were psychologically true and I thought that Dresser shows us our world with its absurdities and we laugh and realize that we are laughing at ourselves.... The story had a kind of surreal quality. I couldn't tell when or where it took place and it made me think. I guess that is the chief reason why I got involved and needed to make it into a movie. It made me think and it was funny....
>
> [T]he basic story was on the page. The characters were wonderful. The situations were funny. The dialogue was great. What had to be created was the world in which all of this takes place.

The animation, Young says, was not a choice but "a necessity." Young had found the perfect location for the film at an abandoned oil refinery and a nineteenth century sugar factory in Puerto Rico, but the original plans fell through when the English company that was financing the film declared bankruptcy. The English company wanted big name stars in the film (Willem

Dafoe, Bill Murray, John Goodman, Alan Arkin, and Randy Quaid were all considered at one point), but those plans were shelved with the loss of financing. The project continued, however, with the help of Joel Ehrlich, Young's friend and producer, who introduced him to a computer graphics artist who said that the background could be supplied with computers. Young felt that with the animation he was "creating an original world that was not Puerto Rico but was in keeping with the themes of *Below the Belt*." Using the Puerto Rican models as a starting point, he could be "more original and freer in my individual conception and not be bound by the real world." He says that at one point it dawned on him that, "My God, I'm making an animated film — like *Shrek*—with real actors."

Young calls *Human Error* "a moral tale, a fairy tale.... It's not the real world ... but everything in it is psychologically true, one of the requisites for any successful story." Fairy tales are real to us because of this truth: cartoon characters, like Shrek, "conform to what happens in life and to human behavior." The animated characters take us into absurd situations, and that is what Young saw in Richard Dresser's play:

> I think that the film we are making is very much like an animated film, but with real people instead of animated characters.... The humor comes out of real situations that are taken seriously. The computer graphics have given us the opportunity to take the story into a super-reality that I believe enhances the story that existed in the play. The movie is very true to the play, but is able to go further in its suggesting that we are living in a world that is going to hell. We are able to dramatize this in a way that a play could not.

The crucial scene in which Bob Young departs from what readers visualize is the party scene. In the play, we do not see the fire, nor do we see the party that Merkin, Hanrahan, and Dobbitt are not invited to. They are welcome only for a short period before all the fun and games begin, and for once they unite against the powers-that-be (unseen and only referred to — much like our corporate giants who rule us with their electricity that might fail at any minute, their computers and their money-making machines).

The film of the party scene is unsettling for the viewer because Hanrahan and Dobbitt do attend the party, which is a rambunctious affair with singing and dancing by half-naked people. The partygoers paint their faces and dance uninhibitedly, creating a sexual tension. In the film, Dobbitt and Hanrahan are titillated and teased to participate, whereas in the play they remain outsiders, unable to connect with the ordinary workers. This seems a shift from the paranoia of Dresser's play. In the play, Dresser lists only Dobbitt, Hanrahan and Merkin, each individually described as "a man."[16] This evokes an image of businesses which make their employees compete with one another, while the film shows how supervisors are often isolated from the workers they oversee. In the film, Dobbitt and Hanrahan are still outsiders at the party: they are the only white people in attendance and seem unable to feel the rhythm of the party or to connect with anyone. Hanrahan attempts to dance with the workers, while Dobbitt looks terrified.

Young says the party scene

> came out of an experience I had in South Africa. On Sundays, the workers would dance and act out farces in front of their co-workers — who sat in the bleachers in the hot sun and their bosses who sat in a shaded pavilion. The costumes were handmade out of available materials and the dances and skits mocked the bosses — thus the masks/effigies of the bosses displayed by the workers [in the film]. Of course they are all of different ethnicities — but not white.

Young made other choices and changes by adding characters and more scenes with additional people. Early in the film, after the opening scene in which a cockroach encounters a stamping machine, Dobbitt tours the factory on his arrival to the compound, and we hear an ambulance siren. We see the workers at the factory rushing to some unspecified tragedy, the music swells, and the scene dissolves into a cemetery where we see "R.I.P. Haney." Haney is the worker whom Dobbitt replaces, and this scene makes it clear to the viewer that something mysterious happened to Haney. Young felt that adding characters was "necessary for enlarging the story," that the play was just "too isolated with just three guys: We have the ability to see the world; why not see the factory?" We see the polluted river, the moat, the party scene, and what the Company is doing to the river. To Young, these added scenes and people add "more reverberations."

Dresser approved the expansion of the cast to include more people:

> It just seemed on stage that the claustrophobic world of these men would be diminished by seeing anyone else. But I think in the film, the claustrophobia is accentuated by seeing the native workers. What I love about the party scene in the film is that the natives are so natural and sexual and open while the three guys are stuck with each other and the lunatic power games they are condemned to play. Their party is no different than their meetings in Merkin's office. By seeing the workers, we get a deeper sense of the vibrant life the guys are missing and how utterly trapped they are.

Another major difference between the play and the film is the ending. In the play, Hanrahan prepares to leave the company to rescue his marriage while Dobbitt and Merkin continue their games. In the film, Hanrahan rejoins the company, only now he is lower in the pecking order, below Dobbitt (and Dobbitt now gets the chair in Merkin's office). Dresser says of the different endings,

> There actually were two endings to the play. When it premiered at Actors Theatre of Louisville, Hanrahan escaped. When we did it Off Broadway, I changed the ending because I felt it violated what the play is saying, that nobody escapes. And that's how it is in the film.

Young feels that the end of the film is the only place where he shows the audience directly what he wants them to think. We see Hanrahan, after he has been re-processed and accepted back into the fold, in what Young calls "a silent scream ... a recognition of his pain, an existential shout of man naked and screaming of how he really feels." This full-screen close-up of Xander Berkely as Hanrahan clearly illustrates Hanrahan's despair and realization that he is trapped in a horror movie. This scene is juxtaposed with Dobbitt as self-satisfied and smug. He's played the game and he's won. He wears his cowboy hat and is puffing contentedly on a cigar. But (now in full ownership of Hanrahan's view) he looks at the river, the effluvium that is adding misery to the world, and watches as young kids scoop up the "water" and begin painting their faces with green, glowing radioactive waste. Then there's a quick switch to Merkin driving a golf ball toward the camera and the audience, and the ball becomes planet Earth. This is what Young calls "one moment of recognition" that this is "a real story and not fantasy."

Young also says of the closing scene:

> The film is ironic and because of the power of film and our ability to take the characters into situations that would be impossible on the stage ... [the ending] goes beyond what was in the play. And the close-up of Hanrahan as he silently screams could not be done on the stage.... This is the only time in the story that we deal with the implications of what is going on. And it is just for a moment, to give weight to the last scene where Merkin hits the golf ball that becomes the world. We wanted this one note that adds weight to what the audience experiences.... It is after all a comedy, and I think that comedy is a way of seeing with proportion. When the king slips on a banana peel and lands on his ass, he and we are grounded in the truth. That is what we intend to have happen at the end: the reality of the kids and Merkin hitting the golf ball that becomes the earth. That should ground the audience in what is happening in the world.

Dresser, as the screenwriter, agrees with the changes made for the film:

> I think the biggest difference between my conception of the play and the film is that film is, by definition, so real and the play is surreal. What that

means in a practical sense is that some of what worked beautifully in the theatre simply felt like marking time in the film. So I cut it. For the film to work, it has to find its own momentum, and with all the talk, the danger was that it would feel like treading water. So there is a brutality in cutting and shaping the material of the play to create a filmic story that has dramatic movement. Having said that, I must point out that this film is remarkably faithful to the play both in ideas and language. And in many cases, Bob wanted to hold onto things that I wanted to cut. It was exactly the opposite of what normally happens between writer and director. He once referred to his "having more respect for the words than the author." Which is quite true. And it made for an interesting creative dynamic. But what we agreed on is the language is the battlefield and there is absolutely no small talk in the movie. Everything that is said is either an attack or a defensive maneuver.

What we envision as readers when we read the play is three men in claustrophobic proximity to each other — each with his own agenda, usually of aligning one of the others with him against the third. After their initial encounter with Merkin and their subsequent bonding scene, Hanrahan and Dobbitt make a pact to be totally truthful with each other regarding what Merkin says about the other. Later, Dobbitt aligns himself with Merkin to protect Hanrahan in the dubious but well-meaning aim of sparing Hanrahan from the pain of finding out that his wife has left him and gone to join a convent.

But what we see as we read — what Dresser wants us to see — is laid out at the opening. Dresser describes the setting as "an industrial compound in a distant land. We see a room with two beds, an office, a little bridge over a stream, and a bit of the surrounding area."[17] The reader visualizes three people in isolation from the wider world. They desperately try to connect with each other but they are restricted from doing so by the sterile, paranoid environment they inhabit. Dobbitt and Hanrahan are Checkers — what they check is never made clear, which adds to the general absurdity of the work force and the play. Robotic people go about their lives everyday, doing their "duty" as they think they should — plying their trade to gain money, self-respect, health benefits, or gratification — but perhaps, Dresser suggests, they never really know what they're doing.

A stage director or a film director sees the play differently than a writer does. A writer may see a scene in her head, but that doesn't necessarily translate into how people will see it on stage or in a film. Many theatres that accept manuscripts do not want extensive stage directions. Shakespeare's stage directions were simple, usually little more than "they exit," "they fight," "they die," and famously in *A Winter's Tale*, "exit, pursued by a bear." It is up to a director to transform the words on the page into a seeable product, which is why so many Shakespearean interpretations differ.

When Dresser was asked if he directs his own plays and whether he'd want to, he replied:

> I have not directed and I can't say I have much desire to do so. For starters, I'm not patient enough to want to go to rehearsals every day. Plus, I have found that good directors bring a point of view that challenges what I have done as a writer and ultimately can make the work stronger. When I have finished writing a script, I put on a different hat and work very hard to protect that script and engage the right director and actors. Hiring the right people and then giving them the freedom to do their work is how I like to operate, and it is certainly what I observed working with Bob.

The relationship between director and writer can be a contentious one, but Dresser clearly feels his collaboration with Bob Young was a positive experience:

> I tend to get very involved in collaborating with directors in the theatre in casting and rehearsals, but I also find it's helpful to get out of the way during the middle part of the process and let the actors make the work their own. This allows me to come in with fresh eyes at the end of the process, which can be of great benefit to the director. This is how we have been working on the film. At every stage of the process, I get together with Bob and we discuss where we are and where we want to go. I loved being on set because I felt that I could be — and was expected to be — an active collaborator in the filming.... I understand why writers want to direct; it often comes out of frustration with how their work is treated by others. I've certainly had that frustration, which is why it is so exhilarating to work with Bob, who is fierce in his dedication to the work and what lies beneath the surface.

When a director and a writer can "connect" and achieve a certain camaraderie and empathy with each other, the collaboration blossoms into something bigger than each of them can produce individually. The words on the paper may be art as well, but a play only really comes to life when it happens on the stage — or in this case, on the screen. (This is not to suggest that Dresser's play has not been successful. It premiered at Actors Theatre of Louisville as part of the Humana Festival, has been produced Off Broadway, and has had many regional productions in addition to having a long-running production in Berlin before touring throughout Europe.)

An example of how writer and director collaborate to create a new vision is presented by the little yellow eyes. They were not in the first film version, but Dresser says, "They are now and were always intended to be." Dobbitt first sees the eyes outside the fence and wonders who or what they are. Hanrahan suggests that they are former workers who fell into the river — or perhaps they were trying to escape the compound. Merkin is unconcerned about them because the Regional Director and others with seniority over him have not told him what to think of them. When they appear inside the fence later in the play, Dobbitt senses them getting closer and becoming more menacing, but Merkin assures Dobbitt that the higher-ups have informed him that because the eyes are now inside the fence, they have been apprehended. One might see the eyes as witnesses to the destruction at the compound. They are "collateral damage"; they are we, the audience, unwitting collaborators with the powers-that-be.

In theatrical productions, Dresser often used twinkling lights for the eyes. Young says he first thought of them as "creatures that represent the consciousness of the world." He thought of shooting them in many ways but found that he was "asking for sympathy for the creatures" and wanted a harder image, one that would make them "more mysterious, more abstract." He didn't want to "empathize with them and make a direct appeal to people's feelings." He sees the film as comic, but also "more like a horror movie." This horror movie idea is emphasized with the opening scene of Dobbitt arriving at the compound. There is ominous music in the background and a wolf-like howling accompanied by disembodied eyes watching Dobbitt. Then Dobbitt is subjected to an assembly line of delousing, and commands to "bend over and spread your cheeks," and "cough." All men can identify with this scene, and the humiliation is meant to tell viewers that he is entering an institution that regards him as less than clean, as less than human. By making the eyes, in Young's words, "no longer concrete, more nameless," we see that Merkin, Dobbitt, Hanrahan and Company are "destroying something, but they don't know what, and it's catching up with them." The eyes see the horror of the world, and perhaps they are innocents who die.

Dresser says the yellow eyes

> can mean different things, but I would agree with your conclusion that they serve as a kind of witness to the destruction of the world. When the play was first done in Berlin, they kept trying to get me to say what the eyes really were. Of course I wouldn't tell them because I wanted them to find what they would mean in their own production.

The eyes really grab the reader's attention, and perhaps one quibble with the film is that the eyes are not as prominent, not as menacing as portrayed in the written play. They are only shown a couple of times in the film. Also, the play ends with the ominous stage directions describing the eyes: *There are more of them and they're much closer.*"[18] In an earlier version of the film, the eyes were included at the end when Dobbitt sees the children painting their faces with radioactive waste. But they are cut in the final version because, Young says, "[I] felt they would take away from the concrete threat of what was happening to the children.... I felt the eyes had done their job and might weaken the ending."

Dresser sounds somewhat wistful about them:

> [The eyes] were so palpably menacing in the stage version ... but it's a very theatrical device. I'm not sure we ever found quite how to make them as disturbing in the film.... What we finally decided on was that the terror at the end is more psychological terror at what happens among the three men rather than what we'd get by using the yellow eyes.

Commenting about what is different in writing for film as opposed to writing for the stage, Dresser referred to the eyes again as "a theatrical device, but they started to seem like a cheesy horror movie device in the film. Writing for film is writing for images, where the audience is manipulated into what they are seeing." He says in the theatre the audience can look at whatever they choose, but "there's much that works in a play that seems over-the-top or slow or stagy or fake in a movie. A look from an actor [such as the close-up of Xander Berkely as Hanrahan] can convey what that brilliantly wrought monologue accomplished on stage."

As with all artists, playwrights make conscious decisions about what they choose to include in a play, but sometimes hidden messages emerge without their being fully aware of them. Dresser addressed this idea in an interview:

> When I write plays I am not specifically thinking of the stage. I'm trying to tell a story and I don't like to deal with the more practical issues until later in the process. Initially, I am trying to just hit a vein and let the work happen without being forced or contained. I don't edit myself much in a first draft either. I believe that in starting a script, everything should feel possible. If, later on, one consolidates the characters and strips down the setting and does all the things one can do to get a production, well, fine. But at least, if you're lucky, the work has a strongly beating heart by then.... I don't tend to think thematically when I'm writing. I am trying to tell a particular kind of story that of course has relevance to me because of its theme. But thinking about themes during the writing process seems quite reductive.

Playwrights write and directors direct (though of course sometimes the lines get blurred between the two). Playwrights, for the most part, want to see what someone else will see when they read the play. They want someone else's vision. When the two visions coincide as with Bob Young and Richard Dresser's collaboration on *Human Error*, something astonishing and moving emerges and shows us the world in a new way.

Below the Belt pulls the reader in with its wordplay and the paranoia of the characters, the dichotomy between their competitiveness and their desire to connect with each other. But in *Human Error*, Bob Young's film treatment, another theme that is sometimes overlooked when reading the play is brought to the fore: the destruction of the planet by corporate interests bent on making money. The Company does not care what they are making except they know they are making money. They do not care what causes the river to glow and then later catch on fire. This element of global antipathy is definitely in the play. The first time the river is mentioned, Hanrahan remarks that the river "positively glows."[19] Dresser means this literally. The river has had so much waste dumped into it that it radiates menacing vapors that may have caused the "little yellow eyes" to become what they are.

While Dobbitt, Hanrahan, and Merkin argue about "trivial things"—who sits in the chair, what Hanrahan has said about Merkin—we see Bob Young's version: "[This is a] world that doesn't work, that's falling apart.... I want the film to make us aware that the male-oriented world is not working." This "male-oriented world" that is "crumbling all around us," is what Dresser exposes in his play and what Young has built into the movie. In Dresser's original play, there were only three men. In the film, there are more people, but women are marginalized when they are present at all. Dobbitt's wife, Catherine, is seen kissing him goodbye early in the film, and then is only seen in Dobbitt's nightmares, gleefully having sex with Hanrahan in one instance. The other women in the film are workers and dancers at the party, a nude bowler that Merkin watches as Dobbitt arrives at the compound, and the voice of a virtual secretary espousing the company motto of "people come first." Maybe people matter in the philosophy, but how important is this platitude if it is delivered by a disembodied voice? Merkin is oblivious to a radioactive leak and is often seen in the film hitting golf balls. (He does miss the ball completely at one point, probably muttering to himself, "Human error.") He gets the last shot of the film, driving a golf ball directly at the viewer, and the ball transforms into planet Earth. "Merkin doesn't see what's really going on around him," Young says. Only production quotas matter to the Company, Young says, bringing this theme into clear focus: "That's about as much thought and care that goes into the way our leaders treat our world." Merkin's reaction to the fire earlier in the play is similar: he is concerned with doing something that will show him to be effective. He doesn't care what that something is, but he wants to *appear* to be doing the right thing that will earn him points with the big bosses (whoever they are).

Young's vision of the world coincides with Dresser's vision. Merkin tells Dobbitt not to lie *to* Hanrahan about Hanrahan's wife's decision to join a convent, but to "lie *for* Hanrahan: He'll survive losing his wife, but once the company cuts bait it's a fast drop to the bottom of the ocean."[20] A man is a man because of his work — his self-esteem and his self-worth depend on this work, not on his relationships with people. The same sentiment is echoed later in the film (a scene that is not in the play) when Hanrahan is being re-processed to work for the company. The virtual secretary mouths platitudes: "The thing is we respect people; we don't care about profits." The smoke screen is the platitudes, the ideas we blindly espouse while the reality is a bait-and-switch. Sure, we value our families, and yes, we care about protecting the environment, but making money comes first so that we can care for ourselves and our families.

When asked whether he sees the film as going further than the play, expanding on its themes, or whether he sees it as a separate work of art, Young responded:

> The film is deeply related to the play. After all, it stems from Richard Dresser's writing, but it becomes another kind of creation.... [W]e treat the film, not like a drama, but more like an animated movie.... It is a fairy tale with a moral ... and a made-up fantasy world, but one that contains the insights of what is going on in our real world.

He calls the film a "long journey," and describes himself as "dim-witted" because it's taken him so long to see some things. But he sees his film as "serving" Dresser: "It is very much [Dresser's] work.... [But] he encourages me to be bold, and I feel privileged to be working on this."

The film happened "partly by chance," Young says, referring again to the circumstances which forced (or enabled) the film to be made with computer graphics. But he says, "I've found possibilities and exercised my imagination. I've discovered certain things, taking the story into deeper territory that I never expected, never knew would be there." He cites as an example the scene in which Hanrahan stands on the bridge over the river around the factory, smoking a cigar and enjoying "his" view. We watch as Merkin drives golf balls across the polluted river. The film's Computer Graphics Supervisor, Chris Healer, asked Young if he wanted to put a skeleton in the water, but Young thought that would be too obvious and decided, "I want to put the camera under water." So he did, not literally since the actors had already been filmed on a blue screen, but with the computer graphics. Merkin drives one of the balls into the river and we see the ball dissolve in the water, "like an Alka-Seltzer," to show the audience how polluted the river is. Then, through the bubbles from the golf ball, we see a forklift on the bottom of the river, and we are slowly shown that there is a figure in the forklift — or at least a suit of clothing in it — but when the camera gets to where the face would be, there is no face; the person has apparently dissolved like the golf ball.

When asked if the film brought out any different themes than he envisioned when he wrote the play, Richard Dresser replied,

> The film deals very strongly with the themes of the play. And that doesn't surprise me because Bob was so intrigued by what the play is saying. He didn't want to change what the play is about; he wanted to find a way to make it work in its own way as a film. And to me what is so brilliant about Bob's approach is he has made those three guys so psychologically real that one is pulled into their world and not allowed out.... I was intrigued by the dynamics of the three characters — they are simultaneously competitive but also deeply in need of connection — and that really is what the story is about ... loneliness and isolation and the need to connect. By setting it in "a distant land" and having it deal with manufacturing and the rape of the environment I was clearly giving it a larger arena but the political nature of the piece comes quite directly out of the most intimate moments.

The audience/readers can also envision new elements that neither Dresser nor Young originally intended. A reader may notice connections to *Hamlet* in *Human Error*: Dobbitt's first decisive act is to attack Hanrahan just as Hamlet's first decisive act is to attack Polonius; Hanrahan's wife goes off to join a convent ("Get thee to a nunnery!"); and Merkin echoes Polonius in discussing the fire and what to do about it: "It could turn an accident into an incident. Or an incident into a disaster. Or a disaster into a tragedy."[21] Regarding these observations, Dresser comments:

> You are finding things in the script that I was completely unaware of. The *Hamlet* comparison is interesting but not anything I had in mind. This story came so clearly out of personal experience that I really didn't have any kind of "source" in mind. Which is not to say I wasn't unconsciously influenced by any number of things in structuring the story.... I often hear observations from directors about my work that seem quite apt but I didn't necessarily intend.

The play could be considered as Absurdist, in the tradition of Samuel Beckett, Bertolt Brecht, and Edward Albee, but Dresser says he doesn't see the play that way:

> I was trying to be very true to a particular psychological dynamic and an attitude toward loneliness and alienation. I guess it just doesn't seem absurd to me. Everything in it seems quite real, including the eyes that one can't quite identify and the nature of the work, which is also hard to identify.

Young also sees the play as realistic: "These guys are us and the way they act and react is the way we act and react."

Bob Young's children Zack and Nick Young and their band Artificial Intelligence have supplied music for this film as they have for some of his other films. When he was listening to a CD of a Franz Liszt piece played by his sons' Bulgarian keyboardist, Milen Kirov, Young says, "I saw the beginning of the movie." The opening scene is of a computerized cockroach and the pounding of a machine stamping out the company's logo over and over. On the other side of the machine are some peanuts, and the first cockroach dances through to the other side to the peanuts. Another cockroach is not so fortunate, and Young sees this as "an analogue of what the film is about.... With heroic music of a big symphony orchestra in contrast to a little cockroach; it's just very funny." The music creates "a tension between the music and what you see," and "choreograph[s] some of the feelings" to make them more forceful. Earlier in the film Hanrahan confronts Dobbitt while he is praying, and Dobbitt says that he is praying for his wife's happiness. Hanrahan asks Dobbitt if he would still pray for her happiness if it entailed having her brakes serviced by a burly mechanic who also might service her. This confrontation between Dobbitt and Hanrahan is accompanied by what sounds like a respirator (it is the radiator in the room), creating added tension between the men and adding to the overall paranoia of the piece. Young says that he doesn't want to tell viewers what to think or feel, though he feels this film is not as subtle as others he has done. He says the music is "trumpeting" the message "as it often does in fairy tales or animated films."

Young has also added fantasy segments which reinforce the bizarreness of the play and add a deeper layer of meaning. In one of Dobbitt's daymares, he gets thrown into a vat at the factory and descends down a long tunnel into "his own private hell" where he is chewed up and spit out onto an assembly line, becoming, in Young's words, "many little Dobbitts," caught in the machinations of the Company. A scorpion with Hanrahan's face and a Merkin-snake threaten him while his wife appears angelically above him, cooing siren-like, "Shall I wait up for you, sweetie?" Then Dobbitt descends further into what Young calls "our version of Dante's *Purgatorio*," which echoes the opening scene of the cockroach and the stamping machine.

In an interview, Young described another scene (cut from the final version because it was "too big an interruption") with smokestacks going limp and later ejaculating which conjures Monty Python, especially Terry Gilliam's animation, but while Young says, "I'm affected by everything," he does not feel any special affinity to that troupe. A major influence he did cite in the interview was the original version of *King Kong*. The film "deeply affected" him, and he feels his career parallels the film in some ways: "I guess I've gone off to the jungle on some romantic mission to rescue — to save — the beautiful girl from King Kong. What I have looked for in the bottom of my stories is some kind of myth."

Whether intended in the film or not, the interaction between Dobbitt and Hanrahan is almost that of lovers wooing each other, reminding viewers of E.M. Forster's words, "Only connect." These men (and Merkin) are desperate for interaction, desperate for connections, but because of the sterile, paranoid universe they inhabit, they are unable to find either. Hanrahan "reassures" Dobbitt about Catherine: "My relationship with your wife was no different from the relationship she enjoyed with many young men."[22] Later Dobbitt attacks Hanrahan with a razor because, at this point, Dobbitt has not been invited to the party. Hanrahan parries with a toilet plunger, culminating in Dobbitt straddling Hanrahan in a decidedly sexual position. Dobbitt's single beep from the intercom summons him to the party and the men bond over Dobbitt's forcefulness. Later, they engage in a literal tango (Hanrahan leading), which echoes the earlier fight. Hanrahan twirls, spins, and even dips Dobbitt — until Dobbitt inadvertently reveals that he wrote Jacqueline Hanrahan's letter.

Dresser says there was no "conscious decision to accentuate sexual tension" between Dobbitt and Hanrahan in the film, but he says the film's scenes are "remarkably similar" to the play's scenes:

> I always thought there was a subterranean element of sexual tension, which is probably similar to what occurs in prison in the play.... They are in desperate need of human connection. They give each other presents [Dobbitt gives Hanrahan a scone] ... and they dance and they part over a misunderstanding. The play and the movie have always been, to me, a kind of love story.

Because the play and film are full of social commentary and political satire, Dresser was asked about the name *Merkin*. One might view it as a direct comment on Americans, and in fact, the *Oxford English Dictionary* defines "Merkin" as a slang term for "American." However, Dresser says, "I definitely did not have [this] in mind. It was the first definition ["a pubic wig"] ... which struck me as the perfect name for a boss."

While this movie began before the George W. Bush administration came into power and the play was published in 1996, Young and Dresser both see the film's events mirrored in today's headlines. While Young made the decision to outfit Dobbitt as a cowboy, no direct correlation to George W. Bush was intended: "When I talked with Bobby Knott [the actor who plays Dobbitt] and found out he was from Arkansas and his natural non-actor's voice had a western twang, I thought we should go in that direction."

There are other echoes of the world at large in the film. At the party, after Dobbitt and Hanrahan have retreated to the safety of Merkin's office, Dobbitt leans over the railing and wonders, "Why don't they like us?" Dobbitt claims earlier that "People have always liked me," and he is constantly trying to make people happy, even praying for his wife's happiness (though Hanrahan exposes the hypocrisy of this prayer). All of these ideas echo the cries of many Americans after 9/11: "Why do they hate us?"

Dresser says though it was Bob's decision to make Dobbitt a cowboy,

> I loved the idea; it's so American and conjures such images of American optimism and a can-do attitude that of course runs right into a buzz-saw when Dobbitt arrives at the compound. At this point, for me, when I see Dobbitt it's hard not to think of President Bush with his truly insane optimism in a self-styled cowboy package. I think that the movie is ever more relevant now with American imperialism [both military and corporate] rampant and Americans scattered around the globe discovering what it's like to be isolated from and hated by the rest of the world. And hungering for some kind of connection that makes them feel their lives have meaning and they are not the monsters the rest of the world makes them out to be. Which of course is the story of Dobbitt, Hanrahan, and Merkin.

Young denounces those "idiots" in charge (he specifically mentions Vice President Dick Cheney and secretary of defense Donald Rumsfeld along with President Bush), as having "as much involvement, interest, and concern about what they are doing with our fate, with the world," as Merkin has in driving his golf ball. Young feels we need to make a "deeper commitment to the future, the planet, to our children," and he is dismayed by the lack of "foresight of consequences."

The headlines are full of Merkins, Dobbitts and Hanrahans acting out their roles on the world scene, either in Iraq, for Halliburton, in Guantánamo or Abu Ghraib. Their indifference to and lack of curiosity about the world around them and their resistance to accept any consequences for their actions is played out by the current U.S. administration. We should not be surprised to hear them attribute the problems American soldiers are encountering and causing in Iraq as "human error." And then they'll go play golf.

Notes

1. Dresser, Richard. *Below the Belt.* In *A Decade of New Comedy: Plays from the Humana Festival*, Volume Two (Portsmouth, New Hampshire: Heinemann, 1996), 157.
2. Dresser, 159.
3. Dresser, 167.
4. Dresser, 183–4.
5. Dresser, 184.

6. Dresser, 185.
7. Dresser, 186.
8. Dresser, 187.
9. Dresser, 188.
10. Dresser, 189.
11. Dresser, 203.
12. Dresser, 198.
13. Dresser, Richard. Interviews conducted by e-mail 13 October, 18 November, 8 December 2003, and 12 May 2004. Subsequent remarks about and by Dresser.
14. Dresser, *Below the Belt*, 161.
15. Young, Bob. Interviews conducted by e-mail 7 October, 8 October, 8 December 2003, 11 May 2004, and by phone 13 October and 14 December 2003. Subsequent references to Young are from the interviews on these dates.
16. Dresser, 155.
17. Dresser, 155.
18. Dresser, 164.
19. Dresser, 191.
20. Dresser, 186.
21. Dresser, 170.

Appendix A: Filmography

Director

1952	*It Takes Everybody to Build This Land*	documentary
1955	*Wonders of the Sea*	documentary
1956	*Secrets of the Reef*	documentary
1958	*Life of the Molds*	documentary
1958	*India* (The *High Adventure* Series)	documentary
1959	*Danger Island* (The *High Adventure* Series)	documentary
1959	*Horizons of Science*—"The Life and Behavior of Microscopic One-Celled Animals"	documentary
1959	*The Living End*	documentary
1960	*Sit-In*	documentary
1961	*Angola: Journey to a War*	documentary
1962	*Trauma* (as Robert Malcolm Young)	feature
1962	*Anatomy of a Hospital*	documentary
1962	*Cortile Cascino*	documentary
1963	*Dialogue: The Influence of Martin Buber in Israel*	documentary
1964	*Nothing But a Man* (with Michael Roemer)	feature
1966	*In the World of Sharks* (with Peter Gimbel)	documentary
1970	*The Eskimo: Fight for Life*	documentary
1971	*The Maze*	documentary
1971	*J.T.* (CBS "Children's Hour")	TV special
1972	*Man of the Serengeti*	documentary
1973	*Navajo Girl*	documentary
1974	*Bushmen of the Kalahari*	documentary
1975	*The Great Apes*	documentary

1976	Soldier's Home (The American Short Story)	TV episode
1978	¡Alambrista!	TV special
1978	Snowbound (NBC Daytime Special)	feature
1979	Short Eyes	feature
1980	Rich Kids	feature
1981	One Trick Pony	feature
1982	The Ballad of Gregorio Cortez	feature
1984	Saving Grace	feature
1986	Extremities	feature
1987	We Are the Children (ABC Movie of the Week)	TV movie
1988	Dominick and Eugene	feature
1989	The Plot Against Harry (with Michael Roemer)	feature
1991	Talent for the Game	feature
1992	Children of Fate (with Andrew Young and Susan Todd)	documentary
1993	Splitting Heirs	feature
1995	Roosters	feature
1995	Solomon and Sheba (Showtime)	TV movie
1996	Caught	feature
1996	Slaves of Dreams (Showtime)	TV movie
2001	China: The Panda Adventure	feature
2004	Human Error	feature

Writer (as Robert Malcolm Young or Robert M. Young)

Specific episodes are listed when credit as a writer is not distributed among the writers working on the production

1963	The Crawling Hand	feature
1965	The F.B.I.	TV series
1966	Mission Impossible— "The Amnesiac"	TV series
1968	It Takes a Thief	TV series
1969	Then Came Bronson	TV series
1970	(Rod Serling's) Night Gallery— "The Ring with the Red Velvet Ropes"	TV series
1971	Cannon	TV series

1971	*Longstreet*	TV series
1973	*Barnaby Jones*	TV series
1973	*Kojak*	TV series
1974	*Harry O*	TV series
1975	*Escape to Witch Mountain*	TV special
1976	*To Fly!* (National Air and Space Museum)	documentary
1977	*Columbo*—"The Bye-Bye, Sky-High I. Q. Murder Case"	TV series
1977	*Force of Evil* (or "Tales of the Unexpected")	TV series
1978	*The Ghost of Flight 401*	TV special
1979	*Women in White*	TV mini-series
1979	*Diary of a Teenage Hitchhiker*	TV special
1979	*Trapper John*	TV series
1983	*Starflight: The Plane That Couldn't Land*	TV special
1983	*(Agatha Christie's) Sparkling Cyanide*	TV special
1984	*Crazy Like a Fox*	TV series
1995	*Escape to Witch Mountain*	TV special

Appendix B: Chronology

1924   Robert Milton Young born in New York City, November 22

1939   Graduates from high school; is accepted at Massachusetts Institute of Technology

1940   Adolph Zucker, president of Paramont Pictures, hires Young to film his Nanuet, N.Y,. estate for $75

1941   Enrolls at M.I.T. with a major in chemical engineering

1943   Drops out of M.I.T.; joins the Navy and serves two years as a combat photographer in New Guinea and the Philippines

1946   Enrolls at Harvard majoring in English literature; co-founder of Harvard Film Society

1949   B.A. Harvard University; completes *A Touch of Time*, a silent comedy about Boston factory worker, with Harvard classmates

1949   Establishes filmmakers cooperative to make documentaries with Lloyd Ritter and Murray Lerner; paints DuArt facilities for weekly wage

1951   Hired by Marineland in St. Augustine, Florida, to make underwater shorts; films *Castles in the Sea* in Marineland tank

1952   *It Takes Everybody to Build This Land*, made for Encyclopaedia Britannica Films, wins Scholastic Teacher Award

1953   Secretary, Board of Directors, DuArt Film Laboratories (until 1973)

1955   Writer/director/cameraman on *Wonders of the Sea*

Appendix B: Chronology

1956 Writer/director/cameraman/editor on *Secrets of the Reef*, named "Choice Film" by *Time Magazine*

1958 Associate director/writer/cameraman on *Danger Island*, C.B.S. Special *High Adventure with Lowell Thomas; Life of the Molds* named one of 10 Best Documentary Films of 1958 in the *New York Times* annual review

1960 Hired by N.B.C. to film four episodes of *White Paper* series; *Sit-In* wins Peabody Award; wins George Polk Award for Heroism

1961 *Angola: Journey to a War* wins George Polk Award; Overseas Press Club Award for Best Foreign Reporting

1962 *Cortile Cascino* withdrawn prior to presentation by N.B.C.

1964 Completes *Nothing But a Man* with Michael Roemer

1968 Accepted by Lee Strasberg's Actor's Studio as actor; director, graduate seminar, Yale School of Drama (and 1970)

1969 Producer/cameraman for Michael Roemer's *The Plot Against Harry*, which is not released for distribution

1970 Director/Cameraman on *Eskimo: Fight for Life* for C.B.S. Special; Emmy—"Outstanding Achievement in Documentary Filmmaking"; American Film Festival, Blue Ribbon; CINE Golden Eagle; Four Christopher Awards; joins Directors Guild of America

1971 Director/writer/cameraman/producer on *The Maze* for Houghton-Mifflin Publishers; misplaced after initial release; recovered in 2002. Directs *J.T.*, C.B.S. Drama Special, Peabody Award.

1972 Accepted at Actors Studio, Directors Unit; "Andy" Award for Best Thirty-Second Commerical, for Volvo

1973 Four Travels in Galapagos Islands; shoots footage for film about Baba Ram Das in Central Park, N.Y.C.; footage held by Ram Das followers for two years, then disappears

1975 John Simon Guggenheim Foundation Fellow for Filmmaking; writes screenplay for *¡Alambrista!*

1976 Given $200,000 from "Visions Project" of KCET-TV in Los Angeles to shoot script of *¡Alambrista!*

1978 *¡Alambrista!* wins Camera d'Or at Cannes, Best First Feature Film; wins Golden Shell at San Sebastian, Best Feature Film

1979 Takes over and completes production of *Short Eyes*

1981 *Cortile Cascino* screened at the Museum of Modern Art in N.Y.C.

1983 *The Ballad of Gregorio Cortez* first film to gain major distribution after premiere at Sundance Festival

1985 Begins production of Obie-Award Play *Extremities* by William Mastrosimone, starring Farrah Fawcett-Majors and James Russo

1988 Films *Triumph of the Spirit* in Auschwitz

1989 *The Plot Against Harry* opens at New York and Toronto Film Festivals

1992 Produces *American Me* for Edward James Olmos; executive producer of *Children of Fate: Life and Death in a Sicilian Family,* which wins Grand Jury Prize and Cinematography Award at the Sundance Festival

1993 Honored at the Harold Lloyd Master Seminar: The American Film Institute; transcript published by the Center for Advanced Film and Television Studies, Los Angeles (September 9, 1993), 1–27, as a part of the Louis B. Mayer Library Special Collection

1994 Films biblical epics (*Solomon and Sheba; Slave of Dreams*) for Showtime in Morocco; *Nothing but a Man* selected for National Register of Films; cashes out IRA account from DGA Pension to raise money for production of *Caught*

1995 Takes over and completes production of *Roosters*

1996 Edward James Olmos wins Best Actor in Feature Film award from National Council of La Raza for *Caught*

2001 Travels to China to make IMAX film about pandas

2003 Collaborates with Rick Dresser on film adaptation of Dresser's play *Below the Belt*

2004 *Human Error* opens at Sundance Film Festival in Frontier section; travels to Canada to film an episode of *Battlestar Galactica*

The Contributors

Edwin T. Arnold, professor of English at Appalachian State University, is co-editor of *Perspectives on Cormac McCarthy* and *A Cormac McCarthy Companion: The Border Trilogy*; the author of several books about William Faulkner and (with Eugene Miller) a critical study of the films of Robert Aldrich and a book of interviews with Aldrich.

Melissa E. Barth, a clinical mental health counselor and professor of English at Appalachian State University, coordinates the English department's professional writing program, having previously served as the coordinator of Appalachian State's women's studies program, the director of its Office of Women's Concerns, and the founding director of its Equity Office, where she worked with faculty, staff and students who had concerns about discrimination isssues. Professor Barth has co-edited *Reading for Difference: Texts on Gender, Race and Class*, as well as several textbooks. When not otherwise engaged in tilting at windmills, Professor Barth enjoys watching the deer in her yard and tending to her cockatoo, cockatiel, two dogs, three cats, a tank of fish, and a flock of 26 laying hens.

Dennis Bohr teaches composition and literature at Appalachian State University and is co-founder of Black Sheep Theatre, a theatre troupe dedicated to performing their own original works. He has written fourteen plays, including *Pope Joan: The Hiss of the Snake; Burn in Hell*, and his one-man show *The English Whore*. With Black Sheep he has performed his work in Northern Ireland, London, North Carolina, and Kentucky.

Zohara Boyd, a Holocaust survivor from Poland, teaches early American literature at Appalachian State University.

Cecelia Conway, professor of English at Appalachian State University, teaches twentieth century American literature (including cultural perspectives, folklore, and film). Author of *African Banjo Echoes in Appalachia* and co-maker of award-winning films, including *Dink: A Pre-Blues Musician* and *Sprout Wings and Fly: A Portrait of Fiddler Tommy Jarrell* (with Les Blank, Alice Gerrard, and Maureen Gosling), she is currently working on the video *Robert Morgan's Lucid Poetry and Prose*.

John Crutchfield is a poet, playwright, performer, and founding member of Blue Shift Theatre Ensemble. He also teaches English and creative writing at Appalachian State University and is editor of *The Cold Mountain Review*.

Bruce Dick is a professor of English at Appalachian State University. His publications include *A Critical Response to Ishmael Reed* and *A Poet's Truth: Conversations with Contemporary Latino and Latina Poets*.

Craig Fischer, associate professor of English at Appalachian State University, is a past member of the Executive Committee of the Society for Cinema Studies and previous assistant editor of *Cinema Journal*. His articles have appeared in *The Velvet Light Trap, Spectator, The National Women's Studies Association Journal, The International Journal of Comic Art, The Comics Journal*, and the anthology *Enfant Terrible: Jerry Lewis in American Film*.

Rosemary Horowitz, associate professor of English at Appalachian State University, is interested in Jewish literature and literacy and has written extensively about Jewish memory. She is currently working on a book entitled *The Storytelling Genius of Elie Wiesel*.

Leon Lewis is a professor of English at Appalachian State University, where he directed the film program from 1975 to 2000. He is the author of *Henry Miller: The Major Writings*; *Eccentric Individuality in William Kotzwinkle's The Fan Man, E.T., Doctor Rat and Other Works of Fiction and Fantasy*, and (with Bill Sherman) *The Landscape of Contemporary Cinema*.

Holly E. Martin teaches ethnic American literature in the English department at Appalachian State University. She received her Ph.D. in Comparative Literature at Emory University in 2002, where she focused on ethnic American literature, including works in languages other than English.

Thomas McLaughlin teaches literature, cultural studies, and writing at Appalachian State University. He is the author or editor of *Literature: The Power of Language, Critical Texts for Literary Studies* (with Frank Lentricchia), *Reading for Difference: Texts on Gender, Race and Class* (with Melissa Barth and James Winders) and *Street Smarts and Critical Theory: Listening to the*

Vernacular. He has just completed a book on basketball as a cultural practice.

Eugene L. Miller has taught at Appalachian State University for 26 years, including five years during which he served as assistant dean of the College of Arts and Sciences. Miller has co-authored (with colleague Edwin T. Arnold) two books on American film director Robert Aldrich. His most recent research involves films, fiction and war correspondence about World War II. Miller teaches undergraduate classes in English, American and World literature and graduate classes in twentieth century British literature; he also teaches in the departmental honors program. Miller was the recipient of the UNC Board of Governor's Award for Outstanding Teaching in 2005.

Alexander H. Pitofsky, assistant professor of English at Appalachian State University, is the author of essays on the novel and eighteenth century literature, history and law in *Studies in Eighteenth-Century Culture, Eighteenth-Century Life, Twentieth-Century Literature, Postmodern Culture, English Language Notes* and other publications.

Roger James Stilling, a professor at Appalachian State University, is a Renaissance scholar, a specialist in the study of speculative fiction, and the author of *Love and Death in Renaissance Tragedy.*

Mark Vogel, a professor of English and director of the English education program at Appalachian State University. Before becoming a teacher educator, he taught at the middle and high school and community college levels. Vogel writes most often on trends in young adult literature, contemporary American literature, and writing theory and practice.

Index

Page numbers in ***bold italics*** indicate photographs

ABC Network 44, 45, 46
Absurdist 234
Abu Ghraib 237
Academy Award *see* Award
acting 12, 21, 33, 37, 85, 88, 90, 141, 164, 200, 201, 221, 237
actor 1, 3, 12, 13, 24, 25, 31, 33, 35, 37, 39, 69, 88, 91, 92, 93, 94, 95, 100, 101, 103, 104, 105, 110, 122, 129, 131, 132, 141, 163, 164, 200, 201, 206, 208, 220, 225, 229, 231, 233, 236
The Actors Studio 13
Adam 139
Adler, Stella 13
Admiralty Islands 10
Africa 17, 18; *see also* South Africa
African-American 5, 47, 59, 60, 72, 82, 112, 120, 121, 132
Alabama 58, 60; Birmingham 58, 61, 65, 70
alambrista 74, 75, 76, 77, 78, 79, 81, 82, 83, 84, 85, 86
¡Alambrista! The Illegal (1977) 5, 12, 24, 25, 30, 32, 34, 74–86, 87, 113, 114, 116, 121, 123; characters: Alberto Ramirez 80, 82, 83, 84; Berto 78, 79, 82, 84; Grace Ramirez 84; Joe (José) 78, 79, 82, 84, 85; Roberto Ramirez 75, 76, 78–86; Sharon 79, 80, 84
Albee, Edward 234
Aldrich, Robert 4
Alexander the Great 168
Alger, Horatio 154
Alka-Seltzer 233

Allen, Robert C. 53
Allies 162
Alonso, Maria Conchita 31, 192, ***207***, 208, 213, 216
Alpert, Richard (Baba Ram Dass) 27
Altman, Robert 5
Alvarado, Tony 32
Alvarez, Lily 85
Amalek 171
Ambriz, Domingo 75
America 12, 18, 45, 56, 70, 71, 72, 74, 75, 76, 77, 78, 79, 80, 81, 82, 84, 85, 86, 113, 121, 124, 130, 131, 149, 157, 180, 194, 200, 236, 237; culture 44; dream 186; imperialism 237; public 59; South 59; Southwest 5; *Zeitgeist* 44
American Film Institute: Harold Lloyd Master Seminar 74, 78
American Geographical Society 17
American Me 38
Americas 195
Anatomy of a Hospital (1961) 47
angel 195, 199, 208
Angels *see* California
Anglo 78, 80, 83, 84, 115, 117, 118, 119, 120, 121, 122, 123, 124, 126, 127, 128, 129, 130, 131, 201
Anglo-American 78, 83
Anglo-Texan 115, 130
Angola 17, 18, 19, 47, 71; Luanda 17
Angola: Journey to a War (1961) 17, 47, 51, 71
"Angry Young Man" movies 45
animation 224, 225, 233, 235

250 Index

Annapolis 10
Anthrax (music group) 157
Apollo Guide 166
Appalachian State University 4, 5, 112; Equity Office 5
Apted, Michael 55
Arama, Shimon 162
Arctic 32, 113
Arizona 74, 83, 85, 202; Phoenix 74, 83; Tucson 200, 203
Arkansas 236
Arkin, Alan 225
Army (intelligence) 17
Arnold, Edwin 4, 5, 43, 46, 186, 189, 190, 245; conducted interview 9–42
Arouch, Avram 164, 172, 173
Arrouch, Poppa 164, 173, 174
Arrouch, Salamo 161, 162, 163, 164, 165, 166, 168, 169, 171, 172, 173, 174, 175, 176; "The Ballerina" 161
art 21, 41, 88, 92, 93, 99, 103, 104, 109, 110, 130, 136, 137, 161, 171, 185, 189, 220, 229, 233
Artificial Intelligence (band) 235
artist 27, 30, 93, 136, 137, 190, 224, 225, 231
artistic 12, 30, 40, 93, 101, 102, 111, 115, 116, 128, 137, 176, 189
Aryans 170
Atlantic City 155
Atlantic Pictures 33
Atropine 146
audience 13, 20, 29, 36, 37, 44, 45, 54, 65, 77, 78, 88, 91, 93, 94, 95, 96, 101, 102, 104, 105, 109, 111, 115, 116, 119, 130, 137, 139, 150, 152, 155, 156, 158, 159, 162, 163, 165, 166, 167, 171, 176, 184, 188, 189, 190, 200, 206, 208, 210, 212, 214, 215, 217, 219, 220, 227, 230, 231, 233, 234; viewer 14, 29, 45, 48, 52, 53, 69, 72, 78, 86, 115, 117, 118, 119, 123, 124, 125, 129, 130, 152, 166, 167, 173, 181, 182, 185, 187, 188, 191, 194, 200, 204, 225, 226, 230, 232, 235, 236
Auschwitz 161, 163, 164, 165, 166, 167, 168, 169, 172, 173, 174, 175, 176; Birkenau 163, 164, 171; Cell block 11, 163
Austin *see* Texas
Austria 170
Avisar, Ilan 172

Award: Academy 55; Camera d'Or 114; Cinematography Award and Grand Jury Prize 55; Emmy 28, 113; George Polk 17, 59; New York Drama Critics Circle 90; Obie 90; Overseas Press Club 17; Peabody 28; Tony 122
Aztec *see* Indian, American

the Babe 188
Babylonian 168
Bachicha, Virginia 85
Bahamas 15
Balickci, Asen 29
Balkans 161, 168; "the Jerusalem of the Balkans" 168
ballad 76, 79, 80, 81, 101, 114, 115, 116, 120, 121, 127, 128, 129, 131; *see also* hero
The Ballad of Gregorio Cortez 5, 112–132, **114**, **125**; characters: Cortez *see* Cortez; Sheriff Fly 122, 123, 124, 125, 128, 129
Ballard, Carroll 32
Baltake, Joe 194
Barnouw, Erik 45, 46
Barrow, Mike 31, 35–6
Barsam, Richard Meran 116
Barth, Melissa E. 5, 74, 245
baseball 180–183, 185–190
Beatty, Ned 83
Becker, Hartmut 163, 164
Beckett, Samuel 234
Begelman, David 77
Below the Belt (2004) 5, 36, 37, 219, 220–223, 224–238; characters: Catherine 222; checkers: Dobbitt 36, 219, 220, 221, 222, 223, 225, 226, 228, 229, 232; Hanrahan 36, 219, 220, 221, 222, 223, 225, 226, 227, 228, 229, 232; Jacqueline Hanrahan 222; Merkin 219, 221, 222, 223, 225, 226, 228, 230, 232; regional director 221, 230; see also *Human Error*
Benchley, Peter 26
Benjamin, Walter 99
Berkely, Xander 227, 231
Berlin *see* Germany
Berlin: The Symphony of a Great City 116
Berrones, Paul 78
Bialy-Wieczorek, Dorota 163
Biltmore House 185
Binding, Karl 170

Index

"Bird of Paradise" (adventure story) 37, 38
Birmingham *see* Alabama
The Black Stallion 32
Blackfoot *see* Indian, American
Blacks in American Film and Television (1988) 72
the Blasters 157
Blechman, Corey 149
blue-collar *see* class
Boddy, William 43
Bogle, Donald 72
Bohr, Dennis 5, 219, 245
Bomba the Jungle Boy 11
Bordwell, David 53
Boston *see* Massachusetts
Bourbon Street Beat (1959–1960) 44
Bourdieu, Pierre 209, 210
Bower, Tom 119, 130, 183
boxing 159, 161, 163, 164, 169, 171, 173, 175, 176
Boyd, Zohara 5, 161, 245
Bracco, Lorraine 181, **183**, 188
Braga, Sonia 192
Brando, Marlon 122, 138; Stanley Kowalsky (character) 122
Brantz, Rennie 5
Breaking Away (1979) 157
Brecht, Bertolt 234
Britain's Channel 4 54
British 116
Broadway 91, 92 (*see also* Off Broadway)
Broeske, Pat H. 163, 164, 165, 171
Brooks, Albert 188
Bulgarian 235
Bull Durham 185, 190
Bus Boys 157
Bush, George W. 236, 237
Bushmen of the Kalahari (1974) 28
Butterfield, Al 14

C.I.A. 17, 18, 19
Cagney & Lacey (1982–88) 157
California 15, 76, 149, 150, 158; Angels (A's) 180, 181, 182, 184, 185, 186, 187; Los Angeles (L.A.) 122, 130, 181, 184
camera 3, 13, 14, 15, 16, 21, 24, 26, 29, 30, 31, 32, 33, 48, 49, 51, 55, 78, 79, 80, 81, 85, 100, 104, 111, **114**, 117, 118, 123, 129, 138, 139, 147, 180, 182, 204, 209, 210, 213, 217, 227, 233; thirty-five-millimeter 46
cameraman 15, 17, 24, 26, 30, 31, 35, 47

Camillo, Marvin Felix 88, 91
Cannes *see* Film festivals
Carlyle, Thomas 13
Carnegie Hall 13
Carroll, Janet 184
Catholicism 27, 50, 201
Caught (1996) 1, 5, 27, 31, 35, **39**, 40, 113, 123, 158, 206–218, **207**; characters: Betty 206, 207, **207**, 208, 209, 210, 211, 212, 213, 214, 215, 216, 217; Danny 208, 209, 210, 211, 213, 214, 215, 217; Joe 40, 206, 207, **207**, 208, 209, 210, 211, 212, 213, 214, 215, 216, 217; Nick 206, 207, **207**, 208, 209, 210, 211, 213, 214, 215, 216, 217
CBS Network 28, 44, 45, 46; "Golden Shop" 46; *Woman!* 46
CBS Reports 46, 51; "Harvest of Shame" (1960) 51
censorship 51
Central Juvenile Hall 122
Chang (1927) 15
Channel 4 Film 167
character 20, 36, 38, 51, 52, 53, 54, 59, 63, 72, 79, 89, 90, 91, 92, 93, 94, 95, 96, 97, 98, 99, 100, 101, 103, 104, 105, 109, 110, 111, 114, 117, 121, 120, 122, 123, 124, 129, 141, 145, 149, 150, 152, 156, 157, 158, 159, 160, 163, 167, 169, 171, 175, 186, 188, 189, 191, 192, 195, 197, 198, 206, 208, 209, 210, 212, 213, 215, 216, 217, 219, 224, 225, 226, 227, 231, 232, 234
Charlie's Angels 140
Chávez, Cesar 39–40, 76, 77, 83
Chavez, Maria Guadalupe 79
Cheers (1982–93) 157
Cheney, Dick (vice president) 237
Cheyenne (1955–63) 44
Chicago Sun-Times 166
Chicano 74, 83, 85, 121, 127, 128, 205
Chicano American 78
Children of Fate: Life and Death in a Sicilian Family (1991) 35, 55
Children of the Sea 15
China 29
China: The Panda Adventure (2002) 29
choreography 181, 235
Christ 152
Christian 167, 168, 195; Democratic Party (in Sicily) 19; Democrats 19; iconography 138

Christian Spotlight on the Movies 167
cinema 100, 104, 116, 135, 146, 171
cinéma vérité 43, 45, 46, 48, 49, 51
cinematographer *2*, 11, 200
Cinerama Holiday (1955) 47
Ciudad Juárez *see* Mexico
civil rights 47, 59, 71, 112; movement 66, 71
civilization 137, 139, 143
Clark, Curtis *2*
Clarkson, Phil 24
class: blue-collar 79, 149, 156, 157, 159, 160; elite 75; middle 61, 87, 89, 200; underclass 75; white 78; white-collar 154; working 61, 149, 156, 157, 158, 159, 160; *see also* social
CloseUp 46
Coal Miner's Daughter (1980) 157
Cobb, Lee 122; Willy Loman (character) 122
Coburn, Arthur *2*, 162, 163
Cold War *see* War
Colorado 81, 82, 83, 220
Columbia *see* South Carolina
Columbia (University) 27
Combating the Gypsy Nuisance 170
comedy *see* genre
Communist 19, 45, 51; Russian Communist Party 19
community 4, 60, 61, 63, 64, 65, 67, 69, 71, 72, 116, 121, 130, 149, 152, 161, 168, 169, 178, 184, 192, 194, 195, 205
concentration camp 161, 163, 164, 165, 170, 172, 174; Auschwitz *see* Auschwitz; Dachau 170; Dieselstrasse 170; Sachsenhausen 170
Congo 17, 18
Conquistadors *see* Spain
Conrad, Joseph 9
Conway, Cecelia 5, 112, 245
Cooper, Merian C. 15, 37
Corbett, Jeff 183, *187*, 188
Corliss, Richard 135
corrido 114, 115, 120, 121, 127, 128, 130, 131
Cortés, Hernán 196, 197
Cortez, Gregorio 113, 115–131; see also *Ballad of Gregorio Cortez*
Cortile Cascino (1962) 3, 5, 19, 27, 35, 43, 48–57, 59; characters: Adriana 48, 49, 50, 51, 53, 54, 55; Angela 20, 21, 48, 49, 50, 51, 52, 54, 55; Beatrice 48; Finnucia 54; Gildo 49; Luigi 49, 50, 54, 55; Salvatore 49; Santina 49, 50, 51; *see also* Sicily
costumes 24, 214, 226
cowboy 118, 119, 121, 123, 236, 237; boots 193; hat 227
coyote (middleman) 75, 76, 82, 83
Cracknell, Ryan 166, 167
Cripps, Thomas 71–2
Crist, Judith 71
criticism 30, 43, 44, 45, 52, 53, 55, 56, 115, 116, 119, 121, 127, 129, 165, 166, 167, 192, 194
Crutchfield, John 5, 87, 246
culture 3, 18, 28, 45, 56, 77, 84, 102, 109, 114, 115, 116, 117, 119, 120, 121, 122, 128, 132, 135, 137, 148, 171, 194, 196, 212, 215; alien 222; American 44; Anglo 115, 118, 128; Asian 64; Aztec 202; border 118, 121, 128; cattle 116, 117, 118, 121, 125, 126, 128; conflict 116, 118; contemporary 5; cowboy 121; Greco-Jewish 168; horse 120; Indian 121; Latino 122; Mexican 115, 121, 128, 192, 195, 197; Mexican-American 192, 194, 195, 197; multi 113; patriarchal 209; politics 212; popular 5, 45, 137, 148, 149, 156, 157, 179; postfeminist 148; South Side's 152; Southern 66; study 5, 121, 140; working-class 157; *see also* class
Curtin, Michael 45, 51
Curtis, Jamie Lee 153, ***153***

Dafoe, Willem 163, 164, 165, 166, 167, 168, 224–225
Dallas *see* Texas
dance 101, 110, 111, 164, 182, 185, 191, 202, 211, 213, 225, 226, 232, 235, 236
Dances with Wolves 121
Danger Island (1959) 16
Dann, Mike 28
Dante 184, 235; *Inferno* 184; *Purgatorio* 235
The Dating Game 105
David 22
Davison, Bruce 105
Dawn 25
Day of the Dead (All Souls Day) 201, 202
Death 38, 133, 137, 138, 140, 141, 145, 146

death 16, 41, 49, 50, 51, 52, 53, 54, 55, 80, 96, 106, 119, 124, 130, 137, 138, 139, 143, 145, 146, 147, 150, 151, 155, 163, 172, 173, 174, 175, 192, 198, 200, 202, 203, 208, 211, 212, 217
Death Camp to Existentialism 112
death camps 169, 170, 171, 172
de Gomez, Rafaela Cervantes 79
del Castillo, Bernal Diaz 196
Del Lords 157
de Rochemont, Louis 47
Derrida 129
designer 24, 91, 92
DeSota, Rosana 119
de Tocqueville 12
Detroit 65
deus ex machina 185
Deuteronomy 171
Dial 126
dialogue 23, 37, 78, 93, 96, 98, 100, 101, 105, 107, 111, 129, 204, 219, 220, 224
Dick, Bruce 5, 58, 73, 246
Diego, Juan 195
direction 2, 4, 15, 24, 25, 26, 30, 32, 33, 39, 47, 55, 87, 88, 105, 111, 112, 113, 149, 150, 162, 164, 165, 182, 189, 200, 229, 231; stage 89, 94, 98, 104, 221, 228, 230
director 2, 4, 6, 11, 13, 23, 25, 33, 34, 35, *38*, 47, 59, 74, 87, 91, 92, 93, 99, 101, 133, 135, 138, 158, 164, 165, 166, 168, 176, 189, 200, 203, 219, 228, 229, 231, 234; art 24; journeyman 34; special effects 163
Directors Guild 2, 3
Dixon, Ivan 24, 58, *64*
documentary 1, 3, 5, 13, 14, 15, 16, 17, 19, 20, 21, 24, 26, 28, 29, 30, 43, 44, 45, 46, 47, 48, 49, 50, 51, 53, 55, 56, 59, 72, 74, 77, 83, 87, 88, 100, 101, 103, 113, 114, 117, 130, 131, 132, 135, 164, 165, 168; *see also* television
Doerfer, John 44
Dominican Republic 44
Dominick and Eugene (1988) 2, *2*, 5, *6*, 149–160, *151*, 162; characters: Chernak (Mike's father) 159; Dominick ("Nicky") 149, 150, 151, *151*, 152, 153, 154, 155, 156, 157, 158, 159; Eugene Luciano (Geno) 149, 150, *151*, 152, 153, *153*, 154, 155, 156, 157, 158, 159;

Father T 156; Frankie (the Squirrel) 153, 159; Guido 152, 153, 154, 156, 159; Jennifer Reston 153, *153*, 154, 155, 157, 158; Larry Higgins 152, 155, 156, 157, 158, 159; Luciano 150, 158; Mike Chernak 150, 151, 152, 155, 156, 158, 159; Mr. Johnson 155, 156; Mrs. Gianelli 158; Mrs. Vinson 155, 158; Sal 153; Theresa Chernak 158
Don Juan 192
Donnelly, Thomas Michael 189
Dorkins, Charles 17, 47
drama 21, 52, 60, 72, 88, 91, 92, 94, 96, 98, 103, 104, 105, 106, 110, 113, 117, 118, 129, 135, 136, 137, 141, 159, 160, 168, 180, 187, 189, 217, 228, 233; melodrama 100, 101, 150, 166, 167, 208; prison 32; race 47
dramaturgical 87, 91, 92, 93, 104
Dresser, Richard (Rick) 5, 36–7, 219, 220, 223, 224, 225, 226, 227, 228, 229, 230, 231, 232, 233, 234, 236, 237
Drew, Robert 45–46
DuArt Film Laboratories 2, 9, 23
Duke University 112
Durham *see* North Carolina
DVD Talk 167

Earle, Steve 156, 157; "Guitar Town" 156
Earth 138, 227, 232
Ebert, Roger 149, 166
economic 3, 62, 66, 67, 69, 71, 75, 76, 77, 208, 209
The Ed Sullivan Show 46
Eden 139, 140
editing 1, 3, 2, *2*, 9, 10, 11, 14, 37, 45, 47, 48, 52, 104, 113, 186, 189, 231
education 61, 124, 135, 149, 152; *see also* film
Edward, Jonathan 10
Egypt 168, 169, 171; King Ptolemy 168
Ehrenstein, David 119, 124
Ehrlich, Joel 225
Eidelman, Cliff 165, 166, 167
eighties (1980s) 54, 156, 157
Eisenstein 11, 131
El Carmen 115
El Dorado 42
El Pachuco 122, 127
El Paso *see* Texas

Elfand, Marty 189, 190
Ellis, John 52
Embassy Picture 130
Emmy *see* Award
English 11, 18, 45, 47, 48, 78, 79, 84, 115, 119, 124, 126, 178, 224
Eros 137, 138, 146
erotic 40, 110, 123, 206, 207, 209, 211, 212, 213, 214, 217; autoerotic 213, 215
Eskimo 27, 29, 32; film 28, 29, 32; Netsilik 113
The Eskimo: Fight for Life (1970) 27, 113
essays 4, 5, 13, 144, 145, 148, 172, 205
ethics 43, 105, 107, 109, 139, 155, 187, 209, 210
ethnic 113, 118, 121, 168, 226; studies 170, 171; literature 5
Europe 115, 168, 169, 170, 176, 194, 229; Eastern 161; Western 45, 168
Eve 139
Extremities (1986) 6, 33, 133–148, **141**, **144**; characters: Joe 133, 134, 137, 138, 139, 140, 141, **141**, 142, 143, 145–147; Marjorie Easton 133, 134, 136–147, **144**; Patricia, 133, 134, 136, 139, 142, 143, **144**, 144, 146, 147; Terry 133, 134, 136, 139, 142, 143, 144, 145, 146, 147
Exxon 26

"The Family" 88, 90
fantasy 235
Farrell, Mike **2**
fascism 12
Fates 145, 146; the Spinners 146; Three Fates: Atropos 145, 146, 147; Clotho 145, 146; Lachesis 145, 146
Faust 92
Fawcett, Farrah 34, 133, 135, 139, 140, 141, **144**
FCC 44
"Female Archetypes in Mexican Literature" 195
femininity 209
feminist 5, 109, 147, 148
Fender, Freddy 101, 102
Ferguson, Larry 189
Field of Dreams 190
fifties (1950s) 16, 43, 44, 45
Filipino 193
film: baseball 189; educational 47, 48; feature 1, 25, 30, 32, 47, 48, 101, 129, 160, 166; fiction 75, 77, 113; Holocaust 161; independent 12, 47, 114, 131, 134, 168; noir 208; nonfiction 131, 132; science fiction 180; studio 34; western 123
film festivals 4; Cannes 114; New York 220; Sundance 1, 2, 55, 220, 223; USA 220; Vail 220
film society 14
filmmaker 2, 4, 6, 7, 10, 11, 12, 16, 26, 29, 30, 40, 46, 47, 48, 53, 59, 60, 71, 72, 73, 77, 113, 114, 116, 130, 131, 134, 137, 159, 160, 166, 168, 169, 190, 208, 217; documentary 3, 5, 87; independent 1, 131, 132, 134
Filmtracks 168
Fischer, Craig 5, 43, 246
Flaherty, Robert 45, 113, 117, 120, 121, 128, 130, 131
Florida 3; St. Augustine 15
folk: ballads 127; legends 127; song 115, 158
folklore 5, 59, 73, 113
Fonda, Jane 93
form 12, 16, 21, 43, 51, 56, 72, 75, 88, 93, 95, 99, 100, 101, 102, 104, 110, 116, 131, 136, 137, 140, 142, 152, 159, 208, 216; art 92, 93, 104; *corrido* 115; dramatic 21; theatrical 88, 100
Forman, Milos 27
Forster, E.M. 236
forties (1940s) 45, 47
Foster, Gloria **64**, 65
France 162
Frasier 53
Freed, Fred 46
Freud, Sigmund 136, 137, 139, 141, 144, 145; *The Ego and the Id* 137; "Eternal Wisdom" 145; "The Theme of the Three Caskets" (1913) 144
Friedman, Peter 55
Friendly, Fred 46

gang 117, 122, 124, 152, 184; Mexican 118; section 61, 70
gangster 25, 159
Ganon, James 122
Gelmes, Joseph 72
gender 135, 194, 212, 213, 215; roles 192; *see also* stereotype
Genessee *see* Idaho
genre 44, 53, 73, 92, 103, 136; comedy

32, 136, 213, 223, 227, 237; documentary 101; dramatic/performance 136; film 123; sitcom 53; tragedy 90, 135, 136, 206, 211, 216, 217, 234
George Polk Award for Heroism *see* Award
Germany 47, 163, 168, 169, 170, 171, 175; Bavaria 170; Berlin 47, 229, 230
Gilliam, Terry 235
Gillin, Linda 79
Gimbel, Peter 26
Gitlin, Irving (Irv) 16, 18, 21, 22, 46, 47, 50
Gitlin, Todd 52
Glengarry Glen Ross 99
God 41, 50, 152, 154, 184, 200
goddess 145, 146, 148
Goethe 92
"Golden Age of Television Documentary" 43, 51
Goldstein, Sam 1
Goliath 22
Goodbye, Columbus 25
Goodman, John 188, 225
Goodman, Walter 135
Gould, Jack 44
The Graduate 188; Benjamin and Elaine (characters) 188
Graff, Todd 152
Grapes of Wrath (1940) 113
graphics, computer 220, 225, 233
Grass (1925) 15
The Great Apes (*National Geographic* 1975) 28, 117
Greco-Jewish 168
Greece 137, 146, 161, 167, 168, 169, 176, 183; Gyppe 170; King George I 168; philosopher 185; Sephardic 161, 168; theater 185; Thessaloniki (Salonika) 161, 163, 168, 169, 175; tragedy 135
Greensboro *see* North Carolina
Grierson, John 45, 116, 117, 131
Grim Reaper 50, 138
Guantánamo 237
Guare, John 27
Gulf Stream 26
The Guns of Navarone 162, 165
Gunsmoke 28
gypsies 161, 163, 167, 169, 170, 171, 173, 175, 177, 178, 179; European 169; Roma 169, 170, 171, 177, 178, 179; Sinti (German gypsies), 169, 170, 171, 178, 179; see also *Triumph of the Spirit*

habitus **210**
Hades 138, 139
Haen, Zion 162
Halliburton 237
Hamlet 234; Hamlet 234; Polonius 234
Harlem 28
Harris, Julius **64**, 65, 82
Harvard 3, 11, 14, 47, 157; Film Society 3
Hawaiian Eye (1959–1963) 44
HBO 53
Healer, Chris 233
Heath, Larry 162, 163
Hemingway, Ernest 5
Herculean 135
hero 10, 19, 20, 71–72, 114, 115, 117, 118, 122, 124, 127, 128, 142, 143, 164, 167, 187; action 152; ballad 117, 118, 123, 127, 128, 129, 132, 235; folk 115; legendary 128, 130, 131; working-class 157
Heyl, Burkhard 163
High Adventure with Lowell Thomas (series 1958–59) 16, 47
Hill Street Blues (1981–87) 157
Himmelstein, David 189
Himmler, Heinrich 170, 171
Hindu Kush 15
Hinson, Hal 71
Hispanic 74, 83, 85, 127, 129, 130
Hispanic American 76, 79, 82, 84
historical 88, 113, 121, 127, 128, 136, 167, 171, 172
Hitchcock, Alfred 54, 100, 143
Hitler 170, 175
Hoboken 113
Hoche, Alfred 170
Hoffman, Donald 121
Holderness *see* New Hampshire
Hollywood 32, 55, 101, 121, 157, 163, 224; film 32, 189, 223; studios 157, 160
Holocaust 25, 161, 163, 166, 167, 168, 169, 171, 172, 176; Americanization of 171; Museum in Washington 169; Studies Symposium 5
Holocaust Testimonies: The Ruins of Memory 171
homosexuals 175

Horowitz, Rosemary 5, 161, 246
horror movie 227, 230, 231
Howe, Desson 66
Hulce, Tom **6**, 149, *151*
Hulk Hogan 157
Human Error 1, 219, 220, 223, 225, 231, 232, 234–238; characters: Catherine 232, 236; Dobbitt 226, 227, 230, 232, 234, 235, 236, 237; Haney 226; Hanrahan 226, 227, 230, 231, 232, 233, 234, 235, 236, 237; Jacqueline Hanrahan 236; Merkin 226, 227, 230, 232, 233, 235, 236, 237; see also *Below the Belt*
Humana Festival 229
Humphrey, Hubert 46

Iago 106
Idaho 180, 181, 183; Genessee 183, 185; Pocatello 182
identity 18, 84, 107, 121, 138, 146, 171, 202, 210, 212, 216
immigrant 2, 76, 86, 113, 114, 117, 130, 152, 160
immigration officers 82, 120
In the World of Sharks (1966) 26
The Incredible Hulk 152; Incredible Hulk (character) 154, 157
independent film *see* film
India (1958) 16
India(n) 169, 170; Punjab 169
Indian, American 28, 29, 125, 195, 196, 201; Aztec 195, 197, 201, 202; Blackfoot 184; Mayan 197; reservation 27
industrialization 118, 120, 128
Inuit 29
Iran 15
Iraq War *see* War
Iron Horse 116, 121
Islamic Ottoman 168
Israel 161, 162, 176
Italy 19, 45, 49, 51, 55, 158, 168; *see also* Sicily
Ivan Dixon (character) 24

J.T. (1971) 5, 28
Jack Daniels 156
Japan 3, 11, 60
Jawetz, Gil 167
Jaws 26; Quint (character) 26
Jekyll and Hyde 154
Jesse James 126

Jesus 27, 152, 194
Jew 12, 25, 80, 145, 161, 163, 164, 167, 168, 169, 170, 171, 175, 176; Ashkenazi 168; gangster 25; Italian 168; organizations 176
Jim Crow 58
John Henry 58, 59, 120; "John Henry, Steel Driving Man" 58; *see also* folk
Joslin, Tom 55
journalism 17, 18, 22
Judas 126
Jung, Carl 136
Jurassic Park films 143

Kabbalah 140
Kael, Pauline 100, 102
Kalahari 28
Kansas City Royals 185, 186
Kelleher, Ed 134
Kelly, Grace 54
Kempley, Rita 55
Kennedy, President John F. 44, 45, 46, 55; Administration 51
Kermode, Frank 133
Kiansis (county) 125; *see also The Ballad of Gregorio Cortez*
King, Dr. Martin Luther, Jr. 58, 70, 71; "I Have a Dream" speech 70
King Kong (1933) 15, 143, 235–236
King Lear 144; Cordelia 144; Lear 144
Kinney, Terry 182
Kintner, Robert 46
Kipling, Rudyard 11
Kirkland, Bruce 149
Kirkpatrick, David 189
Kirov, Milen 235
Knott, Bobby 236
Kopelson, Arnold 162, 164
Korea 60
Korean War *see* War
Kozloff, Sarah 53
Kristallnacht 170
Kuleshov, Lev 99
Kurelek, William 27

Labor Day 130
The Labyrinth of Solitude 197
Lampell, Millard 162, 163
Langer, Lawrence 172, 176
Laramie Project 88
Lassez, Sarah 192
The Last Temptation of Christ 165

Latin 101, 102, 122
Latin America 132, 192, 194, 205
Latino 40, 121, 122, 124, 130, 132
Law, Lindsey 200
Lawrence of Arabia 19
Leacock, Richard 46
Leaks, Sylvester 72
Leal, Luis 195
Learner, Murray 14, 15, 47
legacy 131
legend 59, 87, 114, 117, 121, 122, 127, 128, 130, 131, 132, 195, 196
Levi, Primo 168
Levy, Jocko 164
Lewis, Leon iii, vii 246
life 13, 14, 16, 21, 29, 30, 34, 36, 41, 49, 51, 55, 59, 60, 63, 66, 67, 70, 75, 80, 91, 95, 103, 112, 117, 128, 138, 139, 140, 142, 143, 145, 146, 147, 163, 172, 175, 212, 214, 216, 217, 220, 222, 225, 226
Life Is Beautiful 161
Life magazine 45, 46
Life of the Molds (1958) 16, 47
Lightfoot, William E. 59
Lincoln, Abbey 24, 59
Lincoln Center 90
Liotta, Ray 6, 149, **151, 153**
Liszt, Franz 235
literature 3, 25, 28, 71, 91, 92, 109, 111, 137, 144, 145, 148, 168, 195, 205
Lithgow, John 32
The Living End 16, 47
Loggia, Robert 164
London, Jack 78
Los Angeles *see* California
Los Angeles Calendar 163
Los Angeles Magazine 194
Los Angeles Times 163
Los Lobos 157
Lost Boundaries (1949) 47
Louisiana Story 117
Luanda *see* Angola
Luciano, Charles "Lucky" 152
Lurie, Rob 193

machismo *see* stereotype
MacIntyre, Alisdair 209, 210
Mafia 50, 54, 152
magical realism 191, 200, 201
Maltin, Leonard 149
Mamet, David 99

Man of Aran 117
Man of the Serengeti (1972) 28
Manhattan 88, 216
March of Time 47
marginalized 211, 214, 215, 232
Mariana *see* stereotype
Marianismo *see* stereotype
"Marianismo: The Other Face of Machismo in Latin America" 192
Marina, Doña 196, 197
marine: films 14, 15; land 117; life 13; ocean life 14
Marine Studios 3, 14, 47
Marineland Studios 117
Martin, Holly E. 5, 191, 204, 205, 246
Martinez, Salvador 83
Marx, Groucho 222
masculinity 68, 109, 149, 159, 209
Maslin, Janet 150, 151, 165, 166, 168
Massachusetts 23; Boston 3; Cambridge, City Hospital 47; Institute of Technology (M.I.T.) 3, 10, 11, 14
Mastrosimone, William 135
Matewan (1987) 157
Mayan *see* Indian, American
Mayfield, Curtis 101, 102
Maysles, Albert 46
Maysles, David 46
The Maze (1971) 27
McCarthy, Cormac 4
McCormack, Bob 18
McLaughlin, Thomas 5, 206, 246
media 1, 43, 75, 99, 117, 120, 122, 123, 126, 128, 147, 179, 185, 223
Megadeath (music group) 157
megaphoning 94, 95, 96, 97
Melanesian 11
Melville, Herman 9, 11
Mephistopheles 106
The Merchant of Venice 144; Bassanio 144; Portia 144
mestizo 195, 196
Mexican-American(s) 75, 76, 79, 80, 121, 192, 194, 195, 197, 202
Mexican-Texan 115
Mexico 74, 75, 76, 77, 80, 81, 82, 83, 84, 85, 114, 115, 117, 118, 121, 122, 124, 125, 126, 127, 128, 130, 131, 191, 192, 195, 196, 197, 201; Ciudad Juárez 81; literature of 195; Mexico City 195; Michoacan (Mexican state) 76, 80, 83, 85, 86; New Spain 195; Sons of

Malinche 197; Tepeyac 195; Tijuana 81
Michoacan *see* Mexico
military 10, 18, 58, 60, 64, 159, 170, 220, 237
Miller, Eugene L. 4, 5, 180, 247
Miller, Mark Crispin 52
Milton, John 92
Minow, Newton 44, 45
Miramax 1
mise-en-scène 137
Mississippi 112
Mississippi Burning 165
Mitchell, Martin 101, 102
Moby Dick 11
Mona Lisa 147
Montana 27
Montauk (Gulf Stream) 26
Montezuma 196
Monty Python 235
Mother Teresa 40
MTV 33
Munvees, Frank 26
Murder, Inc. 152
Murray, Bill 225
Murrow, Edward R. 44, 45, 51
music 5, 33, 49, 59, 67, 79, 80, 81, 86, 99, 101–2, 166, 167, 168, 181, 214, 226, 230, 235; Latin 101, 211; Norteña 81, 85; rock 157
musical score 127, 165, 166
Mustang 181, 182, 184, 188
Mutual Broadcasting System 44
Myrdal, Gunnar 12
myth (mythology) 6, 130, 136, 137, 138, 139, 140, 143, 144, 145, 148, 150, 236

Nanook 130
Nanook of the North 113, 117, 120
narcissism 213, 214
narrative 7, 14, 21, 23, 24, 44, 48, 53, 54, 56, 63, 111, 115, 116, 117, 119, 123, 133, 154, 157, 158, 160, 176, 181, 189
narrator 49, 50, 51, 111, 156
Nashville *see* Tennessee
National Farm Workers Union *see* United Farm Workers of America Union
National Gallery 35
National Museum of Art 35
native 11, 79, 93, 124, 226
Native American 121, 185; literature 28
The Natural 190

Navajo Girl (1972) 28
Navy, U.S. 3, 10, 14, 15, 113; intelligence 17
Nazi 12, 161, 162, 169, 170, 171, 172, 173, 174, 175, 176; persecution of Jehovah's Witnesses 169; persecution of Slavs 169
NBC Network 3, 16, 17, 18, 19, 20, 21, 22, 23, 28, 43, 44, 45, 46, 48, 51, 55, 59, 157; *64,000 Dollar Question* scandal 16
Negro 71, 73, 119
Neorealist movement 45
Never Cry Wolf (1983) 32
New Guinea 3, 10, 11, 37
New Hampshire: Holderness 9
New Haven 46
New Jersey 24
New Orleans 23
New York 2, 9, 11, 32; City 1, 35, 113; Film Commission 1
New York Shakespeare Festival 90
New York Times 18, 28, 43, 135, 165; *Sunday Magazine* 1
The New Yorker 100
9/11 237
Nixon, Richard 45
Nogales (border cities) 203
Norma Rae (1979) 157
North (American) 60, 64
North Carolina: Durham 112; Greensboro 112
Northeast 71
Norton, Chris 68
Nothing but a Man (1964) 3, 5, 12, 13, 22, 24, 25, 26, 28, 48, 58–72, 78, 112, 113, 158; characters: Duff Anderson 23, 24, 58–70, 71, 72, **64**; Frankie 60, 67; Josie Dawson 59, 61–70; Lee **64**, 65, 70; Pop 61; Reverend Dawson 61, 65, 69; Will Anderson **64**
Nova International Films 165
NOW–NYC 135
Nucci, Danny 192
Nuremberg Laws 170

ocean life *see* marine
Off Broadway 227, 229
Officers' Club 10, 11
O'Keeffe, Georgia 211
Olmos, Edward James (Eddie) 31, 37,

38, 82, *114*, 122, 123, 124, ***125***, 127, 129, 130, 131, 163, 169, ***169***, 171, 180, 181, ***183***, 186, ***187***, 188, 189, 190, 192, ***193***, 200, ***207***, 208, 212, 215
One Trick Pony (1981) 32
The Online Shopping Center 167
"Opening to the Left" 19
Oxford English Dictionary 236

PBS 53, 130, 200; *American Playhouse* 200
Pacific 11
Palace of Versailles 185
Palermo *see* Sicily
Palestine 168
Papp, Joseph 90
Paramount studio 189, 190
Paredes, Americo 121, 122, 126, 127, 128, 130, 131
Paris 48
Paz, Octavio 197
Pearl Harbor 3
Pennebaker, Donn 46
Pensacola Flight School 10
Perez, José 105
performance 24, 34, 36, 37, 92, 94, 97, 102, 105, 110, 135, 136, 141, 150, 156, 161, 166, 167, 168, 171, 208, 213, 215, 221
Persephone 138
"Phenom"/phenom 181, 182, 183, 184, 185, 187, 189
Philippines 3
Phoenix *see* Arizona
photography 3, 10, 11, 25, 47, 113, 117, 123, 129; director of 112
The Pianist 161
Piñero, Miguel 3, 5, 35, 87, 88, 90, 93, 94, 95, 97, 99, 100, 101, 102, 104, 105, 107, 108, 109
Pitofsky, Alexander H. 5, 149, 247
Pittsburgh 157; Pirates 156; "Steel Town" 157
Platoon 164
play 5, 28, 35, 36, 52, 87, 88, 89, 90, 91, 92, 93, 94, 95, 96, 97, 98, 99, 100, 101, 104, 105, 108, 109, 148, 200, 204, 219, 220, 221, 223, 224, 225, 226, 227, 228, 229, 230, 231, 232, 233, 234, 235, 236
playwright 3, 5, 91, 92, 93, 105, 135, 219, 231

plot 97, 104, 105, 139, 182, 186, 188, 189, 206, 208, 213
The Plot Against Harry 5, 13, 22, 25, 26, 27
Pocatello *see* Idaho
"Poem in October" (Thomas) 7
Poland 163, 168, 171, 176
Police 58, 77, 133, 134, 147, 150, 152, 206
politics 22, 47, 49, 51, 55, 56, 71, 72, 79, 92, 148, 159, 175, 177, 184, 196, 205, 206, 212, 213, 220, 234; cultural 212; gender 212; satire 236; sexual 212
Poltel (Polish Television) 163
Pomerantz, Eddie 27, 35–6, 38, 40
Pope Benedict XIV 195
popular culture *see* culture
Popular Culture and the Shaping of Holocaust Memory in America 171
pornography 223
Porrajmos (the Devouring) 161, 169
Port Marobi 11
Portugal 17, 18, 19, 168
The Postman Always Rings Twice 208
postmodern 112, 131
poverty 19, 23, 47, 50, 51, 55, 59, 66, 71, 154
practitioner 209, 210
Priest, Marty 13
Primary (1960) 46
prison 32, 87, 88, 89, 90, 91, 95, 96, 97, 98, 100, 101, 102, 103, 106, 109, 111, 123, 126, 130, 193, 197, 203, 217, 236; Bedford Hills 88; drama 31; films 101; Manhattan House of Detention for Men (The "Tombs") 3, 35, 103, 109; Sing-Sing 35, 88
prisoners 35, 89, 97, 98, 102, 103, 104, 105, 106, 107, 110, 163, 165, 167, 168, 172, 173, 174, 175
private sphere 209
producer *2*, 21, 26, 32, 34, 45, 46, 47, 52, 53, 112, 122, 162, 165, 172, 189, 200, 225
production 1, 2, 4, 5, 6, 7, 34, *38*, 44, 47, 48, 55, 88, 90, 91, 104, 111, 116, 118, 122, 127, 132, 135, 148, 162, 223, 229, 230, 231, 232; designer 24
psyche 136, 154, 196
psychoanalysis 136, 109, 133, 140, 141
psychology (psychological) 14, 77, 109, 113, 135, 136, 137, 141, 143, 145, 163, 165, 209, 224, 231, 234; problem 135;

realism 200; reality 103; space 209; truth 13
Puerto Rico 3, 88, 89, 95, 98, 109, 110, 224, 225

Quaid, Randy 225
quinceañera 195
Quintero, Jose 13
Quiz Show (1994) 43
quiz show scandal 43, 44
Quonset hut 11

race 3, 23, 47, 112, 120, 170, 178, 182, 195; categories 170; conflict 126; dialectic 110; groups 96; problem 23, 59; purification 170; separation 58; slur 155; tension 58, 71
racism 58, 63, 64, 65, 67, 68, 69, 71, 72, 112, 119, 121, 125
Ragusa *see* Sicily
Ramirez, Armandina 85
rape 33, 98, 99, 107, 133, 134, 135, 137, 140, 145, 147, 148, 234
rapist 97, 138, 140, 146
Rear Window (1954) 54, 100; characters: L.B. Jeffries 54; Lisa 54
Redford, Robert 1, 43, 114
religion 12, 50, 112, 145, 152, 183, 185, 220; ceremony 50; faith 199; fanaticism 194; tolerance 168; values 184
reviewers 55, 68, 90, 100, 101, 111, 121, 135, 149, 159, 166, 167, 168, 193, 200, 208
rhetoric 57, 71, 137, 148
Rich Kids (1980) 4, 5, 32
Rio Grande 114, 126
Ritter, Lloyd 14, 15
Rivera, Tomas 121, 130
Rivers, Johnny 181
Roach, Hal, Jr. 44
Robin Hood 127
Rocky (1976) 156, 162, 165; Rocky Balboa 156
Rodriguez, Valente 198
Roemer, Michael (Mike) 3, 5, 12, 19, 20, 22–28, 43, 47–51, 53, 54, 59, 60, 71, 112
Rolling Stone 166
Romania 170
Rome 48, 126
rooster 191, 192, 193, 198, 199, 201, 202, 203, 204

Roosters (1995) 5, 35, 191–205, **193**; characters: Aden 198, 203; Angela Morales 192, 193, 194, 195, 196, 198, 199, 200, 201, 202, 203; Chata 192, 193, 195, 196, 203; "The Filipino's son" 193, 195, 199, 203; Gallo Morales 192, 193, **193**, 194, 196, 197, 198, 199, 200, 201, 203; Hector Morales 192, 193, 195, 196, 197, 198, 199, 201, 202, 203; Juana Morales 192, 193, 196, 197, 199, 200, 201, 203; Papi (Gallo's father) 191, 193; Zapata (rooster) 191, 198, 201
Rorschach test 167
Rumsfeld, Donald 237
Russia 2, 168, 175; Communist Party *see* Communist
Russo, James 133, 135, **141**

Saab 157
Sachadinanda, Yogi 27
Sacramento Bee 194
sacrifice 35, 68, 90, 172, 186, 191, 194, 197, 199, 200, 201, 202, 203
Saenz, Michael 119, 124, 126
St. Augustine *see* Florida
Salazar, Ludevina Mendez 79
Salonika *see* Greece
Samson Agonistes 92
San Antonio *see* Texas
San Antonio Daily Express (newspaper) 117, 118, 126
San Antonio Light 126
Sanchez-Scott, Milcha 200
Sandoval, John 83
Santa Fe 113, 127
Sargent, Alvin 149
Satan (Great Adversary) 138, 185
Saving Grace (1984) 5
Scarwid, Diana 133, 139
Schindler's List 161, 168
Schoedsack, Ernest B. 15
Schub, Steven 208
Scottish border ballads 114
The Scout 188
screenplay 27–8, 38, 60, 93, 99, 106, 131, 149, 200, 201, 223
screenwriter *see* writer
script 12, 15, 23, 24, 25, 31, 32, 33, 35, 37, 38, 44, 48, 59, 60, 87, 91, 92, 93, 99, 109, 118, 119, 122, 127, 130, 162, 163, 165, 166, 200, 201, 202, 229,

231, 234; playscript 92, 93, 99, 104, 110
Secrets of the Reef (1956) 3, 15, 117
Seger, Bob 156
segregation 58, 60, 62
Serengeti 28
7 Up 55
Seventh Cavalry 162
The Seventh Seal 138
seventies (1970s) 156
77 Sunset Strip (1958–1964) 44
sexuality 40, 80, 96, 137, 140, 142, 147, 181, 188, 192, 195, 206, 209, 211, 212, 213, 214, 215, 225, 226, 236
Shakespeare 6, 144, 145, 228; *see also* individual plays
Shephard, Sam 27
Sheridan, Jamey 182
Short Eyes (1979) 3, 5, 32, 34, 35, 87–91, 94–111, *89*; characters: Captain Allard 105, 106, 107; Clark Davis 89, 90, 94–99, 103, 104, 105, 106, 107, 108; Cupcakes 89, 90, 98, 99, 101, 102, 105, 107, 108, 109; El Raheem 96, 106, 107, 108; Go-Go 102, 103, 104; Ice 93, 94, 108; Juan ("The Poet") 88, 89, 90, 94, 98, 99, 104, 105, 107, 108; Longshoe 95, 96, 97, 105, 106, 107, 108; Mr. Nett 89, 96, 97, 105, 106, 107; Paco 98, 99, 106, 109
Shrek 188, 225
Shreveport, LA 119
Sicily 3, 19, 20, 22, 23, 48, 43, 51, 55, 59, 152; Cortile Cascino (neighborhood) 47, 48, 49, 50, 53, 54, 55; film 35; movie 29; Palermo 47, 48, 50, 53; Ragusa 55; *see also* Italy
Signs of Intelligent Life in the Universe 28
Silkwood (1983) 157
Silva, Trinidad 75, 78
Silverlake Life: The View from Here (1993) 55
Simon, Paul 32, 33
Sit-In (1960) 17, 23, 47, 59, 60, 71
sixties (60s) 12, 26, 28, 43, 45, 60, 71
Smith, Anna Deveare 88
Smith, Huey "Piano" 181
social 69, 77, 109, 116, 139, 188, 209; classes 194; codes 217; commentary 236; concerns 23; issues 11, 134; problems 135; racism 67; reality 103, 104;

redemption 90; relations 137; relevance 43; responsibility 114, 116, 131; scene 64; scientists 44; space 139 (*see also* space); stability 60; structure 5, 60; support 135; workers 146
socialists 19
society 12, 21, 55, 107, 109, 135, 160, 169, 171, 174, 197, 220; Anglo 120
sociological 71, 212
"Soldier's Home" (1976) 5
Solomon and Sheba (1995) 5
Sonderkommando 164
Sony 1; Classics 2
South: the American 12, 23, 59, 60, 71; Deep 60, 112; Old 101; Side 150, 152, 154, 155, 157, 158, 159
South Africa 226
South Carolina 23; Columbia 60
space 13, 102, 111, 139, 142, 171, 203, 206, 207, 209, 210, 211, 213, 214, 215, 216, 217; confined, 216; domestic 206, 215; erotic 211, 213; open 216, 217; physical 206, 208, 209; psychological 209; public 206, 217; sexual 214; sexualized 211, 214; social 139; work 211
Spain 74, 78, 115, 117, 119, 120, 126, 129, 168, 192, 194, 195, 196, 201; Conquistadors 194, 196
spirituality 80, 108, 121, 130, 136, 145, 147, 185, 194, 195, 199, 210
Springsteen, Bruce 157
SS 161, 171; guard 163; Lieutenant Heinrich 163; Major Rauscher 163; members 164; officer 163; see also *Triumph of the Spirit*
stage 20, 88, 91, 99, 100, 101, 104, 167, 184, 185, 188, 226, 227, 228, 229, 231; *see also* direction
Stallone, Sylvester 156
Stanford 149, 154
Star of David 80
Star Spangled Banner 84
Steelbound 88
stereotype 118, 124, 141, 146, 191, 192, 194, 195, 196, 197, 198; gender 194; machismo 122, 191, 192, 194, 197, 198, 199, 200, 201, 203, 205; Mariana 194, 203; Marianismo 191, 192, 194, 195, 197, 204, 205; whore 195, 196, 197
Sterne, Laurence 152
Stevens, Evelyn P. 192, 194, 196
Stewart, James 54

Stilling, Roger James 6, 133, 247
Stone, Oliver 164
Storm from Paradise 171
storyboard 31
Strasburg, Lee 13
Strathairn, David 159
Sua, Murphy 184
Sundance 127; *see also* Film festivals
Surfside Six (1960–62) 44
Surkin, Eddie 163
Survival in Auschwitz 168
Swedish 12
"the system" 7, 12, 72, 107, 120, 221

Talent for the Game (1991) 5, 180–190, *183*, *187*; characters: Bobbie 181, 182, 183, *183*, 184, 185, 186, 187, 188, 189; Dick Bortner 184; Gil Lawrence 182, 184, 185, 186, 187, 188, 189; Iron Jack Kelly 185; Lester 180; Ma Bodeen 184; Reverend Bodeen 183; Sammy Bodeen 183, 184, 185, 186, 187, *187*, 189; Tim Weaver 181, 182, 185, 186, 189; Virgil Sweet 181, 182, 183, *183*, 184, 185, 186, 187, *187*, 188, 189
television 5, 22, 26, 43–48, 52, 53, 55, 56, 72, 86, 88, 95, 105, 106, 148, 152, 155, 157, 163, 165, 166, 177, 186, 209, 212; documentary 43, 45, 55, 56; genre 53, (action) 44, (sitcom) 53, (western) 44
Television: Technology and Cultural Form (1975) 52
Tennessee 59, 125; Nashville 47, 59
Tenochtitlán 196
Tepeyac *see* Mexico
Terry, Megan 27
Texas 81, 112, 114, 115, 118, 121, 124, 128; Austin 127; Dallas 112, 220; El Paso 81; Gonzales 113, 115, 121, 127, 128; Rangers 114, 117, 118, 119, 120, 121, 122, 123, 124, 125, 126, 127, 128; San Antonio 117, 130
The Texture of Memory: Holocaust Memorials and Meanings 171
Thanatos 137, 138, 139; see also *Extremities*
Theater (Theatre) 25, 48, 71, 91, 93, 95, 96, 99, 100, 101, 102, 109, 110, 130, 147, 148, 176, 200, 228, 229, 230, 231; Actors Theatre of Louisville 227, 229; The American Theater Ring 122; Brechtian 94; Greek 185; Los Feliz 130; Rialto 112; "Theatre of Testimony" 88; Theatre of the Riverside Church 88, 90; Touchstone 88; Vivian Beaumont 90
theory 35, 52, 56, 136, 145, 148, 170, 218; literary 5
therapeutic 136
Third Reich 170
thirties (1930s) 2
Thomas, Dylan 7
Tijuana *see* Mexico
Time 135
Time/Life Corporation 46
Todd, Susan 55
"The Tombs" *see* prison
Tomlin, Lily 28
The Tonight Show 46
Toronto 220
A Tour of the White House with Mrs. John F. Kennedy 45
tragedy *see* genre
tragic flaws 208
translation 48, 99, 105, 110, 115, 116, 119, 128; mistranslation 115, 129
translator 110, 119, 120, 123–124, 128, 129, 130, 163
Travers, Peter 166, 167, 168
Tree of the World 140
Triumph of the Spirit (1989) 5, 25, 161–169, *162*, *169*, 172–179; characters: Allegra 174, 176; Elena 174; Gypsy *169*; Jacko 175, 176; Avram, Poppa and Salamo Arouch *see* Arouch, Avram; Arouch, Poppa; Arouch, Salamo
Trujillo, Rafael 44
Trump, Donald 189
truth 7, 9, 12, 13, 19, 20, 21, 22, 30, 33, 51, 69, 71, 77, 94, 96, 98, 102, 108, 116, 143, 145, 162, 163, 167, 223, 225, 227; actual 20; fictive 21; inner 166; literal 21, 30; psychological 13; real 20
Tucson *see* Arizona
TV Guide Online 167
twenties (1920s) 2
Twenty-One 43

Uncle Toby (Laurence Sterne) 152
Underworld 138
United Farm Workers of America Union 77, 83; *see also* Chávez, Cesar

United States (U.S.) 18, 19, 45, 47, 48, 76, 78, 80, 81, 82, 83, 85, 194, 195, 237
University of California 121
University of Pittsburgh 149
The Untouchables (1959–1963) 44
U.S.S.R. 45
Utah 1

Variety 166, 167
Vatican 5
vernacular 156
Vertigo 54; characters: Madeline/Judy 54; "Scottie" Ferguson 54
Verveen, Arie 31, *39*, **207**, 208
Victoria's Secret 134
Vietnam War *see* War
viewer *see* audience
Villasenor, Victor 127
violence 44, 58, 63, 67, 69, 70, 71, 72, 77, 82, 100, 103, 109, 115, 119, 121, 127, 137, 142, 147, 148, 152, 154, 157, 158, 159, 160, 192, 198, 199, 202, 203, 204, 217, 222; criminal 87; domestic 150; nonviolent 72; physical 94; street 152
Virgin Mary 194, 195
Virgin of Guadalupe 80, 195
Vogel, Mark 5, 58, 73, 247
Volvo 26

Wagner, Jane 28
Wall Street (1987) 157
Wallace, George C. 58
War 10, 11, 12, 14, 47, 52, 134, 166, 167, 176, 202; Cold War 45, 55; guerrilla 71; Iraq 52, 237; Korean 60; Vietnam 45, 159; World War II 10, 11, 37, 47, 164
Warner Bros. 44
Washington: D.C. 17, 35, 169; March on 70–71
Washington Post 71
Wasserman, Al 21, 46, 47
Whiplash, Snidely 189
white-collar *see* class
White Paper (series) 3, 5, 16, 17, 43, 46, 47, 51, 59; see also *Cortile Cascino*
Whore *see* stereotype
Wiesel, Elie 25

The Wild One 138
Williams, Raymond 52
Willis, Brett 167
A Winter's Tale 228
Wisconsin 46
"With a Pistol in His Hand": A Border Ballad and Its Hero 121
Wonders of the Sea (1955) 15
Wood, Robin 54
Woodard, Alfre 133, **144**
Woolworth's 112
World War II *see* War
World Wide 60 (series) 47
Wright, Richard 5
writer 2, 12, 28, 32, 35, 36, 37, 47, 74, 88, 93, 112, 113, 148, 162, 167, 169, 178, 189, 223, 224, 228, 229; screenwriter 100, 148, 227
Writers Guild of America 162, 165, 180
Writing Below the Belt 223

Xocotl 202

Yale Drama School 27
Young, Andrew 55
Young, Nick 235
Young, Robert M. (Bob) 1, 2, *2*, 3, 4, 5, 6, **6**, 7, 9–42, **38**, *39*, 43, 46–51, 53–55, 59, 60, 69, 71, 74, 75, 76, 77, 80, 82, 83, 85, 87, 88, 93, 97, 99, 100, 101, 102, 103, 104, 105, 106, 107, 109, 112, 113, 114, **114**, 115, 116, 117, 118, 119, 120, 121, 122, 123, 124, 127, 128, 129, 130, 131, 133, 134, 135, 136, 138, 147, 149, 150, 154, 157, 158, 159, 161, 162, 163, 164, 165, 166, 167, 168, 169, 171, 172, 173, 176, 180, 181, 182, 184, 185, 186, 187, **187**, 188, 189 190, 200, 201, 202, 203, 206, 208, 209, 210, 211, 212, 213, 214, 215, 217, 219, 220, 223, 224, 225, 226, 227, 228, 229, 230, 231, 232, 233, 234, 235, 236, 237; interview with 9–42
Young, Zack 235
YWCA 112

Zakhor: Jewish History and Jewish Memory 171
Zoot Suit (1981) 122, 130
Zorba the Greek 164

www.ingramcontent.com/pod-product-compliance
Lightning Source LLC
Chambersburg PA
CBHW051214300426
44116CB00006B/573